Work That Makes Sense

Operator-Led Visuality

Creating and Sustaining Visuality on the Value-Add Level

Second Edition

GWENDOLYN D. GALSWORTH

Routledge
Taylor & Francis Group

A PRODUCTIVITY PRESS BOOK

Book Design: Brook Kirklin; Iwan Sujono of Eone Design, Sydney, Australia
Book Cover: William Stanton
Editor: Aurelia Navarro

First published 2022
by Routledge
605 Third Avenue, New York, NY 10158

and by Routledge
4 Park Square, Milton Park, Abingdon, Oxon, OX14 4RN
Routledge is an imprint of the Taylor & Francis Group, an informa business

ISBN: 978-1-032-05485-8 (hbk)
ISBN: 978-1-032-05481-0 (pbk)
ISBN: 978-1-003-19774-4 (ebk)

DOI: 10.4324/9781003197744

La Poesía

And something ignited in my soul,
fever or unremembered wings,
and I went my own way,
deciphering
that burning fire,
and I wrote the first bare line,
bare, without substance, pure
foolishness,
pure wisdom
of one who knows nothing,
and suddenly I saw
the heavens
unfastened
and open.

by Pablo Neruda
translated by David Whyte

By The Same Author

Books
Work That Makes Sense: Operator-Led Visuality
Visual Workplace . Visual Thinking: Creating a Workforce of Visual Thinkers
Visual Systems: Harnessing the Power of a Visual Workplace
Visual Workplace . Visual Order Associate Handbook
Visual Workplace . Visual Order Instructor Guide
Smart Simple Design: Variety Effectiveness and the Cost of Complexity
Smart Simple Design: Reloaded

Online Training Systems
Work That Makes Sense: Operator-Led Visuality (also fully in Spanish)
Work That Makes Sense Resource Folio
Leading for an Effective Implementation
Training for an Effective Implementation
Poka-Yoke: Perfect Quality Through Mistake-Proofing (with Dr. Martin Hinckley)

Training Implementation Suites
Work That Makes Sense: Operator-Led Visuality
Visual Workplace/Visual Machine®
Visual Adherence: Visual Standards & Visual Controls
Achieving Zero Defects: Visual Guarantees (poka-yoke systems)
Visual ScoreBoarding: Problem Solving for the Chronic, Complex, and Costly
Becoming a Leader of Improvement-1: A New Role for Supervisors and Managers
Becoming a Leader of Improvement-2: A New Role for Executives
Management by Sight: Visual Displays/Visual Scheduling
Creating and Deploying the X-Type Matrix & Operations Roadmap
Smart Simple Design: De-Complicating the Enterprise Through Variety Effectiveness

VisualEdge Training Packages
The Basics of Visuality
The Building Blocks of Visual Thinking
Automatic Recoil/The Visual Where: Borders
Visual Mini-Systems/Visual Inventiveness
The Four Power Levels of Visual Devices
The Five Reasons for Workplace Visuality
The Visual Machine®: Let the Machine Speak
Machine Lubrication: Visual & Effective
Visual Workplace/Visual Order
Creating and Deploying High-Performance Work Systems
Soft Skills for Visual Workplace Trainers

Contents

THE 18 LEADERSHIP TASKS

List of Photos, Series, Figures & Insets

Section 1: Visual Workplace Basics

Chapter 1. Introduction to the Visual Workplace

Chapter 2. The Building Blocks of Visual Thinking

Chapter 3. Your Implementation Tool Box

Section 2: Smart Placement

Chapter 4. Smart Placement: Logic, Meaning, and Mapping

Chapter 6. Smart Placement Principles (8-14)

Section 3: The Visual Where

Chapter 7. Smart Placement Principles (8-14)

Chapter 8. The Visual Where: Addresses and ID Labels

Section 4: People and Results

Chapter 9. Ourselves and Others

Chapter 10. Results: People and the Bottom Line

Section 5: Drilling Deeper

Chapter 11. Visual Mini Systems & Customer-Driven Visuality

Chapter 12. The Four Power Levels of Visual Devices

Foreword by | **Brent Allen**

Many companies have a full box of improvement tools—lean, six sigma, kanban, 5S, TPM, to name a few. When these are deployed, company leaders get results, often promising results. But these results are also often not sustained. The solution, they are told, is to make sure the effort is *operator-led*. But that goal often seems even more elusive.

A new business paradigm is required.

In her book, *Work That Makes Sense* (WTMS), Dr. Gwendolyn Galsworth provides such a paradigm when she shares her comprehensive methodology for implementing the visual workplace through operators—operator-led. First, operators are shown specific procedures for implementing workplace visuality in their own areas—from smart placement and the visual where, to mini-systems and the four power levels of visual devices. Great examples, great photographs, and systematic step-by-step methods show how. Galsworth teaches that "how" extremely well, providing chapter after chapter of the principles and techniques that operators need to drive out waste through visual solutions. This, the mechanics of visuality, is the first dimension of this excellent book.

The book's second dimension is even more powerful: the cultural change and how leadership is widened to include operators. Galsworth does this better than I have seen anywhere else—in any book, program or methodology—positing a new business paradigm for us to consider. She calls that leadership paradigm: *I-driven*.

At the heart of I-driven leadership is the realization that operators do not know how to lead *because* they have not been given the opportunity to learn to do so.

I know this from my work at Lifetime Products, Inc. in Utah where we manufactured a wide range of innovative lifestyle products. Thanks to 2,500 hardworking men and women, we were leaders in several of those markets. After 30 years as a Lifetime executive and in my role as Faculty Fellow at the Shingo Institute, I am convinced that most supervisors would love to get their operators to take on more responsibility and make more decisions. Their question is how?

Managers and operators want the same thing. But how do we get it? I found the answer—one I had sought for a very long time—in Galsworth's implementation framework. A successful continuous improvement work culture must find the balance point between *structure* and *free will*.

This is at the heart of Galsworth's I-driven approach—her approach to visuality and her approach to creating a work culture for excellence. Her book clearly identifies what category of decisions operators can and cannot make. In the week-long WTMS training for trainers Galsworth led at Lifetime, I saw this in action when operators were presenting a list of visual improvement projects they had identified. She asked them to circle the ones they could do and the ones that were management's. They did, taking on many tasks as their own. I was taken aback. Prior to that, not only operators but managers would have listed **all of them** as management's job. I suddenly realized that the answer to the question who gets to lead is about giving operators permission, time, and authority to lead. To lead what? *To lead themselves.* Once given, operators willingly accept *and* meet that challenge.

The fact that Galsworth's approach has structure—shape, rules, and accountability—provides managers a way to contribute to continuous improvement and to excel. You need to retain structure so the place doesn't get blown up and to communicate an abiding respect for managers and their legitimate role. That same structure allows operators to freely determine *how* they want to fulfill their own need to contribute and excel—operator-led visuality. A spirited and engaged workforce is not about anti-management. It is about a system where both sides of the equation succeed. It is *not* either/or but *both*. This is a great definition of teamwork.

And yet a third element is needed and also found in this exceptional book—the one that gets added to teamwork so the enterprise can grow to a new horizon. That third element is *exactness*.

Work That Makes Sense teaches us that visual devices translate information into exact behavior. That is its primary purpose: embedding and sustaining exactness through visual solutions. And this can only come about in a culture of free will—an I-driven culture. The third element for enterprise excellence— for creating the continuous improvement work culture I have sought for Lifetime—is exactness: the exactness that visuality, and every other improvement method, requires for its success.

Exactness cannot be demanded. The level of exactness required for continuous improvement to become a way of life at a company can only be given voluntarily, through an act of free will.

Free will, structure, and exactness are a shifting balance point. This is the new business paradigm that Galsworth offers us. This is an I-driven enterprise. Once learned and operationalized, this paradigm allows the organization to take on anything, any new improvement effort.

I have been a student of management for 30 years, read countless management books and gone to many seminars. I have never found a better, more powerful system of transformation than Galsworth's. That comes through on every page of this book. She does that better than anybody.

Brent R. Allen
Vice President of Operations (retired)
Lifetime Products, Inc.
Clearfield, Utah

Foreword by **Rhonda Kovera**

Twenty-five years ago, I started a company, Visual Workplace Inc., in order to provide products and coaching to companies wanting to implement the visual workplace and visual management.

It became obvious very quickly that many organizations equated the 5S/workplace organization method to creating a visual workplace. We recognized the difference and work every day to help companies understand the difference. Please don't get me wrong. 5S is a very important first step on every company's journey to enterprise excellence.

That is why we are so delighted with Dr. Galsworth's book, *Work That Makes Sense*. It doesn't just define what a visual workplace is, it shows you step by step by step how to transform your company into a visual work environment. This book describes in detail tools, processes, and outcomes that are so far beyond what is understood as the visual approach by most people that I feel sure that anyone who reads it will never confuse 5S and the visual workplace/visual management again. They will know that *workplace visuality* (Gwendolyn's term) will build your safety, quality, and on-time delivery specifications into the work environment, that visual devices will let you spot abnormalities at-a-glance, and that visual solutions will build standard work and your KPIs into daily operations, and more.

Work That Makes Sense represents an opportunity for all organizations, not just manufacturing, to apply some extraordinary concepts to their workplaces—service professions, education, health care. The tools and concepts in this book provide operators—the experts—with concrete ways to improve their own workplace in a way they can and want to be responsible for. Whether you are an operator, nurse, mechanic, or teacher, the common sense practices in this book and hundreds of practical examples will show you what a visual workplace is and how to apply it to your own world.

In fact, I think you will discover in this book (or already know) what I discovered so many years ago: The visual workplace is its own distinct approach to excellence, with its own distinct benefits, and its own distinct implementation methodologies.

The visual workplace is not the same as 5S. It is greater than that. And it is greater by far than "a place for everything and everything in its place." But even more, you are right in recognizing your own 5S efforts will slide back into disorganization—they will fail—without the visual workplace.

I'd like to say this again: No matter how much a company tries, it will never be able to sustain its 5S or lean outcomes if it does integrate visual information-sharing devices, visual communications, and visual methods.

To go much further, we need a new horizon. And it seems the only way for us to get a new horizon is to make one. We are convinced that this book will go a long way in helping that to happen.

Rhonda Kovera
CEO and Co-Founder
Visual Workplace Inc.
Grand Rapids, Michigan

About | Gwendolyn Galsworth

Gwendolyn D. Galsworth, PhD, is president/founder of Visual Thinking Inc. (VTI) which she formed in 1991 as a training, consulting, and development firm, specializing in the technologies of the visual workplace and visual management. Her early focus was on codifying the field of visuality into a single coherent framework of principles, training, thinking, and application.

Now VTI helps companies around the world transform their bottom lines and work cultures through Dr. Galsworth's methods. The Visual-Lean® Institute is VTI's teaching arm, training and certifying in-house trainers and external consultants, onsite and online, in nine core visual workplace methodologies.

Dr. Galsworth is a Faculty Fellow at the Shingo Institute and hands-on implementer. She began her lifelong work in visual thinking as the head of training and development at Productivity Inc. There she worked closely with Dr. Ryuji Fukuda on adapting Sumitomo's CEDAC® process for western companies, implementing it extensively. She also developed a series of poka-yoke courses for the West at Dr. Shigeo Shingo's personal request. He was her sensei until his passing in 1990. Galsworth was also principal developer and implementer of visual factory, TEIAN (associate-based suggestion systems), and the X-Type Matrix when Dr. Fukuda first introduced it to North America and Europe.

A former Baldrige and Shingo Prize Examiner, Dr. Galsworth is author of seven books, including *Work That Makes Sense: Operator-Led Visuality* and *Visual Workplace-Visual Thinking*, both recipients of the prestigious Shingo Prize. Her books are available on her website and Amazon.

When not onsite or online with clients, or teaching at the Institute, Gwendolyn can be found hiking or working on her next book. She can be reached through the VTI website, *www.visualworkplace.com,* where you can also find hundreds of her podcasts and articles.

Acknowledgements

This is a book for and about value-add associates—you. I had waited nearly twenty years to write the first edition which was published in 2011, and another ten years for this, the 2022 second edition. I could not have written it sooner because I did not know enough about visuality, about the workplace, or about you. Now I do. This book is my gift of thanks to you. Any of its errors are my own and no reflection on those thanks. After more than thirty years of working with you, side by side, sharing what I know, learning what you shared, I can only say it has been magical and rewarding beyond measure. I hope the pages of this book capture some of my respect and affection for you, and my abiding gratitude.

All in all, I feel the luckiest of people. I work in a field I love. Besides encountering brilliant visual thinkers everywhere I go, there are people in my life who are willing to help me with that work.

First among equals: Aurelia Navarro, my esteemed editor. Aurelia has the skills and judgment in her field that allow me to excel in mine. One could want no more from an editor. Except that she is also a friend who supports my work as though it were her own. If I thought Aurelia's mettle had been tested on my previous books, this one, *Work That Makes Sense*, set a new definition of "against all odds." The details shall remain quiet. Let me simply say: Aurelia, without you, this book would never ever have happened. Thank you.

Second: Brook Kirklin, the masterful book designer of this book's first edition; and Iwan Sujono of eOne Design in Sydney, Australia, the expert adapter of this, the book's second edition.

To you who allowed me to enter your companies and assist on your journey to workplace visuality, thank you. Your vision got me started. Your resolve held things fast when the improvement road got bumpy as it seems to always. But it was your willingness to learn and use a new paradigm on your journey to excellence—workplace visuality—for which I am enduringly grateful. You are the pioneers.

My heartfelt thanks in particular to:

Pratt & Whitney and **Hamilton Standard** (Connecticut): Clark Shea, Al Lapa, John Christian, Tom Dancy, Mike Feltrin, John Ghann, Al Lapa, Stanley Mickens, Richard Scorzafava, Gordie, Tom Cormier, Cynthia Matroni, Theresa Paul, Brad Slater, John ("Yago") Yacavone, Howard Ferrara, Ed Brey, and so many others on Pratt & Whitney and Hamilton Standard Teams.

United Electric Controls (Massachusetts): David Reis, Harvey Chambers, Paul Plant, Bob Rando, Fred Ritzaw, Lee Sacco, Bruce Hamilton, Annie Yu, Maureen Hamilton, Pat Wardwell, Bill Antunes, John Pacheco, Luis Catatao, Michael Holmes, Beverly Scibilia, Mildred Williams, Randy Campbell, Cindy Barter, Ellen Brill, Randy Brown, Maria Helena Cabral, Randy Campbell, Theresa Carroll, Carlos Chaves, Bob Comeau, Mike Contardo, Tony Cruz, Maureen DiRusso, George Farraher, Dan Fleming, Krikor Frounjian, Shahag Hagopian, Vee Hagopian, Joan Hurton, Pam King, Doug Kuntz, Jesse MacArthur, Debbie Martin, Frank McKenna, Andrea Minasian, Mary Rose Mix, Manny Monteiro, Judy Moon, Ryta Mullen, Cheryl O'Connell, Lilia Orozco, Janet Prescott, Regina Santos, Manny Sousa, Kelly Tonner, Steve Torres, Hieu Tran, Michael Vailliant, Glen Whittaker, Arthur Barter, Levon Khatchadourian, Joe LePage, Aram Minassiam, Berg Narjian, John Mondello, Fernando Rego, Ed Velosa, Gerry Yuskauskas, Guy Alger, Cindy Allen, Gladys Appleby, Frank Barter, Tom Brennan, John Burke, Bill Colby, Chris Cronin, Judy DeMartin, Mark DeNovellis, Jodie Glennon, Diana Hajain, Don Holm, Chris Jaffier, Don Jones, Joe Lyons, John Machado, George McGary, Al Nashawaty, Charlie O'Hearn, Manny Pereira, Janet Raposo, Bob Sanders, Jim Silva, Joe Silva, Joan Sampson, Dave Smith, Terry Sousa, Bud Tucker, Dave Vaughan, Allan Waugh, Dave Williams, Pat Woods, and so many others on the UE Team.

Fleet Engineers and sister company, **Lee Industries** (Michigan): Wes Eklund, Brett Balkema, Tim Olt, Kenny Cain, Laura Dewald, Steven Hascher, Dan Herzhaft, Craig Tobey, Dennis Johnson, Larry Kaufman, Gary Buys, Roscoe Clark, Greg Hancock, Al Stone, Jeff Hamm, Robert Oldaker, Garry Boos, Mark DeWitt, Roger Stalzer, Stefanie Bennett, Bruce Boos, Cindy Boos, Harold Coleman, Patti Falbe, Mike Hart, Diane Schmiedknecht, Terry Verhulst, and so many others on the Fleet/Lee Industries Team.

Denison Hydraulics (now Parker Denison/Ohio): Ken Theiss, Joseph Linehan, Steve Harvey, Bill Cornell, Paul Baker, Larry Moore, Rick Ell, Dorothy Wall, Sheila Bowersmith, Michael Church, Ron and Judy Lake, Dave Dobbins, James Justice, Mel Foreman, Mark Bell, and so many others on the DH Team.

Royal Nooteboom Trailers (Holland): Henk Nooteboom, Marc De Leeuw, Roy Kuipers, Frits Foekens, Frank Bogels, Max Janssen, Kees Smeeman, Coby Herman, Henk Hop, Victor Geertruida, Jan Peters, and so many others on the RNT Team. **Lifetime Products** (Utah): Richard Hendrickson, Brent Allen, Cliff Holstein, Lance Bosgieter, Jared Steele, Sandy Turbyfill, and so many others on the Lifetime Team.

Alpha Industries (now Skyworks/Massachusetts): George Levan, Ken Bushmich, Annie Yu, Ellen Babson, George Cassello, Russ McGibbon, Earl Scranton, Sau Tran, Bernice Pereira, and so many others. **Curtis Screw** (New York): Carl Falletta, Bruce Kilbin, Dave Stanley, Kent Young, and so many others. **Greene Rubber** (Massachusetts): Patricia Broderick, Eladios Cruz, Ed Davis, Janine DeGusto, Carlos Gomes, Sheila Morton, Daniel Rossetti, and so many others on the Greene Rubber Team.

Parker Hannifin (California): Curt Williams, Matt Furlan, Troy Gerard, and so many others. **Lockheed Martin** (Texas): Larry Pike, Mark Swisher, Michael Joyce, Marty Harnish, Margie Herrara, John Casey, Robert Boykin, and so many others. **Rolls-Royce Aerospace** (global): Peter Dobbs and Stephen Pollard. **Plymouth Tube** (USA): Rick Keller, Donald Van Pelt, Jr., and so many others on the PT Team. **Harris Corporation** (Illinois): John Saathoff, Sue Osier, Janet Jones, Carolyn Rabe, Pat Humke, Deanna Butler, Beverly Sparks, Janet Jones, Carolyn Rabe, Buzz Harlan, Melody Sparrow, Larry Penn, Dewayne Bullock, Lynn Vollmer, and so many others on the Harris Team. **Delphi Automotive** (Indiana): Jim Luckman, Jerry Hall, Junior Oliver, Francis Davis, and so many others on the Delphi Team. **Scania Trucks** (Holland): Lars Stenqvist, Henk Heijden, and others on the Scania Team.

Trailmobile/Canada: Tom Wiseman, April Love, and so many others. **Seton Name Plate** (Connecticut): Beverly Nichols, Richard Mini, Joyce Clark, John Barrett, David Martin, and so many others. **Hitchcock Industries** (Minnesota): Ronn Page, Carleton Hitchcock, Jonathan Hitchcock, Mike Suchy, Melanie Haggard, Tim Auelt, Wes Gustafson, Ron Halliday, Adam Koronka, Mike Robbins, Ken Trottier, Troy Zuelzke, and so many others. **Delphi** (Mexico): Armando Botti, Socorro Garza, Florencia Martinez, Mark Brown, and so many others. **Sears Parts & Repair Services** (California): Angie Alvarado, Frank Lopuzinski, Georgeann Georges, Marv Thaxton, and so many others. **Schlumberger** (Kansas): Barry Landon, Mark Metzger, Joseph Wilson, and so many others. **Wilson Transformer** (Australia): Jon Retford, Steve Damm, Mauro Stefani, and so many others. **Vibco Vibrator** (Rhode Island): Karl Wadensten, Linda Kleineberg, Susan Heater, Lucy Manley, and so many others on the Vibco Team.

Friends in the business world who helped along the way: Shigeo Shingo, Ryuji Fukuda, Sherrie Ford, Martin Hinckley, Richard Schonberger, Jeff Madsen, Don Guild, Chris Rutter, David Visco, Tony Manos, Anne Marie Chester, Robert Miller, Joy Brisighella, Irek Bilinski, Izabela Starnawska, Mary Price, Ken Snyder, Ross Robson, Jake Raymer, Shaun Barker, Brad and Emily Jeavons, John Kim, Brenton Leitch and Gaye Parsons, Keith Hornberger, Paul Harbath, Michel Greif, Annie Yu, Steve Reed, Paul Olsen, Don Dewar, Phil McCready, Oscar Roche, Ben Chopping, Colette Choryan, Karen Toland, Sarah Howe, Jon Tudor, Brian Levitan, Norman Bodek, Don Fitch, Joe Rizzo, Louis Stephenson, Jeff and Sue Naylor, Tricia Moody, Marley Lunt, Malcolm Jones, Cherie Collins, Elaine Thorndike, Aleta Sherman, Lavon Winkler, Todd Allen, Cynthia Christie, John Croft, Alice Lee, Michel Baudin, Miguel Aguilar, Jorge Falcon, Liz Garibay, Anya Sauceda, Luis Gasca, and Claude Kennedy.

David Whyte, poet and author, whose early encouragement led me to find my own voice and speak it. He is also the source of the image: Far too many of us leave the better part of ourselves in our cars when we go to work, with the window slightly cracked so we can reclaim it at the end of the day.

Jeanne Walters, Rhonda Kovera, and Carol Shaw for their trust and support.

The Visual Thinking Team: Robert Nava, Eva Camilo, Victoria Adong, Cindy Lyndin, Horatio Fairburn, Georgia Spence, Leslie Carver, Harald Hope, Jill Pruett, Linda Faes, and Merlin the Cat and his friend Regan.

Personal friends who care and cared for me: Kathryn and Andrew Kimball, Mataare, Jacqueline and Robert Miessen, Dawn Bothie, Barbara Paster, Mary Lenetti-Donini, Debaura Shantzek, Rosemary Tomkinson, Rania James, Jan Caviness, Sara Kane, Marcy Roban, Judy Barry, Sarah Sporn, Diana Brynes, Diana Asay, Pamela Thomas, Marilynn Considine, Carolyn Perry, Annette Mason, Sharon Ward, Janabai Raymundo, Clifflyn Bromling, Tonya Bednarick, Camilla England, Sally Schwager, Dr. Wei Li, and John Clegg.

My remarkable teacher, Swami Chetanananda, with a lifetime of gratitude.

My family, for all that you are to me: Gary Galsworth, Robert Weigler, Ondine Galsworth and Forrest Boone Brewster, Daniel Galsworth, Roberta Spivak, Martha Millwood and Jessica and Julianne, Stacy Joyce, and Karen Cathcart—and to my splendid parents, Geraldine, George, and Donato.

Philip Hylos, Edmund Noch, Samuel Bear, and Anderson Merlin for their wildly creative participation in my life and the flawless, unwavering guidance of their hearts. It is your song I sing.

Gwendolyn Galsworth
2022

Introduction | Second Edition

Work That Makes Sense (WTMS) is a book—an implementation manual—on operator-led visuality. It asks and answers the central question of the people revolution launched in the 1980s when western companies first encountered the so-called *Japanese Miracle*: How much will your value-add associates contribute if you let them. How far will they go to help you improve the company if you teach them?

Since this book's publication in 2011, there has been a resoundingly positive response from hundreds of companies that have read these pages and put the WTMS methodology to diligent use. The same response, only louder, has come from companies that combined this book with the online training system that puts WTMS methods, values, concepts, practices, and principles on their feet, fully narrated, across 15 instructional modules. And all this has been echoed dozens more times by myself and our team of WTMS affiliates who facilitate so many client implementations of operator-led visuality.

Most companies in the world have grown accustomed to the concept that hourly employees can help the enterprise meet its goals by ... following standard operating procedures, learning to not make mistakes, participating in lean and 6 Sigma blitzes, and coming up with imaginative inventions (sometimes in two seconds) that everyone finds thrilling.

Many operators who make such contributions are, on their part, also thrilled—thrilled by their own ingenuity and by the appreciation and recognition they receive. Sometimes there is also a monetary reward. But as decades of research show, monetary reward is far down the list of motivators, if on the list at all.

Impressive though these contribution are, I say—with over 30 years of hands-on experience in the field—that you can ask a great deal more of your operators. They can not only give more, they want to.

From early on, I saw that it was not enough to simply provide hourly associates with a little extra time to be inventive in, or with an occasional spot on a blitz team—often welcomed time off from the otherwise dreary drudge of their actual day-to-day work. It was also not enough to merely hold brainstorming sessions and capitalize on those frontline employees with imaginations rich enough to conceive of breakthrough ideas that received headline press in the monthly newsletter.

The challenge—the requirement—is to provide all employees, especially on the frontline, with tools that exercise, train, develop, and refine minds to think, assess, and create relevant solutions to the problems encountered in the daily life of the company. *Everyone/Every Day* is only a slogan if the company does not also: 1) pro-actively teach new competencies of thinking to that same "everyone;" and 2) provide structures of emotional intelligence to support the growing of these competencies so they are sustained and sustainable.

This is what WTMS is and does.

WTMS takes the possibility of operator contribution seriously enough to include an improvement time quota, by policy, in its implementation framework so that more than "two seconds" are provided for associates to develop improvements that not only change the work process and dramatically improve quality and on-time delivery but often also save limbs and lives.

WTMS teaches associates a process called *visual thinking,* with a built-in measure that provides value-add associates with immediate feedback on the power and effectiveness of each of their visual inventions. The measure is called *motion.* Motion is caused by missing information—the enemy is invisible. Using motion as their metric, hourly employees can assess for themselves if their visual solutions need to go further—or work to spec as is. Ideas without a metric are only a hope. With a metric, they become practical and progressive. They can be iterated. In a WTMS workplace, your employees become scientists of motion and engineers of their own work. In such a company, work and improvement are the same thing. This edition's new chapter, "Results: People and the Bottom Line," provides ample evidence.

In the decade since the first edition of WTMS, there has been a great deal of discussion around the principle of *respect for every individual* as a gauge for assessing a company's work culture—a real-time function and reflection of our emotional intelligence and that of the company in which we work.

For the most part, that respect principle has been attached to a split between respect-we-are-owed (because we are a member of the human race) on the one side—and, on the other, respect-we-earn (because from time to time we achieve something of worth that others recognize). But respect is not a simple binary principle. The above differentiation barely scratches the surface of respect's true meaning, overlooking as it does the respect that already resides at our core that is neither earned nor owed.

The respect to which I refer is a deep and abiding yearning in each of us to contribute—the inborn longing to share, the innate hunger to create something of value, not just in our everyday lives but also at work. For many of us, especially at work.

Deep in the mystery of our childhood—and then of our adolescent heart—was a profound belief that whatever "I" turned out to be, "I will be excellent at it. I will shine. I will make something of my life. I will be its hero!"

Listen closely and you will hear that same conviction whispering inside each person who goes to work for the first time, holding fast to the belief that people will respect them for their willingness and for the potential they already know they possess. They might not get "respect" at home where so many problems wear them down. But they are convinced they will find it at their new job where everything is fresh and possible—where there is a real chance to do and to contribute.

Too often, however, that hope-filled quest gets squelched by the very work newcomers are assigned, dimming over the years until it is barely detectable. But it never disappears completely. There is a hero within each of us who wants to create, master, excel, share, and contribute. We want this not for recognition but simply because that is who we are.

Horses are magnificent creatures. Racehorses win races. If you asked the crew responsible for caring for them to tell you *why* they think horses race, they will—to a person—say the same thing: Horses race for themselves. They win because they love to win. No prize spurs them on. No whip.

My father loved horses. They were a part of my growing up. But it wasn't until a highly experienced horse trainer said the following to me that I began to finally understand that *why*. "Gwendolyn," he said, "Horses race to feel the wind in their mane. They race for the long stretch of their stride. For the feeling of strength and power. They race because they are sovereign. That is simply who they are."

I developed the WTMS methodology after I spent the 1980s failing at traditional 5S and the 1990s changing it. My evolving approach became a 5S hybrid when I added "select locations" ahead of "set locations." This inclusion made the telling difference because it added *thinking* to 5S. Value-add associates now had to assess, judge, and decide where the things of the workplace ought to be located—instead of merely framing them in paint or tape where they had always been parked. *Smart Placement* was born. Along the way, I also made surprising discoveries about why value-add associates would—or *would not*—engage in improvement activity.

During this same period, Todd Allen, a wonderful business friend of mine who knew and liked my work, phoned. I was surprised when he asked if I could put together a process that would teach operators how to get orderly *and* visual but that did not use the term "5S." I was more than curious. Why Todd? What's the allergy to 5S? "Frankly," he said, "Most of my current clients have been so disappointed in 5S that they have forbidden me to use the term at all. Operators are disappointed too."

I understood. At its roots, 5S is a compliance mechanism. That is why 5S is so often and comfortably linked to audits. Companies in Japan use other programs for employee growth and engagement: Kata, Teian, Quality Circles, and so on. Though some non-Japanese companies implemented 5S to their satisfaction, there were still many western managers who did not recognize 5S's non-developmental nature. Operators, on the other hand, did. Operators wanted to contribute more to their companies than compliance.

Todd's request rang true and launched me on a design pathway that resulted in a highly visual methodology that gave operators not just ways to create and own improvement solutions—but also ways to invent new outcomes and re-invent themselves. Its name was *Work That Makes Sense,* the process by which operators became improvement *contributors*—visual thinkers.

This book is not a management overview of the logic and application of visual technologies. I have written other books on that important topic, with several more to come. This book is an implementation manual for operators, for people who work on the line in direct interface with customers or materials or both. They work on what is called the *value-add level*.

It is a book that speaks to, honors, and supports the vision, knowledge, skill, resolve, imagination, and intelligence of the people on the value-add level of the enterprise—whether factory, bank, military depot, hospital, or open-pit mine. It is written in the voice of "you and I" that allows me to speak directly, in conversation with hourly employees. Many times as I wrote the first edition a decade ago, and this past year as I prepared this second edition, *I felt as much as heard the exchange*. It was a palpable and deeply moving experience.

Yes, at the core of each of us is a deep and abiding need to contribute—a longing to share, to create something of value, and to improve our lives and the lives of others. Not just in our everyday life but also at work—in fact, especially at work. That understanding is the reason for and purpose of this book on operator-led visuality.

There is a hero within who wants to master, excel, and contribute. That hero is us.

At the start, at the end, and at all points along the way, I hope you find this book useful to your purposes and inspiring to your mind and heart and actions. Let the workplace speak.

Gwendolyn D. Galsworth
Visual Thinking Inc.
2022

Visual Workplace Basics

Many people believe they know what a visual workplace is—yet it is so much more than is commonly understood. In a thriving visual workplace, one of the greatest benefits is work that makes sense.

In this first book section, we enlist the support of your company's management and recognize the expertise you already bring to your work. Then you get an overview of visuality, including basic definitions and principles, and the *Ten Doorway Model*. We show you how visual devices translate vital information into exact behavior—your own or other people's.

Then you learn about eight elements—or building blocks of visual thinking—on which a visual workplace is built. The first is *I-driven*, a principle you will find throughout this book that affirms that what *you* do, think, say, feel, and create matters—a lot. We return again and again to these eight elements as the visual learning and applications continue.

Next you learn the basics of getting ready to launch a visual conversion in your own area of work. Likewise, your supervisors and managers start to learn about Leadership Tasks they must undertake to ensure your efforts are well-supported as you create dazzling visual inventions in your area.

As part of this, you learn about five hands-on tools for achieving three main outcomes: achieving a visual showcase, producing measurable bottom-line results, and adopting an ongoing attitude of learning. Let's begin.

Chapter | One

Introduction to The Visual Workplace

A Word at the Start to Managers

This is a book for operators. Your company may use a different word: value-add associates, hourly employees, line workers, or simply employees who convert materials or deliver services. Whatever the name, I wrote this book for them.

How many times have you heard company managers—even yourself—proclaim that *people* are your organization's most valuable resource? That employees on the value-add level are the experts of their work, and that they must be allowed—empowered—to organize their own work and work area to better suit their needs and the needs of high performance? This, you were told, is the doorway to a spirited, engaged, and aligned workforce—and to the empowerment indispensable to enterprise excellence.

But what does this really mean? How does a company create an empowered workforce while strengthening the bottom line?

This book provides the answers, telling you both the what and the how: what true empowerment is and how the organization achieves it. But in this book I discuss these over-arching concepts with two important differences. First, I discuss them as part and parcel of a visual workplace. Second, I discuss them directly with your value-add workforce, the people you say you want to empower or empower more. Whether you refer to these hardworking, inventive individuals as associates, technicians, operators, hourly employees, touch labor or workers, they are in the words of Rolls-Royce: *experts*.

Every great change requires three things: inspiration (a vision of the horizon), a vehicle (the means for getting there), and a pathway (the map or method to get to the destination). These three elements are described in this book in the context of workplace visuality. In more than 35 years of hands-on implementation and research, I have never found a more dynamic, creative, and reliable process for operator-led visual conversions than the *Work That Makes Sense* (WTMS) methodology discussed in this book.

What does that conversion look like? Work areas aglow and alive with the tangible intelligence that visual devices provide when they are inventive by value-add associates who have learned to embed the operational details of their performance into the living landscape of their work. That landscape speaks.

This is the subject of this book; and it is addressed to your value-add employees. These eager and intelligent contributors will find an abundant array of visual workplace concepts, principles, tools, methods, encouragement, teaching, and examples in these pages. And they will use them successfully *only if* ….

The *only if* belongs to you, managers, executives, and supervisors. Success will happen:

- *Only if* you become an active part of the WTMS process;
- *Only if* you provide value-add employees with the WTMS training and supplies they need—along with enough quiet place for them to think and experiment—in order to convert their own work areas to the high level of operational functionality that WTMS is designed to achieve;
- *Only if* you designate time for visual improvement that is separate from time for production in order that a visual conversion can realistically happen in the face of pressing production demands;
- *Only if* you demonstrate your commitment by actively supporting these actions, releasing needed resources, and encouraging people in these tasks;
- *Only then* can you look forward to a workplace that speaks with the relevance, timeliness, precision, and tangible completeness that the language of visuality and the WTMS method can provide.

These *only ifs* are the reason you are the first person I address as this book begins. You are essential to the success of the WTMS process and to the return on the investment you made when you purchased this book. As you and I both know, that investment is one of money and hope. Throughout this book you will find blue panels of notes that are designed to guide your thinking and actions—your thinking as a leader and your actions of commitment and engagement. I encourage you to read and consider all those blue panels and do your best to practice and apply them.

Which brings us to the final *only if*.

You will learn how to become the ally of the change that you say you want *only if* you read and absorb this book from cover to cover. Do not just scan it. Whether you are an executive, supervisor, or manager, *your involvement is indispensable to the success* that the WTMS process is designed to deliver. Here is the anchor point of that: Your knowing and sustained support of the release and empowerment of the human will that is resident in the people who work where value gets added in your enterprise. The human will is the *power* in em*power*ment. Only with the transformation of their role from doers to thinkers to implementers will you gain the stability, growth, and prosperity you long for and require. That is the transformation that can happen *only if* you actively and knowingly advocate for and support it.

A Word at the Start to Value-Add Associates

The *Work That Makes Sense* method described in this book is specifically designed to help you reduce struggle and gain control over your work and the outcomes your work is meant to produce. I like to say it like this: WTMS is designed to give you a sense of control over your corner of the world.

Since your managers and supervisors are partners in this process, there are blue panels of notes for them throughout the book. But you are the reason this book was written. You are the hero of its pages.

In them, you are invited to consider a new way of seeing—and a new way of solving. I call that new way *visual thinking*. The destination is called a visual workplace ... a workplace that speaks.

In a visual work environment, you and your colleagues will find what you need when you need it, know correct quantities and mixes at a glance, meet every deadline on-time, and perform complex tasks with precision and confidence—because you have designed it way. You have made your work visual.

At its core, workplace visuality is a language: the language of excellence embedded into the living, physical landscape of work. Because it is a language, it will gain popularity, common usage, and power as more and more people in your company begin to "speak" it. I hope it will become your language too.

Fellow traveler on this wondrous journey, let's get started!

You are the Expert

You are an expert at what you do. You know your job. Whether that job is in a bank, lumber mill, medical facility, military depot, processing plant for food or chemicals, restaurant, oil field, engineering or marketing office, retail outlet or automobile factory—you are good at what you do, whatever you do and wherever you do it.

Yet that does not mean that everything at your work always happens as expected or according to plan. Not everything is always perfect—not in your company or, for that matter, almost any other company; and not everything is perfect in your work area, not yet.

Generally speaking, knowing your job means you know *what is supposed to happen*. And on most days it does. But there are other days when it just does not. In fact, sometimes what is *not supposed to happen* happens for so many days in a row that work seems more like trouble than a job you know well—a struggle instead of a flow. On days like that, work can begin to seem like some kind of insanity. It just does not make sense.

Oh sure, there are reasons for that—and you know them. If someone were to ask you, you could list plenty of them. In fact, on some level, all the reasons that things go wrong are right. That is not gibberish. It is just a way of saying: You are right about knowing what causes most problems in your area. To which you might say, half-jokingly ... *at least I am right about something!*

The fact is you are not only an expert at the work you were hired to do. You have also become expert at spotting the problems that keep you from that work.

The real question is: What to do about those problems? Will you become skilled at endlessly solving those same problems? Or will you become an expert at eliminating them—not just during your shift but permanently?

This is a book about finding those answers and building them into the very process of your work. In that way, the work itself tells you when you are right, when you are wrong—or on your way into or out of either. The workplace learns to speak. You turn it into a visual workplace—and you are about to learn how.

- How to convert an information-starved workplace, step-by-step, into one that is information-rich.
- How to take the struggle out of your work day and put sense back in through visual information sharing.
- How a robust set of principles, concepts, terms, and methods can help you identify problems at your work that are caused by missing information.
- How to minimize or even eliminate problems completely through solutions that are visual.
- How to use a set of hands-on implementation tools so you and others can create visual solutions and put them actually into place in your work area.
- How to use the natural power of the mind to identify the need for visuality and meet that need.
- How to create work that makes sense by designing a workplace that talks to you in a precise, accurate, complete, and practical language—a language you understand because it is your own language, your own visual language—and that visual language will make sense.

In short, you will become a *visual thinker*.

What is a Visual Workplace?

We start by defining a visual workplace. A visual workplace is:

A work environment that is self-ordering, self-explaining, self-regulating, and self-improving—where what is supposed to happen does happen, on time, every time, day or night because of visual devices.

If you remove the last four words—*because of visual devices*—you remove the engine that drives that definition and its outcome too. Without visual devices, the outcome of *on time, every time, day or night* becomes impossible. Why? Because it is visual devices in the workplace that ensure that what is *supposed* to happen *does* happen. That is their primary purpose.

Here is the definition of a visual device:

A visual device is a mechanism or thing that is intentionally designed to influence, guide, direct, limit, or even guarantee our behavior by making vital information available as close to the point-of-use as possible to anyone and everyone who needs it, without speaking a word.

Photo 1.1 In the early days, gas was pumped out of a tank into a glass cylinder that sat on top of a metal column, as shown here. The glass allowed the buyer to see if the gas was dirty (a big problem at that time). It also allowed the seller to see the gas level. When the seller put the hose in the car, gas flowed down into the car by gravity. Marks etched on the glass cylinder showed the seller and buyer exactly how much gas had been bought.

Photo 1.2 The modern gas pump is so highly visual that, with a little help from you, it easily substitutes for the gas attendant and the cashier.

Photos 1.1 and 1.2. show us an old-time gas pump and a modern one. Early on, visual information sharing was almost absent. Then as the technology became more complex and the number of people needing gas soared, the need for visual devices also increased. The modern day gas station is flooded with visual devices that make it possible for even the most untrained driver to complete the transaction of *gas-for-money* safely, precisely, and with no supervision. Just try to get the kind of gas you need in the right quantity without the help of visual devices and mini-systems. Impossible!

Consider the car itself (Photo 1.3). Examine it closely. Look inside the car where the driver sits, under the hood, under the chassis, and in the trunk, and you will find no less than 144 visual devices that help you drive the car, maintain it, and, when it breaks down, repair it or pay

Photo 1.3 The car is a visual machine.

someone to do it for you. Over 110 million cars and trucks use U.S. roads and highways every day and all of them are *Visual Machines*®.

Visual devices make roads and highways safe and practical for us, our family, and our friends. For bus, taxi, and truck drivers everywhere, these devices form a vital part of their workday. Visuality on our roads and highways create as a gigantic adherence mechanism, providing a common language of at-a-glance rules that makes our economy—and the prosperity that follows—possible. Why not also at work?

Look at the Photo Series 1.4 of roadway visual devices and appreciate the sanity and safety they bring to our everyday life. As you do, realize that these devices did not fall out of the sky. They did not happen by accident. They happened by design, intentionally. They were invented and then implemented.

Photo Series 1.4

As a visual thinker-in-the-making, do the following as you consider roadway devices. In your mind's eye, erase the visual devices from all the roadways on the planet. Now imagine the impact of that for our world. Imagine the problems, delays, accidents, insurance claims, heartache, and expense in an everyday world without visual devices when we drive. That is why they are important in the workplace too.

In the language of visuality, there is a single word for these headaches: *motion. Motion* is defined as *moving without working.* Motion is footprint of the enemy. The enemy itself is missing information—information deficits. You may be familiar with the term *waste*—well, motion is like that, only much more specific, as you will soon learn.

The Translation of Information into Behavior

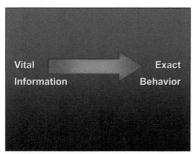

Figure 1.1 The crucial formula for all work in every company.

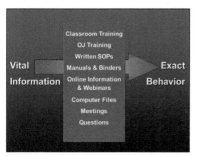

Figure 1.2 Management believes these tactics will reliably ensure exact behaviors; they cannot.

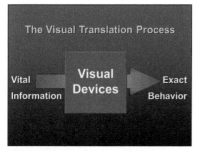

Figure 1.3 Visual devices reliably and repeatedly convert exact information into exact behavior.

The world of work shares a single basic transaction that is repeated millions of times a day: the translation of vital information into exact behavior—human or machine behavior (see formula in Figure 1.1).

But operationalizing this formula is not that simple. Workplace information changes quickly and often: schedules, customer requirements, engineering specifications, operational methods, tooling and fixture needs, material location, and the thousands of other details on which the daily life of the enterprise depends.

To share that information, most companies depend on classroom instruction and OJT (on-the-job training), meetings, coaching, binders of SOPs, reference manuals, online instruction, and more meetings—supported by lots of supervisors and managers who answer and ask many questions (Figure 1.2). These are indirect tactics for sharing critical information. Only a few of them work.

Still, the belief (and hope) is that once we get the right information, we will do the right thing, the right way, on time and safely. We want to believe that everyone will perform in keeping with that information and good things will result, namely perfect products delivered on time and perfect services presented with a smile. We assume, incorrectly, these indirect tactics result in exact behavior. They do not.

The truth is more like this—you begin your day determined to produce outstanding results. Then the unexpected happens. You grab the wrong material (or the wrong material is delivered and you did not know it). You make the wrong model (because you could not quite decipher the work order). You use the wrong tool (because the right one could not be found). You over-heat the part (because the gauge on the oven behind an I-beam); and so on and so forth. You intended to do the right thing—but the wrong thing happened.

What would it be like if the physical workplace itself could share that vital information instead of binders meetings, micro-supervision, questions, and so on? What would your work day be like if the floors, instead of just holding you up, actually helped you do your work, actively and precisely? What would it be like if the walls assisted you—as well as tools, tables, shelves, carts, materials, machines, and the other "things" in your work area? What if they became active partners in helping you reach your daily work outcomes—safety, quality, cost, delivery—day after day, week after week, year after year? What if they could share their vital information visually, without speaking a word?

This is exactly what happens when you create a visual workplace. When you populate the physical work area with visual devices, you make an active partner out of that area. You ensure that the complete, accurate, and precise information you need is available when and as you need it, as close to the point-of-use as possible. The workplace speaks.

Look at Figure 1.3. Visual devices become the translation point between vital information (your standards) and the exact behavior or outcome that information is supposed to produce. Instead of the indirect tactics described above, the physical workplace itself—these devices—influence, guide, direct, limit, or even guarantee that we do the right thing safely, precisely, completely, repeatedly, and reliably.

They transform your physical work area into a gigantic mechanism for adherence, with an impact that is equally gigantic. And it is also simple. You are free to do your work excellently well. This is precisely why you came to work in the first place: to master and execute excellence—to do ordinary things extraordinarily well.

Visual devices are the translation point between vital information and the exact behavior which that information is supposed to trigger. Your journey to a visual workplace begins and ends with them.

Visual Devices Are Everywhere

Visual devices are everywhere in the community, helping us do the right thing, on time and safely, without speaking a word. They guide, direct, and protect us so seamlessly that we barely even notice them. Yet they are powerfully a part of our daily life. Look at the terminal gate at a large metropolitan airport in the United States you see in Photo 1.5.

Notice the yellow marking (line) in the center; in the language of visuality, this is known as the *flow line* or *critical path*. See the black letters and numbers in the yellow cross bars at the end of that flow line (easier to see in Photo 1.6)? We call those: *addresses*. The white markings on the left of the flow line are called *borders* as are the red-hatched areas on each side. These are all visual devices—flow line, borders, and addresses. Together, they make up a visual mini-system: a system of visual devices, all aimed at a common outcome.

Photo 1.5

> *Question 1:* What is the purpose of the yellow bars at the end of the flow line? Why are they there?
>
> *Answer 1:* They hold the names of the plane types that use this gate: 727, DC-10, 757, 747, and 777. Each yellow bar indicates the exact spot the plane (by type) must stop its front wheel.
>
> *Question 2:* Why? Why is it important for each plane to stop with such precision?
>
> *Answer 2:* So that the jet way (the passenger bridge to the right) can quickly and easily connect with the plane's passenger door. Why? So passengers can leave the plane quickly and safely and get on with the reason that brought them to this airport in the first place—a flight connection, business in town, or Grandma's birthday party. That can happen with precision because of this visual system.

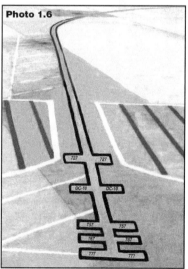

Photo 1.6

Other visual devices at this gate are: white hatch marks on lower left pinpointing the catering function, white hatch marks on upper left marks the spot for baggage handling, and red-hatched areas to the left and right warn us that nearby turbine blades may be rotating.

Let's Think

Think some more about what you see here. Think about how these devices function on the micro level and what their macro impact is. Here are three points.

1. The visual devices in this system enable the pilot and ground crew to have a "conversation." Sitting 20-30 feet above the tarmac with the nose of her plane blocking the view, the pilot cannot see her plane's address—the stop point (Photo 1.7). But the ground crew can; and they share that information with the pilot by means of another visual device: signal wands (Photo 1.8).

2. This splendid system of devices is built directly into the "floor" or tarmac and allows the two stakeholders—pilot and ground crew—to connect accurately and quickly so they can do the right thing for their customers, the passengers on the plane.

3. This visual mini-system does not just benefit pilot, crew, and customers—it also benefits the airline. Because passengers can get off the plane quickly and safely, another group can board just as smoothly; and the plane flies to a new destination. That is the way the airline—and the airport—make money. Nearby towns and cities benefit as well as the entire regional economy. Whether you are a pilot, are on the ground crew or work elsewhere in the airport, when planes take off and land safely and on-time, you get another dose of job security.

These important outcomes are anchored in the visual mini-system at this gate and the way it builds vital information directly into the process of work. That is the power of a visual workplace.

Photo Series 1.9 contains many airport-based visual solutions, including the large photo with a visual device similar to the one we just discussed—that yellow flow line now doubled. Once a workplace (in this case, an airport) learns how to speak visually (without saying a word), you can bet that visuality will spread and deepen. In this series, the examples show the tarmac, runways,

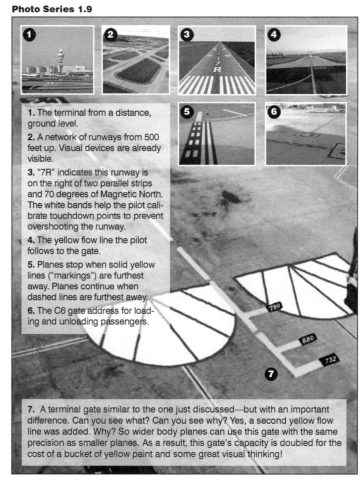

Photo Series 1.9

1. The terminal from a distance, ground level.

2. A network of runways from 500 feet up. Visual devices are already visible.

3. "7R" indicates this runway is on the right of two parallel strips and 70 degrees of Magnetic North. The white bands help the pilot calibrate touchdown points to prevent overshooting the runway.

4. The yellow flow line the pilot follows to the gate.

5. Planes stop when solid yellow lines ("markings") are furthest away. Planes continue when dashed lines are furthest away.

6. The C6 gate address for loading and unloading passengers.

7. A terminal gate similar to the one just discussed—but with an important difference. Can you see what? Can you see why? Yes, a second yellow flow line was added. Why? So wider body planes can use this gate with the same precision as smaller planes. As a result, this gate's capacity is doubled for the cost of a bucket of yellow paint and some great visual thinking!

and the airport terminal itself. They are all speaking the same visual language.

Next time you go to the airport (especially in a larger city), notice how visual devices help you from the moment you enter the airport property. The next time you fly, get a window seat and watch as the plane taxis. You will see lots of visual devices for pilots, ground crew, and support services (Photo 1.10). These devices work so seamlessly, we hardly notice them. We simply obey—we and the thousands of other people who use that airport daily. We do the right thing because it is so easy to know what it is.

Photo 1.10

Together, these devices create a level of operational excellence that would be impossible to achieve without them—everything and everyone functions to plan safely, accurately, precisely, completely, and on-time. What is true for the airport is true for so many community locations. If they are visual, they are almost certainly also safe, well-run, productive, and prospering. We live in a visual world because we are visual beings (and not the reverse). Keep your eyes open and you will see visual devices everywhere!

Before we look more closely at the pre-visual workplace, let's clear up a possible misunderstanding. The purpose of a visual device is to carry a message—vital information. But such a device can and often does use one of our five senses other than sight. Please read Inset 1.1 for more on this.

Inset 1.1. Visual versus Sensory Devices

Calling the devices you see in this book "*visual*" is a bit inaccurate. Why? Because such devices can use any or all of our five senses—not just our sense of sight—to share information and deliver the message. Take a look.

1. Sight. Our most frequently used sense is sight. We are visual beings therefore we live in a visual world. The highways are thick with road signs like the one you see here, telling us vital things.

2. Sound. The ringing phone delivers the message that someone wants to talk to us. In the workplace, beepers on trucks and forklifts warn us when they are backing up and may be heading our way.

3. Smell. Gas in its natural form is colorless, (nearly) odorless, and highly combustible. You cannot see it, can hardly smell it—and yet it can kill. In visuality we say: it carries no message, no warning. That is why a rotten-egg smell (sulphur) is intentionally added to gas—so we can remember to turn stove off or detect a leak before a fire or explosion. The smell became a "visual" device.

4. Taste. A toddler puts everything in her mouth, including that bottle of poison you forgot to throw out. After too many babies were harmed, a bad taste (and often smell) is now routinely added to send the message: "UGH! Don't drink me!" An opposite message is sent when cherry flavor is added to otherwise bad-tasting medicine. Our kiddos lap it up.

5. Touch. Small, raised bumps embedded in walkways (called "tactile paving") are commonly used on crosswalks and train platforms to alert

the visually-impaired of danger. The blind receive this message through the tips of their canes and/or through the soles of their shoes. The message is sent and received. Their behavior aligns.

The Pre-Visual Workplace

By now, you get it. An airport is a workplace and the visual devices we see there ensure that what is supposed to happen does happen. They ensure work that makes sense. So why not bring them into your own company, into your own work area, onto your own bench or desk?

Photo 1.11 A visually capable work area.

The vast system of visual devices that make our airports safe, productive, and profitable can do the same there, though the exact devices will differ because your operations differ.

To make sure you understand the power of visuality, let's use our imagination. Remove the visual devices you just studied from the airport gate (Photo 1.11). In your mind's eye, erase the yellow flow line, addresses, and white and red borders. What does that gate look like now? Probably like Photo 1.12. And what is the impact of that?

Photo 1.12 A recipe for motion.

Would it still be as safe to work at that gate? Would it be as productive? For you? For your customers? Would passengers still have a satisfying experience, safely and smoothly coming and going as their needs required? Would that huge white airplane you see in the upper left even be able to land at an airport where gate operations were not visual? What do you think?

Now ripple your mind out and remove all the visuals you saw in the airport photo album. Turn that airport into a pre-visual workplace—where there are no visual devices and zero visual information sharing. What would that mean? What would be the impact of that?

How many planes per day could land or take off safely in an airport that is not visual? Even if the government did not require such devices, would you risk flying in or out of that place without them? Would other people? Think about the consequences of an airport without visuality, and then the consequences for the community it supports.

Now apply that same logic to your own work area—the place where you spend 35-40 job hours a week (plus overtime). To what extent does that location speak to you—in a language that makes the meaning of that place and the work that goes on there clear, correct, precise, complete, and available at-a-glance? To what extent is your work area visual right now?

In today's world, information is the bedrock of our daily life, so much so that we hardly notice it until it is not there anymore. Easy access to information is vital to our way of life, and visuality is the main way we access it. Think again of our roads and highways. They are populated with visual devices that powerfully and precisely guide and direct us on our way. We barely notice them because they are so much a part of what we expect—what we have come to rely on—to help us do the right thing, and avoid the wrong thing. The result? We can get where we want to go, safely, and on-time.

Why Not At Work?

Why not bring the power of visuality to our banks, hospitals, factories, mines, military depots, engineering and marketing offices, retail stores, restaurants, utility plants, processing facilities, schools and universities, movie lots, and construction sites? Why not bring visuality to the entire world of work?

In a pre-visual workplace, we are forced to rely on words alone (whether written or spoken) to convey information and meaning. As a result, we stay busy reading, or talking and listening (they are called "meetings")—or talking too much and listening too little (also "meetings"). You know how that goes. Even when the information we need is in a report or binder—or, heaven help us, somewhere in a computer—it is never really close enough. It is not where we need it—at our fingertips, at the point of use.

If you ever spent an hour searching your computer for a file you worked on only yesterday, you know exactly what this means. The information is in there *somewhere*, but you cannot find it and so you cannot use it. And even if you do find it, you really only need part of it, not all 15 screens.

Photo 1.13

The pre-visual workplace is always hungry for information, starved for the information that is either there "somewhere" or not there at all. In either case, information is missing—details that can usually only be found in the mind or memory of someone else. But what if that colleague is out ill or just began a two-week vacation? What if he or she is at yet another meeting or just got promoted? What happens is: We are stuck. When all is said and done, the result of missing information is this: We cannot do our work ... not all of it ... or not yet ... or not exactly, completely, safely, or on-time (Photo 1.13).

I began this chapter by declaring you an expert at what you do. I know this is true and so do you. But in an information-starved work area—a pre-visual workplace—you will never get to show that to me, to you or to anyone else. Instead, you are going to do a lot of wandering around and asking questions—and a lot of listening to answers that are not really the answers you need. Or you just might decide to skip all that and guess—take a chance out of desperation or determination to get on with your day. Or you may decide to do nothing and simply stop and wait.

Yes, you are good at what you do—but in an information-hungry, pre-visual work area, chances are slim that you are going to get to do it.

Regardless of the type or size of your organization, information drives your day. If a single employee anywhere in the company cannot get the exact information he or she needs, when and as needed, the organization has a rip in it. Like an otherwise strong fishing net (Photo 1.14), the size and number of these rips—of these information deficits—will determine the level of struggle we will have to deal with.

Photo 1.14 Information deficits are like fish that escape from a torn fishing net. If fishermen do not fix their nets, they will lose a lot of fish.

The *Ten Doorways* we are about to discuss show that each of us can learn to minimize or even eliminate those deficits for ourselves and for others—no matter the organizational level and no matter the cause.

The Ten Doorways: Creating a Workforce of Visual Thinkers

This book is about how you, a value-add associate, can become a visual thinker and what that means to the enterprise. But that alone will not turn your company into a fully-functioning visual workplace. To become a robust visual work environment, your enterprise must engage everyone in making a visual contribution. Each employee must open a door that leads to higher and more complete levels of visual information sharing relative to their own work.

Everyone must become a visual thinker: you, your supervisor, your manager, the material handlers, executives, planners, schedulers, doctors and nurses, machinists, assemblers, engineers, buyers, marketing and sales staff—everyone. And when everyone inside your company is involved, it is time for your supply chain to get on board.

That is why I say there are ten doorways into a fully-functioning visual workplace, each one opened by a specific organizational level or group. I developed this ten-doorway framework (Figure 1.4) in order to show that each group participates—and has to participate—in creating a fully-functioning visual workplace and a workforce of visual thinkers. These doorways also tell us precisely which category of visual function (which visual method) each group is accountable for—which doorway each group owns.

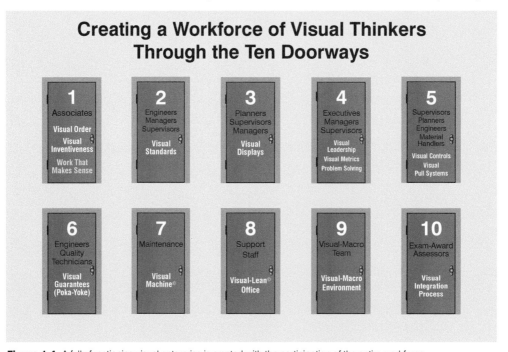

Figure 1.4 A fully-functioning visual enterprise is created with the participation of the entire workforce.

For example, engineers and supervisors own *Doorway 2: Visual Standards*. But that does not mean that you and other value-add associates are not allowed to create visual standards. You are allowed—and almost certainly will and should. It simply means that the company holds managers, engineers, and supervisors responsible for developing and distributing accurate, precise, and complete technical and procedural standards across the organization—and then making them visual.

As an area associate, you own *Doorway 1: Visual Order/Visual Inventiveness*, the subject of this book —*Work That Makes Sense*. But that does not mean that engineers and supervisors—and all other employees—are not expected to also implement visual order (the visual where) in their respective work locations. They are! And they definitely will as visuality picks up speed and focus in the enterprise. But your group will take the lead in operations—because, above and beyond everyone else, the visual where is critical to *your* work. You have an urgent need to know where the things of your daily work are.

The point is the ten doors we are about to scan are not restrictive or exclusive. Anyone in the company can contribute a visual solution for any doorway. But specific groups are held accountable for making sure that specific categories of visual function are implemented in the enterprise, no matter what.

Now let's take a short walk through each of the ten doorways.

Doorway 1 • Value-Add Associates • Visual Order/Visual Inventiveness/ Work That Makes Sense

The first doorway belongs to you. As a value-add expert, you focus first on installing the *visual where* in your area. Knowing precisely where things are, at-a-glance, removes a ton of struggle. The borders in Photo 1.15 make the exact placement of cable reels easy. The device in Photo 1.16 ensures that we will pick the right part. After the visual where, start inventing visual solutions to help work make more sense for yourself and others. In Photo 1.17, Pete, a welder, uses a magnetic tag to alert the forklift driver he needs a load of 1990s next. You will see hundreds of operator-level visual solutions in the chapters to come. Doorway 1 is the home of the *Work That Makes Sense* method.

Photo 1.15   **Photo 1.16**   **Photo 1.17**

Doorway 2 • Engineers, Managers & Supervisors • Visual Standards

Doorway 2 is about making the two types of operational standards visual: 1) technical standards (your product and process specifications), and 2) procedural standards (your work methods and SOPs). Supervisors, managers, and engineers own this doorway because they are responsible for providing accurate, precise, complete, and timely standards—and then, in a visual workplace, making them visual. Photo 1.18 is a visual standard showing the right and wrong way of taping an electrical wiring harness. Photo 1.19 shares the SOP for crushing a part.

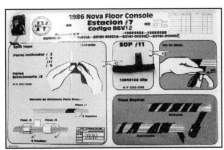
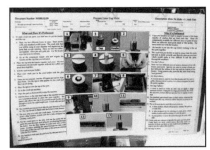

Photo 1.18   **Photo 1.19**

Doorway 3 • Planners, Supervisors & Managers • Visual Displays

In Doorway 3, supervisors, managers, and planners create visual displays (visual scheduling and production control boards) so they can track what needs to be done, in what quantity, by when, where, and by whom. There are as many formats for visual displays as there are needs for them. The display in Photo 1.20 tells us the release schedule for ECNs (Engineering Change Notices), with a spot for follow-up needs. Photo 1.21 is a maintenance display for all current work orders, arranged by what is completed (green), what is new (yellow), and what is overdue (red). We call this: "Telling the truth quickly—as that truth changes."

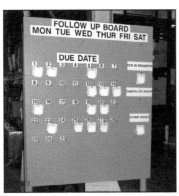

Photo 1.20

Photo 1.21

Doorway 4 • Executives, Managers & Supervisors • Visual Leadership + Visual Metrics + Visual Problem Solving

Company leaders are responsible for: 1) maintaining focus on the vision, mission, and goals of the enterprise, 2) driving towards them through measures (key performance indicators), and 3) solving problems permanently. Doorway 4 shows leaders how to make these happen visually. This threesome is visuality's response to the need for *hoshin* (Japanese for "compass") in every enterprise. Photo 1.22 shows the gap between our last best performance (100% on-time delivery) and today's (93%). Such metrics drive the company's annual plan, for example, using the X-Type Matrix (Photo 1.23). The matrix then gets translated into an Operations Roadmap for action on the value-add level (Photo 1.24).

Photo 1.22

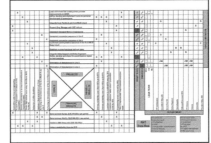

Photo 1.23

Photo 1.24

Doorway 5 • Supervisors, Planners, Engineers & Material Handlers • Visual Controls + Visual Pull Systems

Determining the order and flow of materials into your area is the role of planners, engineers, supervisors, and material handlers. They own Doorway 5. Their first task is material quantity, consumption, replenishment, and control. Photo 1.25 shows a red-line visual control that limits the box quantity this area to 18—a small, useful start.

The second task is to implement visual pull systems—creating pull by limiting quantity or volume. Photo 1.26 shows a 4-part kanban square that ensures there is always enough (and just enough) material to operate. "Don't worry," this device says, "you won't run out. But you also can't hoard material. We took away the room."

Photo 1.25

Photo 1.26

Doorway 6 • Engineers & Quality Technicians • Visual Guarantees

Engineers and your Quality Department are responsible for product and process quality. Doorway 6 focuses on the smartest, surest, quickest way for that to happen: visual guarantees (*poka-yoke* devices). First, your quality techs learn how to build 100% source inspection into the process of work; then they teach you how to do it. The result? You become masters of cause on the attribute level. No more mistakes.

Photo 1.27 is a masking template that prevents us from picking the wrong drill bit in final machining. The device in Photo 1.28 makes sure we assemble all 72 clips—because they are pre-counted and waiting for us on this board.

Photo 1.27

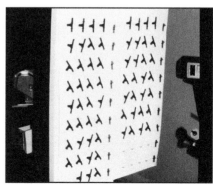

Photo 1.28

Doorway 7 • Maintenance Department • Visual Machine®

If production in your company relies on machinery, your Maintenance Department can stay very busy. In Doorway 7, Maintenance seeks your help in getting the machines to speak through visual devices. When machines become visual, everyone knows how to run and maintain them—at-a-glance. And when a visual machine needs a fix, we know it almost before the machine does. Plus, because the machine speaks, maintenance can make its repairs more quickly. The green in Photo 1.29 shows us, at-a-glance, the acceptable PSI range for this bladder gauge. The device in Photo 1.30 helps to make sure dull tools get sharpened and sharpened tools get returned—visually.

Photo 1.29

Photo 1.30

Doorway 8 • Support Staff • Visual-Lean® Office

Research shows that nearly 70% of all costs begin in company office and support areas. Doorway 8 helps office staff make their areas speak so they too can tell at-a-glance what is right, what is wrong, what is fast, what is slow—and how to make corrections. When pull is added to that equation, lean is added to visual. The result is the visual-lean office, a visual conversion that applies the first six Doorways, to office settings. In Photo 1.31 we see the visual where for hole-punch. David Zanardo, in purchasing (Photo 1.32), hangs his address over his desk that includes the products he is responsible for buying—so we know these vital details at-a-glance.

Photo 1.31

Photo 1.32

Doorway 9 • Visual-Macro Team • Visual-Macro Environment

9

Visual-Macro Team

Visual-Macro Environment

As work areas gather speed on the visual journey, the company forms a special team to coordinate visuality across the enterprise. That is Doorway 9 and your visual-macro team (Photos 1.33 and 1.34), comprised of ace visual thinkers who pay attention to the big picture. They identify the need for, and then create, visual linkages between departments, and pinpoint visual best practices-in-the-making. They take on cross-department projects. Thanks to them, visual information sharing deepens and a common visual improvement language grows within the company. Value-add associates—you!—also sit on this team. I hope you say *yes* when this opportunity comes along.

Photo 1.33

Photo 1.34

Doorway 10 • Exam-Award Assessors • Visual Integration Process

10

Exam-Award Assessors

Visual Integration Process

Doorway 10 houses the *Visual Integration Process*, a framework developed for companies well-advanced in visuality that want to make sure visual practices are tied together and continue to grow for maximum success. Doorway 10 examiners assess each area (Photo 1.35) using a set of audits, based on specific visual principles and practices (Photo 1.36). Assessor teams include master visual thinkers from all levels of the organization, including yours—value-add associates. Doorway 10 ensures that visual thinking and the visual transformation process grow and align across many sites.

Photo 1.35

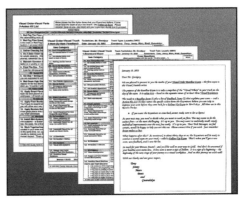

Photo 1.36

There they are, the Ten Doorways and how these doorways are used to create a workforce of visual thinkers in the enterprise, with each company function making powerful visual contributions to take the struggle and guessing out of their own work. The result is an enterprise populated by hundreds, even thousands, of visual solutions—not just on the production floor but equally in support offices, sales and marketing, the lobby, and the board room. Then, sooner or later, visuality jumps organizational boundaries into your company's supply chain.

Imagine what it would mean for your company to become a fully-functioning visual work environment—what that would mean for your internal and external customers, for the work that gets done in your company, and for the people who do it. Imagine what that would mean for you.

The Benefits of a Visual Workplace

As you are beginning to understand, a visual workplace is for everyone who works in your company because it is created by them. The benefits of this are many. Here are seven.

Benefit 1: Work Happens. When vital workplace information is wrong, incomplete, confusing, late, or simply missing ("information deficits"), problems occur, even chaos. But when that same information is clear, correct, precise, complete, on-time, and available at-a-glance, you—and the people around you—can get on with work. So the first benefit of creating a visual workplace is simply this: work happens.

Benefit 2: Sense of Safety. The second benefit of a visual workplace is that people learn they can depend on themselves for good outcomes—and they can depend on others as well. When the work environment is rich with vital information that you and everyone else can access at-a-glance, each person begins to feel a new sense of safety—safety in body, mind, and heart. We reach a new level of trust with our work environment and with the people who work there. In this way, visuality puts us powerfully in the driver's seat of our own work. And there's plenty of room on that bus for everyone.

Benefit 3: Visual Thinking. Third, when a problem arises due to missing information (information deficits), you and your colleagues are able to spot that right away and eliminate it quickly through visual solutions. In this way, you and those around you become scientists of your own work and masters of cause. You become visual thinkers.

Benefit 4: Partners with the Physical. The fourth benefit of workplace visuality happens because—through visual devices—you have made a partner out of the physical workplace (Photo 1.37). For example, you learn to expect more from the floor than simply its capacity to hold you up. You start to see the physical objects in your area in a new light—the desks, carts, benches, machines, tools, parts, shelves, cabinets, walls, and so on. Instead of "just things," you realize that each of these items can help you in your work if you give it a voice to speak—if you make it visual. This understanding deepens our appreciation and use of the inanimate things that populate our lives. They become partners.

Photo 1.37 Maryanne made a partner out of the top of her desk when she fixed her ounces-to-liters conversion chart directly on it, along with a sample materials label. (Seton Name Plate/Connecticut)

Benefit 5: Bottom Line. The results of the above are powerful improvements in product and process quality, lead time, safety, employee morale, on-time delivery, and cost. Visuality impacts measures and metrics—your key performance indicators (KPIs)—directly and significantly.

Make no mistake: When you share vital information visually, what is supposed to happen *does* happen. You and your entire work area perform better than ever, in ways that inspire others and go straight to the bottom line.

Here is a sample of actual Doorway 1 results from several companies already on the visual journey:

- 15%-30% increase in productivity
- 70% reduction in waiting
- 70% reduction in material handling
- 54% reduction in walking
- 96% improvement in quality

- 68% reduction in storage requirements
- $2,555,000 scrap reduction (annualized)
- 7,132 hours/machine downtime eliminated (annualized)
- 60% reduction in floor space requirements
- 100% elimination of rework

Pretty impressive—thanks to associates like you who learned to think visually. See Chapter 10 for more results.

Benefit 6: Companywide Alignment. Benefit six happens when visual solutions in your area get linked up with those in other areas. The organization becomes connected as though it were a human body. Like your own physical body, the company knows what is happening in all of its parts and can begin to function more holistically. When all work areas are visually connected, communication between them becomes smoother, more accurate, more precise, complete, and timely. Alignment follows. The enterprise knows—and can know—itself.

Look at Figure Series 1.5. Here you see an organization from the perspective of an individual (A) and a bunch of individuals (B). Clearly, while everyone is busy, there is no enterprise alignment—and without alignment there can be no empowerment. But an aligned and empowered workforce is perfectly evident in (C), with everyone engaged in working for common outcomes.

Benefit 7: Unity. The seventh benefit of workplace visuality is the big picture: visuality liberates information and, as a result, it liberates the human will.

When we take information out of our minds, filing cabinets, and computers—and install it, instead, into the physical workplace in the form of visual devices and mini-systems, we can move through our work day with confidence, skill, and flow. As we do, we contribute to our own well-being and the well-being of others. We feel powerful because we are powerful. A deep part of ourselves brightens and engages.

Figure Series 1.5

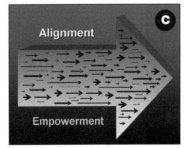

A. Here is a well-intentioned individual in a company without workplace visuality—pedaling in a direction she thinks is a good one for the organization.

B. Here is a bunch of well-intentioned individuals in a company without workplace visuality—each pedaling in a direction each thinks is a good one, many in opposite directions.

C. Here is the same company after implementing workplace visuality across many of the Ten Doorways, with an aligned and empowered workforce, pedaling in the same direction.

That part is called *our will.*

That *will*, which each of us has in equal measure, is the part that decides—decides to act or not to act, decides to improve or not to improve, decides to participate or not to participate. That *will* needs information to embrace its power. That is why the *will* often gets dusty, testy, or even distorted when information is scarce, wrong, incomplete, or too late. Stressed and confused, we lose touch with our true self—our true *will*—and begin to feel powerless to change, impact or improve our lives. In the face of that stress and confusion, some of us withdraw, become passive, and appear not to care. Others strike out, become aggressive and seem to care too much—in the opposite direction.

These two situations are not polar opposites. They are symptoms of the same problem: information deficits, missing information. Visual information sharing cures both—an antidote to a divided *will*. When we liberate information through visuality, we liberate the human *will*. Liberated, that *will*—our *will*—is free to decide ... to decide, for example, to support the corporate intent, to say yes to the company's vision, goals, and objectives. Or to elect not to. Either way, the decision is powerful and life-changing.

Saying yes means that we join in and align with what the company wants because we see there is good in it for us too. This is not giving up on our own vision; it is realizing that, in helping the company succeed, our own vision can be made more real. This is a moment of mighty agreement. It cannot happen if we do not feel safe in body, mind, and heart. It cannot happen in an information-scarce work environment.

Benefit seven is the result of adding all the previous benefits together. You get something that is both the result of and greater than that sum. You get unity—an organization so aligned, synchronized, and energized in its own excellence that it demonstrates the higher values of human endeavor—generosity, harmony, common purpose, shared destiny, a growing excellence, and a built-in flexibility that allows the enterprise to succeed beyond usual definitions. Prosperity in the fullest measure of that word blossoms.

Such a company becomes a touchstone and inspiration to other companies and to society at large, pointing the way to a new horizon of possibility. We learn from that kind of organization, even as it continues to learn and grow from the higher role it has embraced.

This may appear to be a grandiose claim in a simple book about workplace visuality. But it is not. It is a truth that many companies have repeatedly experienced. Not always in the fullness of that promise—of what is ultimately possible. But always with a promise that the next stage of excellence can emerge if the company keeps going, and the next stage after that, and the next and the next.

So you are invited to begin—to begin to learn about and apply the visual concepts, principles, tools, and methods presented in this book. This is an invitation to become a part of something greater by becoming greater yourself as you help that great thing happen: a fully-functioning visual workplace where what is supposed to happen does happen on time every time day or night—because of visual devices. Become a visual thinker.

> You miss 100 percent of
> the shots you don't take.
> Wayne Gretzky

Chapter | Two

The Building Blocks of Visual Thinking

There are two definitions fundamental to this chapter. You have seen the first before—the definition of a *Visual Workplace*:

> *A work area that is self-ordering, self-explaining, self-regulating, and self-improving ... where what is supposed to happen does happen on time every time, day or night—because of visual devices.*

The second is the definition of *visual thinking*:

> *Visual thinking is your ability to recognize motion (the footprint) and the information deficits that trigger it (the enemy)—and then to eliminate both through solutions that are visual.*

When you understand both terms and how they work together, you understand how to achieve a fully functioning visual workplace in your own area. To do that, you must first understand the *Eight Building Blocks of Visual Thinking* (Figure 2.1).

One Simple Reason: Too Many Questions

There is one simple reason why a visual workplace is needed: People have too many questions. Some of these questions are asked, but most of them are not. When people don't ask questions, they do one of three things: (1) they do nothing and just

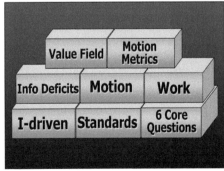

Figure 2.1 The Eight Building Blocks of Visual Thinking.

wait until the answer shows up, (2) they go hunting for the answer, or (3) they make stuff up and go with their own best guess. Sometimes that "stuff" works out. Many times it does not.

You may wonder why people don't just ask the questions they have. That answer lies in the mysteries of the human heart. Some of us don't ask questions because we don't want to appear ignorant or uninformed. Others don't ask because they know that nobody has the answer anyway—so why bother. Still others have *not* been told the truth in the past (intentionally or not), so they have learned not to trust the answers they are given. Still others of us don't ask:

- Because we've come to resent having to ask questions in the first place—especially the same questions over and over again—such as "What do I do next?" or "Where is the material for this job?" or "What are the specifications for this order?" Ordinary questions like these can rob us of our dignity if we have to ask them repeatedly.

- Because the person we must ask (who may also happen to be our boss) is, for example, half our age and brand-new to the company—whereas we have worked here twenty-three years—or twice our age. Our personal pride keeps us from asking.

These are not uncommon reasons for people to hesitate to ask questions; and there are undoubtedly other reasons. But when the above conditions combine, we might find ourselves faced with asking the same old questions, twenty times a day, of a person half our age who thinks his/her main job is to answer such questions. So we refuse to go after the very answers we need. Instead we get angry, go numb, do nothing, or—as mentioned—just make stuff up.

If we repeatedly cannot get plain, accurate, and complete answers to our questions, we may start asking other kinds of questions. Eyes skyward, we might ask, for example: "Is this what I am here for? This?! Chasing down tiny answers to the same old tiny questions I asked yesterday, and the day before that, and the day before that? Oh dear heaven, is this all that my life is about!"

For those less philosophically-inclined, the inner protest might sound more like: "What the heck is this? Chasing down the same stinkin' answers, day in and day out! I've had it! I'm outta here!"

Neither person may actually quit. We all have bills to pay and loved ones to support. Besides we may genuinely like our job and the company we work in—if only the struggle would stop, if only working here made more sense!

So we stay—or at least our hands and our feet do. But we may leave the better part of ourselves in the parking lot, in our car with the window slightly cracked so that part is still alive and waiting when the workday is over and we get in to drive home.

This is not what we signed up for when we agreed to this job. It is not how most of us want to earn our daily bread. Most of us want to earn our living in a meaningful way, doing our work, and expressing excellence. Faced with the insanity-of-tidbits, some of us go numb; others go ballistic.

At the center of this situation is an issue that affects and shapes much in our daily work life, not just in the United States but in the world of work around the globe. That issue is: "Who gets the power?" That is: "Who gets the power to have the answers—when and as they need them—complete, accurate answers that are on time without special effort?"

Not so very long ago, our society learned that *information is power.* That is exactly why many people feel disempowered when asking questions, and others feel far too powerful when answering them. One way or the other, asking/answering questions has become a play of power—highly destructive to the journey to excellence. More about this in a few pages when we talk about *information hoarders.*

Since the primary purpose of a visual workplace is to make answers to vital workplace questions readily and easily available, without speaking a word, we better look at the question of *questions* carefully.

Building Block 1: I-Driven Visuality

When we study all the workplace questions that anyone can ask, we discover only two questions drive them all. (*Why*, the third driving question, belongs to executives and is discussed in a different book.)

The First Driving Question: The Need-to-Know

The first of these two driving questions is: *What do I need to know?* That is:

> *What do I need to know that I don't know right now in order to do my work, or in order to do my work better? What information do I need?* (Figure 2.2)

Figure 2.2 The first driving question.

Need-to-know questions can be very basic. If you work in a factory, an urgent need-to-know question might be: "Where are my pliers?" In a hospital, it might be, "Where is that patient's chart?" In an accounting office, it might be, "Where is that report I was working on yesterday?"

Yes, these are plain questions—but just how many people will you have to ask to get the plain answer: "There! There are your pliers." "There! There is the chart." "There! There is your report." All the while you mutter, "What is it doing there anyway?"

For more plain questions, look at the boxes below (Figures 2.3 to 2.5), listing typical questions across three kinds of workplaces.

FACTORY *Need-to-Know Questions*	**HOSPITAL** *Need-to-Know Questions*	**ACCOUNTING OFFICE** *Need-to-Know Questions*
• Where are my pliers? • What am I supposed to run next? • Where is the material for that order? • Where are the fixtures for that changeover? • How do I change over this machine? • When will that sub-assembly be ready? • Who's on vacation today? • Where is my supervisor?	• Which patients do I look after today? • Where are their charts? • When will the doctors visit today? • Does this kit contain everything I need? • How many beds will be freed up this week? • Who is my supervisor today? • Where is my supervisor?	• Where is the report I worked on yesterday? • When exactly is that report due? • What appendix do I include? • Who do I give this correction to? • How do I deliver this confidential file? • How many more reports need to be completed today? • Where is my supervisor?
Figure 2.3	**Figure 2.4**	**Figure 2.5**

Plain as they may sound, these are the kinds of questions that drive workplace visuality. How? Because once you track down the answers to your need-to-know questions, you then translate those answers into visual devices. That is when you embed the answers, visually, directly into your work area, into your value field—so you never ever have to ask those questions again and no one ever has to answer them! Keep going from there—through cycle after cycle of translating your questions into visual answers—and you will build a robust visual work environment.

Photos 2.1 and 2.2 are reminders of need-to-know solutions you saw in Chapter 1.

Visuality is I-Driven

Please notice that the first driving question does not read: "What do WE need to know?" It reads: "What do *I* need to know?" That *I* is you.

If it did read "what do *we* need to know," then you would face yet another challenge before you could convert your answers into visual devices: a meeting! If the question read "we," you would have to meet with others in your area to discuss and decide which are the most important need-to-know questions, what the possible answers are, and is it really necessary to bother with a device anyway. You would meet, present, discuss, analyze, plan, probably vote—and certainly meet again. And there is no guarantee that enough people would agree that you need to know what you know you need to know—let alone agree on the form of the visual device that would embed the answer. A dreary prospect at best.

Photo 2.1 Rick Ell built this tooling fixture, color-coded by model. Now he can tell at-a-glance which tool to use when he changes over his machine.

Photo 2.2 This is a masking template trimmed in black that prevents us— 100%—from taking the wrong machining drill bit. A second template, in blue, has different cutouts for a second model. A third template is green ... and so on.

But the question does not say "we." It says "I." That "I" is you. You are in the driver's seat of your own visual inventiveness. Good idea! After all, you know which questions you need answered better than anyone—because they are *your* questions. And you know your work. That means you also know what stands in the way of getting that work done. So there is no requirement for you to present, discuss, analyze, plan, or vote on anything. Doing so would probably defeat the very purpose of your asking in the first place. Simply ask the questions that drive you (crazy) and answer them. Then translate those answers into visual devices—so you never have to ask those questions again. To that we all say: "Hurray!"

We have confidence in that "I" and so do you. That "I" is us, too. The starting place for all workplace visuality—for you and for us—is the "I." (This holds true for all ten of the Ten Doorways presented in Chapter 1.) That is why we say: *The visual workplace is an I-driven process. Work That Makes Sense (WTMS) is an I-driven methodology.* Because this is so important, let's make the point again, using other words:

- The visual devices you create are triggered by *your own* need-to-know.
- Your *need-to-know* drives the visual devices you create.
- You, and you alone, are the person who decides what your need-to-know is and what the visual device will be that answers it.
- As long as your device does no harm to, and does not interfere with someone else or their work, other people do not have to agree with you.

- In the visual workplace, *you* are in control of *your* corner of the world.

And if you are concerned because you share your bench or desk with others, we will discuss ways of handling that later in this book (see *Prototype Mini-Systems* in Chapter 11).

Figure 2.6 The second driving question.

The Second Driving Question: The Need-to-Share

As you read through the above discussion, did you find yourself thinking: "I" "I" "I"—that sounds pretty selfish. Where do other people fit in? What about teams? What about "we?"

Good point. But don't worry. The "we" in a visual workplace enters powerfully into the picture with the second question that drives workplace visuality: "What do I need to share?" That is:

What do I know that others need to know that I need to share in order for them to do their work— for them to do it safer, better, faster or at less cost? What information do I need to share? (Figure 2.6)

Notice this second question is still formed around the "I." It is still I-driven. But instead of you driving the question, this time you respond to it. The second question drives you. Where? To the next level of visuality in your area, triggered by the needs of others. Your focus, which was squarely on yourself before, is now turned outwards to others. "How may I help you?" is another way to say this.

At the heart of this second question is the recognition that each of us has knowledge and know-how that other people need in order for them to do their own work better and more safely ... whether those other people are co-workers, a supervisor or manager, internal suppliers and customers, or external suppliers or customers. They are all our colleagues, our work companions. We are all on the same team, whether we will ever sit together in the same room. They are all customers of the information you know. Here are some common need-to-share questions, across the three work settings we looked at before (Figures 2.7 to 2.9).

FACTORY	HOSPITAL	ACCOUNTING OFFICE
Questions from Others that Trigger the Need-To-Share from You	*Questions from Others that Trigger the Need-To-Share from You*	*Questions from Others that Trigger the Need-To-Share from You*
• Planner: What are you working on now? • Planner: When will it be ready? • Supervisor: Where is the order you just completed? • Accounting: When will my report be ready? • Co-Worker: What's my next changeover and when. And where did you put the fixture I need that you used yesterday? • Quality: Where are those defective parts you told me about?	• Co-Nurse: Which patients are mine today? • Newcomer: Where do you keep the blankets? • Nurse from other area: Where is the emergency kit? • X-Ray: When are you sending in Mr. Smith? • Admission: How many beds will be freed up by the end of the week? • Social Services: Is Mrs. Riley ready to go home?	• Operator: Who buys sintered metals for the J-190s? We're almost out. • Supervisor: When will that report you owe me be ready? • Purchasing Officer: Who gets these corrections I just made? • Co-Clerk: How many copies do I make of this joint report and who gets it?
Figure 2.7	**Figure 2.8**	**Figure 2.9**

As you again see, these are simple questions, often repeated. Why should anyone have to struggle to get their answers? Here are two need-to-share visual devices (Photos 2.3 and 2.4). Read each caption to increase your understanding. Who knows? You may be able to use these very solutions to share information, visually, in your own area.

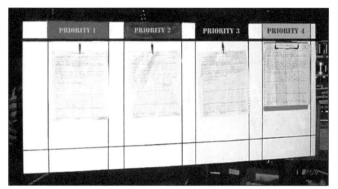

Photo 2.4 Two associates created these boards for newcomers and visitors that share, at-a-glance, the components made in their cell.

Photo 2.3 Supervisor Paul Plant needed a reliable way to share work order priorities with his department—this visual display shows priorities: 1, 2, 3, 4.

More About the Need-to-Share. Sometimes people don't ask us directly for the answers they need. Instead we see them wandering around our work area with no apparent purpose. As you'll learn soon, they are in *motion* (moving without working). Motion is the sure sign that information—an answer—is needed. When you observe that happening, politely inquire: "You seem to be looking for something. Maybe I can help?"

Bingo! Now you'll get the question. Next you'll give the answer. Then—just as with the need-to-know—you'll turn that answer into a visual device so that neither that person nor anyone else ever has to ask you that same question again; and you will never need to answer it again. Why? Because you will have embedded that answer into the physical workplace where it will be available to anyone and everyone who needs it, at-a-glance, without speaking a word.

This is exactly what happened to Sheila Bowersmith, a first-rate machinist and master visual thinker at Denison Hydraulics when she saw Karen, the new planner, wandering around her area. Sheila quietly asked if she could be of help—and the rest is history. Read Photo Series 2.5 for what happened next.

Photo Series 2.5 Sheila Bowersmith: The Need-To-Share

Karen asked, "Could you tell me what you're running right now?" Sheila told her and then decided to never have to answer that question again. So she taped a yellow rectangle on the side of her CNC machine, welded a heavy clip at the top, and put whatever order she's running there. When her machine was idle, a big NONE was visible so Karen—and anyone else—would know (see red circle). (Denison Hydraulics/Ohio)

The point is not that we don't like other people or don't like answering their questions, it is simple this: We want our work life (and theirs) to be about something greater than chasing down informational tidbits. Visuality, starting with the two driving questions, clears the way for that, allowing us to pay more attention to our actual work function—and beyond.

Please read the "First-Question-Is-Free Rule" in Inset 2.1 and apply it. This rule can help your managers and supervisors as well as you. Like you, they spend a lot of time asking and answering the same questions over and over. Tell them about the "First-Question-Is-Free Rule." I'll bet they get excited too.

Inset 2.1. The First-Question-Is-Free Rule

Some people mistakenly think their real job is to answer questions. That may be true for customer-service reps and reference librarians. But for everyone else (including managers and supervisors), learn and apply the *First-Question-Is-Free Rule* and turn those questions into visual answers.

Step 1. Notice. Notice the first time you are asked a given question. For example, if you are a team lead/supervisor, someone might always ask at the start of the shift: "What am I supposed to make/do now?"

Step 2. Answer. Answer the question the way you always do—clearly, completely, and politely—but with this difference. As that person walks away, say to yourself: "That's one."

Step 3. Wait. Wait until you are asked that same question again—by that same person or anyone else: "What am I supposed to make/do now?" As before, you answer clearly, completely, and politely.

Step 4. Create. As that person walks away, say to yourself: "That's two! The first question is free. And now that I've heard that same question a second time, it's time to create a visual device so I never have to answer that question again—and no one ever has to ask it!"

Linking the Need-to-Know and Need-to-Share

As with all visual information, the impact of answering your need-to-know and need-to-share questions by creating visual devices does more than simply embed those answers into the physical landscape of work.

Because other people in your area are also creating visual solutions, a remarkable multiplying effect occurs. The result is an impact far greater than the number of devices in a given work area. Similar to dropping a pebble in a stream, the ripples last longer and reach further than the initial splash.

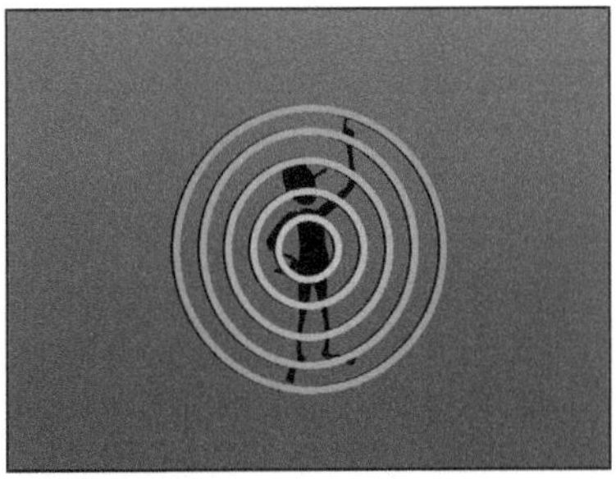

Look at the ripples (concentric circles) in Figure 2.10. This is an image of you applying the first driving question: What do I need to know. The visual solutions you create not only make the answers visible and handy, they also define your improvement reach and impact. Another name for that is your *locus of control.*

Figure 2.10 Begin by answering your need-to-know questions and gain control of your corner of the world.

Now let's do the multiples. We started with you, a single "I", answering the need-to-know. Figure 2.11 shows what happens when other visual thinkers-in-the-making join you. A fabric of visually-capable work stations begins to populate your department. Each visual thinker uncovers the various forms of motion that make work a struggle for him or her and then eliminates (or minimizes) the information deficits that caused them. The result is a new level of individual competency and pride within each of the company's many work areas—independent yet aligned.

Time for the second driving question: *What do I need to share?* With that question, you reach beyond your work station boundary to discover information you can share visually with others. Those visual devices define your sphere of influence, providing missing answers for people outside your immediate area, as you just saw with Sheila's solution. Notice how far that influence extends (purple circles; Figure 2.12).

Soon other visual thinkers join you in generating need-to-share devices. Doing this creates a common focus, improved performance, and good will across the organization. This visual network of connections weaves the enterprise together—area by area, person by person, and visual device by visual device (Figure 2.13).

Summing Up the "I"

When you begin to implement visuality in your own work area, you start—you must start—by responding to your own need-to-know. Why? Because those are the questions that you need most and know best! As you build a firm foundation of visual answers to this first question, you get more and more control of your corner of the world. Then you turn to others and help them get the answers they need. You share the vital information they need through visual devices you create on their behalf.

The I-driven approach is a deeply team-minded process. It asks each of us to take personal responsibility for both ourselves and others. Just remember that the "I" resides in all of us. So when other people in your area begin inventing visual solutions to their need-to-know, they are using their own "I" as the anchor. The same applies to your supervisor. She plugs into her own "I" to create visual devices that serve her need-to-know because it's *her* need. Then she moves on to *her* need-to-share which inevitably touches you and your need-to-know.

Ditto for managers, engineers, marketing people, and the CEO as each of them starts participating in the visual conversion of your company. The "I" becomes the anchor for each of them—their "I." The result is not chaos or anarchy as some might fear. The result is a splendid self-ordering, self-explaining, self-regulating, and self-improving work environment that makes sense to each and every person in it. The result is a visual workplace, true, wide, and deep—a workplace that speaks. And you have made it so.

I-driven is the first building block of visual thinking.

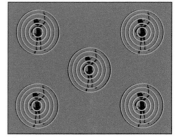

Figure 2.11 As others in your area (or other areas) join in and answer their need-to-know questions, a fabric of visually-capable work stations develops to support company and area-specific outcomes.

Figure 2.12 When you shift to the need-to-share, you reach out visually and help others so their work is safer, better, smarter.

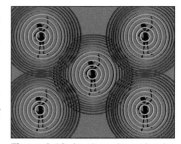

Figure 2.13 As others also undertake to create need-to-share devices, the entire area—and soon the whole company—gets visually linked and aligned.

Building Block 2: Standards

Let's look again at the definition of a visual workplace:

> *A visual workplace is a self-ordering, self-explaining, self-regulating, and self-improving work environ-ment—where what is supposed to happen does happen, on time, every time, day or night—because of visual devices.*

The second part of this definition states that in such a workplace: "what is supposed to happen *does* happen." What exactly does that mean? What *is* supposed to happen?

The answer is your standards. Your standards are supposed to happen. That brings us to *Building Block 2: Standards*.

Your Standards Are Supposed To Happen

When we use the term *standards* in workplace visuality, we are not referring to the time or accounting standards used in bids, quotes, and contracts. Instead, we mean the information that defines exactly *what* we are supposed to do and *how* we are supposed to do it—the *what* and the *how*. More precisely, the *what* refers to your technical standards and the *how* refers to your procedural standards (see Figure 2.14).

Figure 2.14 What is supposed to happen.

Your Technical Standards. A technical standard is a product or process specification, dimension, or tolerance—the detailed re-quirements found in engineering worksheets and drawings. These requirements are the precise values you add as you convert mate-rial into a product your customer wants to buy (or as you develop and deliver a service).

Here are examples of technical standards:

- outer diameter (OD)
- inner diameter (ID)
- pressure sensitivity
- coil resistance level
- cut length
- heat-treat temperature
- gloss level
- exact degree of radiation for this patient site
- dilution level for Taxotere (a chemotherapy drug)
- required response time on a fire claim
- required end-of-the-month sales figures

Once you identify the specification (the technical standard), your next step is to make that spec visual. When you do, you visually anchor it—that technical standard—in the physical landscape of work.

Look at the example on the next page of a visual guarantee (or poka-yoke device—one of the four power levels of visual devices discussed in Chapter 12). It reliably captures a certain type of quality defect and prevents it from traveling downstream (Photos 2.6 to 2.9). This is a technical standard translated into a visual device—and a very powerful one at that.

Photo 2.6
Problem: On some plungers, the outer diameter is too large to slide inside the bushing without rubbing. This hard-to-see defect was rarely discovered before Final Test. (See bushing in next photo.)

Photo 2.7
Challenge: Develop a way to ensure that no defective plunger travels downstream.
Solution: Embed the answer to the question "Is this a good plunger?" as deeply as possible into the process itself. Create a visual solution.

Photo 2.8
Visual Solution: First a plate is mounted on the blue bin with a hole drilled in the center the size of the bushing. Then the bushing (the mating part) is mounted in the hole.

Photo 2.9
With the bushing in place, the operator drops each plunger through the bushing as a size check. If the plunger slips through, it is to spec. If it gets stuck, it is set aside. In both, the attributes "talk" to each other.

Your Procedural Standards. A procedural standard is a method or an SOP (standard operating procedure)—a pre-set sequence of steps that tells you how to do or make something or perform a task. Procedural standards tell you exactly how to achieve your technical standards. In fact, procedural standards are the *how*. They create outcomes.

Do you need to form a 2-inch aluminum ingot into a .50 millimeter thick coil? Follow the step-by-step road map that is your procedural standard.

Do you want to insert an I.V. precisely into a patient's arm? Follow the SOP for that. Same with programming that CNC machine in the radial department. Follow the SOP for that. Here are more examples of procedural standards:

- How to rivet a bolt
- How to set a feed rate
- How to weld a rounded joint
- How to changeover the winder machine (in less than nine minutes).
- How to tighten a six-nut wheel in final assembly
- How to verify a chemotherapy regimen
- How to close out the monthly books

Once you identify a problem SOP, make it visual. When you do, you anchor that SOP into the physical landscape of work. Here is a simple and very effective example (Photos 2.10 and 2.11).

Photo 2.10

1. Problem:
The terminal endings of the electric harnesses are delicate and easily damaged if they hit the floor, making them unusable.

2. Cause: The endings often get banged on the floor when they are hung unevenly and too low on the storage poles.

Photo 2.11

3. Need: Invent a way to make sure we hang harnesses evenly and high enough when we store them on the poles so no terminal ending gets damaged. That is our new SOP.

4. Visual Solution: Show where "too low" is on each pole with red tape to remind us not to let any harness hang below that point.

Combined, your procedural and technical standards are at the heart of all operational excellence. They cause reliable, repeatable, cost effective, and high quality work to occur—the absolute bedrock of all outcomes and the core of all profit-making in the enterprise. They create outputs your company's customers want to buy and will buy—and that is exactly "what is supposed to happen."

Standards are the second building block of visual thinking.

Building Block 3: The Six Core Questions

Take a closer look at your technical standards and procedural standards ("what is supposed to happen"). Notice that they are made up of a specific set of answers—the answers to one or more of only six questions. In visuality, we call these the *Six Core Questions*:

- Where?
- Who?
- How?
- What?
- How Many?
- When?

Answers to these questions represent the details of every standard. They also represent all possible answers to the two driving questions—your need-to-know and need-to-share. When you answer these six questions visually (translate them into visual devices), the details of both types of standards are visually embedded into the process of work, available at-a-glance to you and anybody who needs them. The workplace speaks—at last able to tell us *where* things are, *what* needs to be done, by *when*, by *whom* (or by *which* machine or tool), in *what quantity*, and precisely *how*.

See Photo Series 2.12 for visual answers for each of these six questions. The *six core questions* are the third building block of visual thinking.

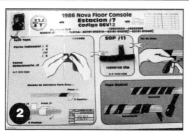

Photo Series 2.12: Six Core Questions

1. **Visual Where.** This temporary standing sign tells us exactly where the J-190 brackets are now, even though they will be moved in an hour.

2. **Visual How.** This clear, crisp SOP visually shows us the right and wrong way to tape a wiring harness. (Notice the chart is in Spanish and dated 1986.)

3. **Visual When.** This standing sign in front of the epoxy cure oven tells us (among many things) the duration of the epoxy cure cycle, at the exact point of use.

4. **Visual What.** This sign stands in front of a large Mandelli machining center, showing us what the unit looks like before and after that operation.

5. **Visual Who.** Leave your name tag in place of any special (and expensive) tool you take so the person who needs it next can find you—and so you know that we know that you had it last.

6. **Visual How Much.** Sheets of cut vinyl slide off this machine and stop, thanks to the edge on this wooden offload platform that operators built. Before the sheets simply rolled off the machine into irregular piles that operators then had to organized and neaten. End of the motion called "double-handling."

Building Block 4: Information Deficits

Once we understand the six core questions and their importance, our task becomes simple: Find the missing answers to those questions and convert them into visual devices. Another term for these missing answers is *Information Deficits,* the fourth building block of visual thinking.

Look at the work bench in Photo 2.13, the *Before.*

Photo 2.13 Cut-saw work bench *Before.*

> ***Question:*** How many *six core questions* are answered there?

> ***Answer:*** None! There is no where there nor what, when, who, how many, or how. This area is full of missing answers—full of information deficits ... full of motion. Because this a cut saw area, it is also very dangerous. That motion is called "risk."

In Photo 2.14 (the *After*), we see the same area. Now it is not just neat, clean, and safe; it is also highly visual, the way it is supposed to be. Motion has been minimized.

Photo 2.14 Cut-saw work-bench *After* the answer to the where question was installed.

Missing Answers Trigger Motion

Motion is triggered when answers vital to work are missing, wrong, late, incomplete, unavailable, or simply not known. Another way to say this is: I do not know—and I do not share (Figure 2.15).

Information deficits have a powerful negative impact on a company. First (as already discussed), when vital workplace information is repeatedly not available, we become immuned to a sense of urgency

Figure 2.15 The two conditions that trigger motion.

at work. No one wants to wander around all day, chasing down the same bits of information. It is hard to imagine a more degrading experience or one that is more a waste of time. And if these tidbits should be held by a select few individuals who withhold them from the many, insult is added to injury. (See Inset 2.2 for more on this, *Information Hoarders.*)

The damage done to the bottom line through missing information is disastrous and huge. A company's performance measures tell the story—its KPIs (Key Performance Indicators). From ordering errors, defects, rework, scrap, and the chronic late deliveries these trigger—to the number of machine repairs, long changeover times, and material handling mistakes, to accidents, long cycle and manufacturing lead times, error-laden sales reports and collection activities, information deficits hurt the entire business. Their power is in their absence—the absence of answers.

Like holes torn in a fishing net, something of value escapes with every missing answer. These rips may start so small that we do not notice the escaping fish because they are so tiny. Over time the holes get bigger as the information deficits multiply. Not only does the loss of so many small fish add up, but now the big fish escape as well (Photo 2.15).

Photo 2.15 Visuality repairs the net.

Learning to See. What to do? The first step in minimizing (even eliminating) this sorry state of affairs is to learn to see what isn't there: those holes—information deficits in the workplace. But that can be a hard task when chasing down missing answers becomes a routine part of the work day and a way of life in some companies. We barely notice these chronic abnormalities and instead write them off as business as usual. The result is this: When our work area overflows with information deficits, we simply get busier and busier and try harder and harder. We hardly have time to notice that we do not get much work done.

Information deficits are the fourth building block of visual thinking.

Building Block 5: Motion

Building Block 5 is *Motion.* Motion is defined as "moving without working."

Motion comes in a thousand familiar and unfamiliar forms and disguises. Here's a sample: wandering, wondering, searching, guessing, checking, checking again, handling, handling again, or simply waiting.

Sometimes when motion gets really thick, the only thing you can do is *stop.* That makes stopping yet another form of motion (Figure 2.16).

But the most common and dangerous forms of motion are connected with questions, a familiar topic already. Look at the red box in Figure 2.16: asking questions, answering questions, interrupting to ask, being interrupted to answer, and waiting for answers.

Questions have a peculiar multiplier effect that makes them very dangerous. Here's what happens.

When you interrupt someone to ask a question (no matter how urgent or genuine)—or when someone interrupts you to ask a question—two people are automatically in motion, you and the other person.

Forms of Motion

• Searching	• Counting
• Looking For	• Counting (again)
• Wandering	• Asking
• Wondering	• Answering
• Guessing	• Interrupting
• Checking	• Waiting
• Re-checking	• Re-Doing
• Handling	• Re-Working
• Handling (again)	• Re-Testing
• Moving (again)	• Stopping (again and again and again)

Figure 2.16 Common (and dangerous) forms of motion

The motion caused by questions is like a contagious disease—you start by asking one person a question; if he/she does not know the answer, he/she then asks a second person. If that second person does not know the answer, chances are he/she will ask a third person. And so on until a whole roomful of people are contaminated, until they are all in motion. You could say they all had *motion-sickness.*

Shall I go on? Research shows that when we get interrupted, it can take up to 12-15 minutes for us to get back—not to work—but to the level of focus and attention we had before the interruption. Yikes!

Information deficits/missing answers are *corporate enemy #1.* Motion is their footprint. By definition, missing answers are not there. They are invisible yet powerful because they cause motion. Visual thinkers become scientists of motion, tracking the footprint of an info deficit—and then eliminating that deficit through a visual solution, and with it, its motion. (See Inset 2.3 for why I use the term *motion*, not *muda*, *waste* or *non value-adding activity.*)

What Motion is Not

Before we go further, let's understand what motion is not. You are *not* in motion if you are taking a break, at lunch, chatting with a friend, calling home, in the rest room—and things like that.

Those are important ways for us to maintain our humanity at work and our sense of community, safety, and personal comfort. Please do not think that I want you to turn into some tireless work robot—an Energizer Bunny who just keeps doing it, doing it, doing it. Simply understand that the above activities are *not motion*. So engage in them. They are not the enemy.

Do It or Don't Do Your Work. Notice your motion and you are a step away from detecting the information deficit that caused it—that caused you, for example, to spend 15 minutes looking for your pliers.

But maybe you are thinking: "Wait a minute! If I need my pliers to do my work and I go looking for them, how is that bad? How is that the enemy? How is that motion? I have to have my pliers if I'm going to get my work done!"

First, you are right: You do need to find your pliers so you can do your work. But also recognize that *looking for your pliers* is not the same as *using your pliers*. It is not the same as working. The correct logic runs like this: "If I am looking for my pliers in order to be able do my work, then I am obviously not yet doing that work while I am looking for them." That's all I am saying.

There is a name for that—for anything you are forced to do or you cannot do your work. It is a name you already know: motion. Motion is anything you have to do or you could not do your work—but it is *not* your work.

> ## Inset 2.3. Motion versus Non-Value-Adding/Waste/Muda
>
> The definition of motion I use throughout this book is the same as Toyota uses in its *Seven Deadly Wastes*: *moving without working*. In visuality, however, I use motion to define problems triggered by information deficits and the unintentional placement of function. While you might think that the terms muda, waste, and non-value-adding activity are used to mean the same thing, I do not use them interchangeably. Here's why.
>
> **Non-Value-Adding Activity:** Many years ago, I noticed that the term "non-value-adding" caused heartache for people whose jobs were, in fact, non-value-adding: inspectors, expediters, rework operators, material handlers, supervisors, and managers—to name a few. Far too often, when these fine individuals heard me call their jobs "non-value-adding," they concluded that they, as people, were "non-value-adding." Nothing is further from the truth. But when I saw how my words affected them, I decided not to describe people's jobs that way anymore.
>
> **Waste:** Waste is a general term. Motion is specific; it is always caused by a specific unanswered question and almost always tied to a specific person—me or you. It is my legs that carry me all over the area trying to answer the question: Where are my pliers? I own that question. I own that motion. The term *waste* is very broad and non-specific. I prefer the term *motion.*
>
> **Muda:** Muda means "waste" in Japanese. I prefer to use a word that does not need translation and, as mentioned, has a more exact meaning.

Here are other examples of motion—the activities that associates like you are forced to do just to be able to do their work:

- Before she can start her work, Mary must remove a pallet of pumps because they are wrong.
- Victoria has to re-check the spec or risk making the wrong order.
- Jose-Luis is forced to count the units again because someone "borrowed" his order sheet.
- Nurse Betty has to go to the pharmacy for a new batch of medications because the batch ID label is missing from the first one.
- Hank has to find his pliers before he can begin to assemble the unit.

Another powerful way to bring home the multiplier impact of motion is to realize that time is its shadow: *Time is the shadow of motion* (Figure 2.17). Every time we have to chase down an answer, the clock is ticking. All the time we are looking for a missing tool that same clock is ticking. It is the clock of our life and the life of the company. However much we may want to work—without that answer, without the tool—we cannot. Either we never get our work started, or, once started, we have to stop. Chasing down answers eats up our day.

Figure 2.17 Time is the shadow of Motion.

It is a numbing experience and witness to motion's destructive power in the workplace.

Motion is the fifth building block of visual thinking. You'll learn other powerful ways to spot it before the end of this chapter.

Building Block 6: Work

Did you notice? I spent over two pages explaining that motion meant moving without working—but I never told you what *working* means. I'll do that now to strengthen your understanding of motion.

Working means *moving and adding value.* That is, we must move in order to add value—in order to convert material or procedures into products or services that our customers want to purchase.

Value is not added by accident or by magic. We don't work on Star Trek's Starship Enterprise, at least not yet! On the Enterprise, when Captain Picard wants a cup of tea, he doesn't have to boil water—nor does his staff. He simply stands in front of the replicator (not a vending machine) and says aloud "Earl Grey tea, hot!" Earl Grey tea, piping hot, instantly materializes from the inside out, along with an exquisite Wedgewood tea cup and saucer that hold it. *Q* (a rather eccentric ET in Picard's world) doesn't even need to say "cup of tea" when he wants one. He merely thinks it. No, our world isn't like that—not yet.

In our world, if we want a cup of tea or an F16 fighter jet, we must *move* in order to create it—in order to add value. We must engage our muscles and our mind in order to build a sub-assembly, grind a housing, load the cable, check a part, administer a medication, or produce a proposal. Yes, we must move in order to add value. We must work. So that means that motion is moving and *not* adding value.

Work is the sixth building block of visual thinking.

Building Block 7: Value Field

When and where do you add value? The answer is: When—and only when—you are in your *Value Field*. Only then can you add value. Only then can you work. It is as simple as that. Your value field is a specific location. It is where work happens.

Look at Photo 2.16: the running track at Tuft's University in Boston. That track is a runner's primary value field. No matter how much time a runner spends working out at the gym, finding the right running shoes or eating the healthiest foods, only when she runs on the track is she in her primary field of value.

Photo 2.16 Running track at Tufts.

Only then is she about the business she has trained for, year after year. Look at the visual details built into that track surface! Olympic careers begin and can end with those details. Move a hurdle up or down an inch, and some Olympic hopeful breaks an ankle and says goodbye to the Games.

It is the same way for you. Since you can only add value when you are in your value field, anytime you are not there, you must be in motion. And you can only do your primary work when you are in your primary value field.

Noticing whether or not you are in your value field is another powerful way to spot your motion. Here is that logic again:

1. Since motion is the opposite of work, and
2. Since you can only do your work when you are in your own value field,
3. Then you know that if you are not physically in your value field, you are in motion—because you cannot be working.
4. Therefore anytime you are not in your value field, you are automatically in motion. (Reminder: Even though you are not in your value field during a break or the like, you are not in motion.)

Photo Series 2.17 shows three views of the assembly bench value field created by Bill Antunes (United Electric Controls, Massachusetts). It is worth a close read.

  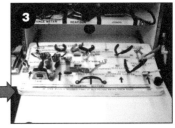

Photo Series 2.17

Bill Antunes, a master visual thinker, solders his subassemblies on this white bench. His primary value field is in the center, with a secondary value field on the left and another on the right for his tools.

Here is a close-up of Bill's solder arm, mounted on a shelf. At night he pushes it back and pulls down the white board that holds his work order during the day.

His hand tools are to the right in another pull-out shelf. Bill doubled the shelf's thickness and cut holes for each tool for easy pick-and-put. We see so many of the eight building blocks in this system.

Primary or Secondary Value Fields

Here's the tricky part: We almost always have more than one primary value field. In any given department, work can take place in several locations. This is especially true in assembly areas and machine centers where there are several actual locations for adding value—for working. There are also *secondary value fields*: other key areas within your department that support that main work.

At first, you may find it challenging to separate the two—your primary from your secondary value fields. This may be because you have never thought about your work like that before. For example, if you are a machinist, you will quickly understand that your machine is your primary value field—that is where the material you load is converted into something of greater value for your customer. But the dies rack, changeover tools, and test station support that. They are your secondary value fields.

Again, if you run six machines for sequential operations or for six models, all six machines are your primary value fields. If you are a medical technician in X-ray, then clearly the X-ray machine is the point from which you measure all motion. It is your primary value field. But if you are a nurse, your primary value field may be less clear. Is it the patient, room by room, or the main nursing station where you undertake so many valuable services on behalf of the patient? It is the same issue for managers and supervisors: Is your main value field your desk? Or is it the areas you walk through as you assess and coach, and monitor and expedite?

The important thing right now is to raise these questions and think. Discuss your thinking with others and listen to their responses. With enough time and input, the distinctions become clear. Be patient with yourself and others. They are learning too. The right logic will surface. Think. Probe. Consider.

Value field is the seventh building block of visual thinking.

Building Block 8: Motion Metrics

The final building block of visual thinking is *Motion Metrics*. (The term "metric" is another word for "measure;" both of them mean "a standard unit of measurement.") A *motion metric* is a mechanism or yardstick that we use to track or measure motion—to find out how much motion there is.

You can track your motion several ways, including the one we already discussed at length—tracking the number of questions you ask or are asked. Here are four more (Photo Series 2.18): your own eyes, a stop watch, a pedometer, and/or a frequency check sheet.

Photo Series 2.18

Your Own Eyes
Use the power of your own observation.

Stop Watch
Measure time away from your value field.

Pedometer
Measure distance traveled from your value field.

Frequency Check Sheet
Track how many times you leave your value field—and why.

When you track your own motion, you get rock-solid evidence of the level of struggle in your daily work. Here are four examples from the same company, Harris Corp. (Illinois).

- Janet, an assembler in electrical cables, watched her pedometer rack up 4.2 miles in walking in a single day—and she never left her department.

- Her colleague, Linda, who was confined to a wheelchair, used a frequency check sheet that showed that she left her value field (her assembly bench) 42 times in three days for work-related reasons. She said she had not realized she was in motion because never before thought of those side trips as a problem. Linda also said that she always felt the pressure.

- Deanna, the supervisor in that same area, kept track of the questions she asked and she answered per shift. By the third day, she had already piled up 72 questions she had answered, and 123 she had asked. She now knew for sure that the motion called *questions* was eating up her time.

- Down the aisle in the same company, Buzz, lead operator in Final Test with 27 years on the job, saw his stopwatch rack up 2 hours and 35 minutes that he spent outside his area on a single shift (not counting breaks or lunch). "No wonder I can't get my work done," he flashed.

Motion metrics give us a concrete way to see for ourselves why we cannot get a full day of work done.

Measure Your Motion

Here is what I would like you to do. Pick a motion metric and track your motion for one week. At the end of that week, study what happened and why. Then look for ways to reduce your motion through visual devices. A few pointers:

- Track your own motion—and no one else's.
- You do not have to share what you discover with anyone else, unless you decide to. Your motion, for the time being, is strictly your own business.
- The important thing is for you to recognize that you are in motion at least part of the time you are on the job. Notice that and notice why. Thanks!

Motion metrics are the eighth building block of visual thinking.

Putting It All Together

This concludes our detailed discussion of the *Eight Building Blocks of Visual Thinking*—and how they work together to help us eliminate motion and the information deficits that cause it. *The Cycle of Visual Thinking* in Figure 2.18 sums this up. Please keep it in mind as you move forward.

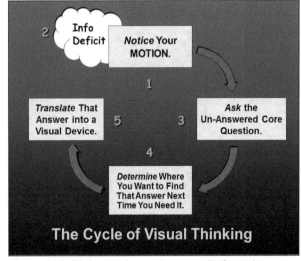

Step 1: Notice your motion.
- Look! I just left my value field. That means I'm not working anymore. I must be in motion.

Step 2: Name the information deficit.
- Hmmm, if I am in motion, it must have been triggered by an information deficit—a missing answer. What was it?

Step 3: Ask the un-answered core question.
- Which of the six core questions is linked to that information deficit of mine? Which question do I need answered?

Figure 2.18 Eliminate motion step by step, cycle after cycle.

Step 4: Decide where to physically install the visual device that captures the missing answer so it is both exact and handy.
- Where should I locate the new device? How close can I get it to the actual point of use?

Step 5: Translate that answer into a visual device.
- Now I will turn that answer into a visual solution—and I won't ever need to ask or answer that question again because the answer will be firmly installed as close to my value field as possible.

Excellent! Then, at the least sign of new motion, the visual thinker starts the cycle again. That visual thinker is *you!*

Using the knowledge you just learned is exactly how you—and you colleagues in your area and throughout your company—can take the struggle out of the workday and begin to populate the work environment with dozens, hundreds, even thousands of visual devices and visual mini-systems. The result is an enterprise of splendid visual functionality, self-ordering, self-explaining, self-regulating and self-improving—where what is supposed to happen *does* happen, on time, every time, day or night, *because* of visual devices.

About the Visual Examples in This Book

A visual workplace is a physical workplace. You actually see visual-information sharing devices with your eye—or perceive the information they share through one or more of your other senses (see page 11 for more on the senses). That is one of the reasons why this book contains over 600 visual devices—so you can see them and understand directly how the visual paradigm works!

In addition, although the majority of the examples in this book are from manufacturing, visuality is a universal language. It makes information in any work setting available at-a-glance—knowable, usable, and transparent whatever in an office or agency, a bank or hospital, military depot, chemical or food processing plant, or open-pit mine. There is no company or person that visual information sharing cannot help. As a universal language, everyone can learn to speak it, inventing sensory solutions to the information deficits they encounter there.

So as you move through the pages, examine the principles and concepts in this book's many visual solutions. Appreciate them from the viewpoint of your own workplace, whatever that is. Then develop devices and systems that *make your workplace speak.*

> Things do not change.
> We change.
> Henry David Thoreau

Chapter | Three

Your Implementation Tool Box

Knowledge and Know-How

To this point, you have learned a good deal about basic visual concepts and the building blocks of visual thinking. Your knowledge of what operator-led visuality (WTMS) is and why it is important is vital as you start improving your work area visually.

But you will need more than knowledge. You will also need know-how: how to implement WTMS so it moves forward, takes deep roots, and keeps growing. Knowledge and know-how. Know-how and knowledge. They go hand-in-hand every step of the way, each strengthening the other as your visual conversion unfolds (Inset 3.1).

> **Knowledge vs. Know-How**
> - Knowledge is the *what*: What principles, concepts, definitions, methods, and practices are needed.
> - Know-how is the *how*: How to put these principles concepts, definitions, methods and practices in place—how to implement them.
>
> **Inset 3.1** You need both.

The know-how needed for a successful WTMS visual conversion in your area is a shared responsibility. You and other area associates own a large part of it. The rest belongs to company leadership: supervisors, mid-level managers, and senior managers (whether "senior" means plant manager, hospital administrator, depot commander, company owner, or CEO).

This chapter focuses squarely on: What you and your colleagues do—and what supervisors, team leaders, managers, and executives do—to effectively implement, grow, and sustain WTMS in your area.

These two sets of tasks are crucial but different. The main pages of this book are always addressed to you, the operator-experts. Leadership (management) tasks appear as blue insets throughout the same pages.

The Three Outcomes

There are three outcomes that define success as you and your co-workers convert your area to visuality through WTMS. They are:

1. Achieve a visual showcase.

2. Achieve trackable bottom-line results.

3. Adopt an attitude of learning.

Outcome 1: Achieve a Visual Showcase

The first thing you want as a result of implementing WTMS in your area is a *Visual Showcase*—a work area where you have drilled deep into the details of your operations and made them visual. I say it like this: *Implement visuality one-foot square and one-mile deep.*

A work area that has reached the showcase level shows us what a well-developed visual work environment looks like and how it functions. When we visit such a showcase, our own eyes tell us why visuality is important. We understand simply by looking. Newcomers and visitors understand too—along with people from areas in the facility that are not yet visual. And when they do, they get inspired and want their own areas to look and run like that also, as well as the entire enterprise.

I often hear it put like this: "I want one like that!" To make sure you remember your progress, your management will take photographs of your area regularly (see *Leadership Task 1*). So the first outcome you focus on is achieving a visual showcase.

Leadership Task 1: Take Photographs

Take plenty of *Before* photos—before associates change anything. Do this for all areas, all shifts. Begin today. Then take another set of photos week-by-week (on the same day of the week, if you can, at about the same time) so you have a moving history of visual improvements as they happen. Take photos weekly even when nothing has changed. No matter. Over time, you will collect the story of the visual journey in the area.

- As a rough guideline, take ten different shots of each department per week.
- To better track an area's visual progress, pick a single spot and regularly take a set of weekly photos from there. Like a tree changing across the four seasons, these photos allow us to see the area visually transform over time (Photo 3.1).

Photo 3.1 Spot point.

Outcome 2: Achieve Trackable Bottom-line Results

As each area makes its way to showcase level, it is important to be able to see visuality's positive impact in terms of trackable, bottom-line results. Management usually takes the lead in tracking this since tangible proof of return on investment is one of their main measures. But you can certainly participate—and, in the case of self-directed teams, take the lead.

Over time, the benefits of visuality must positively impact your performance measures—quality, delivery, cost, and safety (QDCS). You may know these as KPIs (Key Performance Indicators). As your visual rollout gains momentum, look for improvement in them.

Here is one way you or your supervisor can do that: Collect KPIs just before the visual conversion begins in your area (we call that *the launch*). Continue to do this week-by-week, comparing the actual results as you go along (see *Leadership Task 2*).

Within six to nine weeks of launch, you are likely to see a positive drift in your KPIs, often sooner. That steadily increases over time thanks to the visual devices you and others create; information deficits dissolve as a result. In five to six months, expect to see results in your area as good as (or better than) those shared in Chapter 1. Remember?

- 15%-30% increase in productivity
- 70% reduction in waiting
- 70% reduction in material handling
- 54% reduction in walking
- 96% improvement in quality

- 68% reduction in storage requirements
- $2,555,000 scrap reduction (annualized)
- 7,132 hours/machine downtime eliminated (annualized)
- 60% reduction in floor space requirements
- 100% elimination of rework

Leadership Task 2: Your Baseline Set of Metrics

Before you launch the Work That Makes Sense (WTMS) methodology in the targeted areas, collect a baseline set of measures (or metrics) for each of these areas. Collect the current level of Key Performance Indicators (KPIs). In most companies, these are routinely collected anyway. All you need do is print out the latest results and put it in a binder. Do this again often but not less than twice a month.

In six to nine weeks (or sooner), you will begin to see a positive drift in the direction of those measures. What needs to increase will begin to increase. What needs to decrease will start to go down. That is when and how you and others begin to realize that the WTMS improvements underway in each department are translating into better performance and improved bottom-line results.

Other metrics: Two additional metrics (another word for "measures") show visuality's positive impact: (1) management's tracking of improvement time utilization (see the *Leadership Centerfold* in this chapter), and (2) associates' tracking of motion metrics via a stopwatch, pedometer, frequency check sheet, or questions asked/answered (for a review, see Motion Metrics in Chapter 3/Building Blocks of Visual Thinking.)

These are impressive bottom-line results and not uncommon for an effective I-driven visual conversion on the value-add level. So the second outcome you focus on is achieving trackable bottom-line results.

Outcome 3: Adopt an Attitude of Learning

Most of us already realize that learning is our life-long job, no matter what company employs us. The third visual workplace outcome targets the conversion of our mind, heart, and beliefs as we convert the work area to visuality through WTMS.

Continuous improvement is an opportunity to both streamline the physical workplace and help ourselves grow as individuals. As we change the process, the process changes us—and we learn. We learn, for example, what works and what does not, what we like and what we do not like, and what we get right and what we get wrong. As importantly, we learn the difference between demands and preferences.

Safety, for example, is always a requirement. We demand it. But the way I like to have my workbench laid out is a preference. I favor my way—but your layout is also "interesting." I know that I am an adult and so are you. Therefore neither of us need to get bent out of shape if the other person does not agree with us exactly. We just learn to stay open and sort things out.

For Outcome 3, we adopt an attitude of learning. We learn to stay open so, for example, we can appreciate mistakes as opportunities to learn. We may even get so interested in mistakes (including our own) that, instead of hiding them or blaming them on others, we study them and become scientists of our own work. We come to realize that mistakes are part of what makes improvement a journey, not a destination.

When you learn to adopt an attitude of learning in the face of change, you can learn to stay open and bear the discomfort of not knowing the exact result. Over time, you learn to accept things about yourself and others that may surprise you. Where acceptance is beyond your reach, you can become willing to adopt tolerance. You may learn, for example, that:

- You prefer to be in a leadership position, out in front of a change; or
- You like to hang back, with a wait-and-see attitude; or
- You get cranky because you're not so sure you want things to change in the first place.

Whatever your personal preference, though, I encourage you to stay open and remember that not all other individuals will be like you. Allow yourself—and others—to change.

As Gotama, the Buddha, told a student a thousand years ago when she asked how to navigate life's tricky parts: (1) Show up; (2) Tell the truth; and (3) Stay open. That was the Buddha's way of saying—adopt an attitude of learning.

So these are the three outcomes that tell us if our visual workplace implementation is a success:

- Achieve a visual showcase
- Achieve trackable results
- Adopt an attitude of learning

Which is most important? All three. They are equally vital to your success. Now let's look at the five tools in your *Implementation Tool Box* that will help you get going and get growing.

Your Implementation Tool Box: The Five Tools

With those outcomes firmly in mind, you are ready to begin to learn and implement. You use five key implementation tools to help you and your colleagues stay inspired and to focus, target, and drive workplace visuality so your visual improvements sink deep roots, keep growing, and become sustainable.

The five tools are:

1. Your Vision Place (to help you stay inspired)
2. Your Laminated Map (to help you stay focused)
3. Your Hit List (to help you target)
4. Your Supplies (to help you invent)
5. Your Blitz (to help you drive)

1. Your Vision Place (a tool to help you stay inspired)

Name a place where you have actually been where: *what was supposed to happen did happen because of visual devices.* Name your *Vision Place.*

Maybe it's a nearby factory, hospital or accounting office—a place where high levels of visuality make you dream about your own work area someday looking and functioning like that. You can make that your vision place. The purpose of a vision place is to inspire us on the outside until we have a vision place of our own on the inside—inside our own company and inside our own work area.

If there is no hospital or factory like that near you, find a community location that is highly visual—the post office, for example, or county library. Or the following restaurants and retail outlets, famous for the

many user-friendly visual devices that help customers and employees alike: Friendly's Ice Cream Parlor, McDonald's, Home Depot, Staples or Lowe's (Photos 3.2, 3.3). Or if you live in Orlando, Florida, Disney World is the vision place of choice (Photo Series 3.4).

Photo 3.2 Lowe's visual checkouts.

Photo 3.3 McDonald's: Visual McKing.

There are only three requirements for choosing a vision place: (1) It is highly visual; (2) You have actually been there yourself—physically in person (not just heard about it or seen it on video); (3) It is within easy driving distance (10-15 miles)—so you can visit it often to remind yourself what visuality looks and feels like in action until a vision place exists in your own work area.

Photo Series 3.4 World-class Vision Place: Disney World.

Choose your vision place now and write it down so you remember. Then, if your visual efforts get stalled or you forget what you are working for or why, visit your visual place—and you'll say, "Wow, this place runs like clockwork. It's so smart. They've made everything visual. Hey! I want one like that!"

You saw this phrase—"I want one like that!"—when we talked about *Achieving a Visual Showcase*. See the connection? Your visual showcase becomes a vision place inside the company once you achieve it. Let your vision place be a constant source of information, inspiration, and understanding on your own journey to a visual workplace.

2. Your Laminated Map (a tool to help you focus)

When faced with a large job, some people get overly ambitious and want to do everything at once, only to end up getting nearly none of it done. Others faced with a large project, start feeling so overwhelmed even before they start that they *never do start*. The same can happen when we are faced with converting our work area visually through WTMS. There is so much that needs to be done.

That is why the *Laminated Map* is in your Implementation Tool Box—to turn big projects into bite-sized tasks. The right use of the laminated map allows you to say "yes" to the few and "wait" to the many. It helps you decide where to begin in six easy steps. Here are those steps (Figure Series 3.1).

Step 1. Get a paper map of your work area and laminate it.

Figure Series 3.1 Laminated map step-by-step.

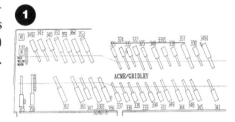

If you do not have an architectural drawing of your department's floor plan, a hand-drawn map will do—as long as it is large enough (minimum 20 inches by 30 inches or go bigger) and *somewhat to scale* (precise dimensioning is not important).

- Your laminated map does not need detail, such as equipment layout, electrical outlets, plumbing, coolant systems, or the like (but if your map already has those, that is also no problem).

Step 2. Draw a boundary around the entire outside of the area.

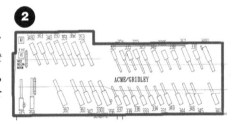

Working with your colleagues, use a dark, *non-permanent* marker to draw a complete boundary around your department, whether it has walls or not. (If you make a mistake, use water and a Q-tip to change it.)

Step 3. Divide the floor plan into its natural work areas.

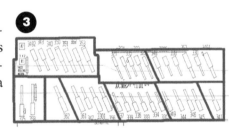

On your map, divide your department's floor plan into its natural sub-areas or sections, based on any combination of factors that makes sense to you—product types, functions, and/or customers, etc. Use your dark, non-permanent marker to draw a boundary, border, or outline around each sub-area.

- Make sure every square foot of your floor plan is bordered or outlined, even closets, staircases, sinks, hallways, aisles, and restrooms (if they are within your department's boundary). Just include each of these within one sub-area or another. This is because, in implementing visuality, every square foot of the physical work environment will eventually be made visual. So everything is included as targets for converting to visuality.

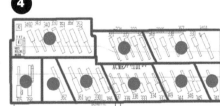

Step 4. Put a blue-dot sticker in each sub-area.

Place a removable blue dot in every sub-area on your laminated map. A blue dot means: *We have not committed to implement here—yet!* See Inset 3.2 for a list of what each dot means.

Inset 3.2 What the Color Dots Mean

● = We have not committed to implement here *yet*. ○ = Smart Placement & the Visual Where are in place.

● = Let's get started—we have a long way to go! ● = A Visual Showcase is achieved and sustainable.

Step 5. Decide where to begin.

With a blue dot in each sub-area, you and your colleagues are now ready to decide where to begin to roll out visuality in your area. Select the sub-area or areas to target first.

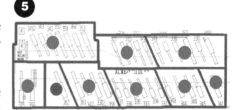

When you have selected your target sub-areas, switch out the blue dot for red ones. Red means: *Let's get started—we have a long way to go!* This is where you will begin to implement visuality, systematically.

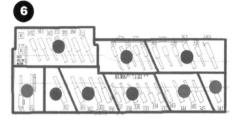

- To start, limit red-dot areas to two or three so you and others feel in control and not overwhelmed by all that needs to be done. Slow and steady wins the race.

Step 6. Begin to implement visuality—and keep going.

Now you are ready to begin to apply the WTMS method, step-by-step. Change the dots, color by color, as you reach each of the visual color-dot milestones in a given targeted area.

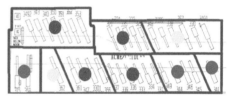

- The blue dot in a sub-area gets changed to red as soon as you begin to apply visuality to it. Dot changes make it easy to track the improvement progress in your area.

- If you wish, mark the date of each color change on the dot itself. TIP: Take photos of your map as the dots change color; the camera's date stamp tracks the process.

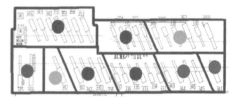

- Post your map on your area's bulletin board. (See *Leadership Task 3* and Photo Series 3.5.)

Leadership Task 3: Visual Workplace Bulletin Boards (Photo Series 3.5)

Each area targeted for WTMS needs a Visual Workplace Bulletin Board for posting various items and notices: the department's Laminated Map, training schedule, Visual Hit List (explained below), Improvement Time Tracking forms (explained below), and other special announcements. With an eye towards uniformity across all targeted areas, work out the format, size, look, color, feel, and location of this board. Make it self-explaining and easy to spot, use, and update—in other words, make sure it is visually functional and appealing.

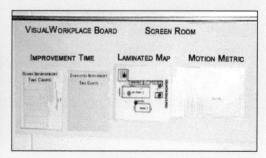

Leadership Centerfold: Your Improvement Infrastructure ~ Six Tools

In the hope for quick and easy solutions to all workplace challenges, we sometimes mistakenly think that improvement success is simply the result of good ideas, carefully implemented. Just as buildings require infrastructure to function safely and well, so your visual conversion requires an internal structure. Management needs to put this behind-the-scenes framework in place before the first associate is trained or the first brilliant visual solution invented. Called the company's *Improvement Infrastructure*, it is management's insurance that steady progress will continue to be made, learning applied, and hard-won gains sustained. As with buildings, the absence of a strong internal framework may go unnoticed until the building (or, in this case, your visual implementation) begins to fail. By then, there is often little that can save the situation. We are left to shake our head and wonder why more strength and reliability were not designed into the structure at the outset.

The six elements or tools below are what I use to help my clients make a successful journey to a visual workplace. When effectively implemented, these tools enable an organization to reach the ultimate destination—a fully-functioning visual enterprise that is also sustainable.

Leader Tool-1. Your Vision Place

Leader Tool-2. Systematic Methodology

Leader Tool-3. Excellent Transfer Materials

Leader Tool-4. Your On-Site Leadership

Leader Tool-5. Your Laminated Map

Leader Tool-6. Your Improvement Time Policy

Two of these six (Vision Place and the Laminated Map) are included in the Implementation Tool Box for associates discussed in this chapter. As managers, you use the same two but, as you read here, with a strong leadership emphasis. The other four are exclusively your responsibility: Systematic Methodology, Transfer Materials, Onsite Leadership, and an Improvement Time Policy.

Leader Tool-1: Your Vision Place. Vision comes first, then transformation. Even though you may have never experienced a comprehensive visual workplace first hand, you have visited places where what was supposed to happen did happen because of visual devices; and, from what you saw, it happened remarkably well. Before you begin the visual journey, choose a location that can serve as your vision place—your touchstone for inspiration—until one exists within your own company (Photo 3.6).

Photo 3.6 Visuals at Lowe's.

Leader Tool-2: A Systematic Methodology. Vision without a road map is only a hope. Select an improvement method with a proven track record for bottom-line results—in this case, related to workplace visuality. Then follow it carefully for at least *three cycles* before you change or remove anything. In that way, you will learn to understand and value the method as given, adapting it knowingly only after you have clarified your local needs. There are many such protocols but for your journey to a visual workplace, our method of choice is the Work That Makes Sense process—structured, principle-based, systematic, and sustainable—with hundreds and hundreds of outstanding visual solutions to learn from and a crisp, robust set of steps to follow.*

Leader Tool-3: Excellent Transfer Materials. How will you transfer visual workplace knowledge, know-how, and excitement to others? How will you inform and inspire others? You need a robust materials package to do so. For visuality, that package needs to include proven content that teaches a systematic method—including concepts, principles, models, frameworks, tools, and practices.*

As importantly, these materials must include scores, if not hundreds, of color photos of splendid visual solutions and explanations, not just from your industry but from many industries. Outstanding instructional materials are indispensable to learning and implementing visuality—and producing sustainable and inventive visual transformations.*

Leader Tool-4: Onsite Leadership. Company conversions do not happen overnight or by accident, not if gains are to last. Your company will need a compact team of high-functioning, emotionally sturdy individuals to lead, coach, and support your visual transformation. These individuals mostly work behind the scenes to plan, support, assess, and troubleshoot the rollout before and during the conversion process. They are responsible for the progress of the rollout, in terms of work culture and the bottom line.

I call this team the *3-Legged Stool*—each leg represents a different person (or group), willing and qualified to be held accountable for a core aspect of the visual conversion and its success. They work together to support the seat of the stool—the targeted areas. The three legs are: the Visual Workplace Champion, Coordinator, and Steering Team (Figure 3.2). (Feel free to change these names to better suit your company).

Leg 1: The Visual Workplace Management Champion is the sponsor of the visual initiative—the person who authorized it and signed off on the resources (dollars, time, and people) needed to support the change. In a union shop, the champion often works hand-in-hand with union leadership. In addition to resourcing the visual conversion, he or she visibly supports the process, providing it with regular top management feedback, and going to bat for the implementation if the need arises. Once the process launches, the Champion's supporting role is largely behind the scenes.

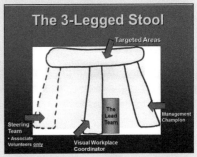

Figure 3.2 An accountable team.

Leg 2: The Visual Workplace Coordinator is the one responsible for: a) the logistical and administrative details that support the implementation; b) coordinating activities between departments (such as maintenance and technical support); c) collecting and graphing improvement time usage; and d) serving as an internal coach to the process.

The Lead Team. Because the Coordinator job is a large one, he or she usually designates a group of two to four people to lend a hand (see small gray box next to the Coordinator's stool leg in Figure 3.2). In some companies, the Lead Team's role becomes more strategic; for example, each team member can be assigned to a targeted area to act as a visual coach and a management liaison. Whichever the case, this team can become an increasingly valuable asset to any serious implementation.

Leg 3: The Visual Workplace Steering Team is formed about three to four months after the initial launch and is made up of an hourly volunteer from each area participating in the visual conversion.

The exact names of Steering Team members depend on who volunteers. This team's mandate is to: a) stay in touch with how the implementation is unfolding within each area and across departments; b) look for ways to strengthen efforts; and c) recommend plant-wide standards and policies to the Management Champion so that visuality sinks deep roots in the enterprise and spreads.

Add a fourth leg to the stool if your company has its own in-house trainers to strengthen and support the visual roll out.*

Leader Tool-5: Your Laminated Map. A conversion can stumble into serious early problems if a decision is made to implement too fast and too wide. No organization knows how to handle or absorb unlimited change right out of the starting gate. The company has yet to learn what to change as well as how to change.

(continues next page.)

(*My company, Visual Thinking Inc., offers outstanding onsite and online training systems in Work That Makes Sense. "The best training materials on the planet," I like to say, as well as an exceptional train-the-trainer process for in-house and external trainers and consultants. See the Resource Section in the back for details or contact us through our website: www.visualworkplace.com.)

The tool called the *laminated map*—this time used on a strategic or enterprise level—can be a big help in focusing resources and pacing the rate of change. In creating this laminated map, you follow the same steps described in this chapter for associates, but for the entire company.

Briefly, managers border all departments on a facility's map; then they decide to which areas to say *yes* ("we'll implement there first") and to which to say *wait* ("We'll implement there later"). The same color-dot system that associates use on their scaled-down map applies here. In this way, managers can regulate the flow of resources that support the initiative, focus on achieving a showcase (a vision place, internal to the facility), and prepare—after their own hands-on WTMS learning—for an easier and more effective conversion in subsequent areas.

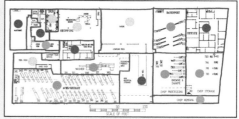

Figure 3.3 Company-wide Laminated Map on its way to green.

Tool-6: Your Official Improvement Time Policy. Any company committed to the journey to excellence is already running full tilt. A company that is not yet on that journey also runs full tilt—but for less positive reasons. If either company does not establish an official improvement time policy, very little improvement will ever happen in that enterprise.

In the battle between operations and improvement for time, operations will always win. That is as it should be since the company is in the business of delivering the products and services that its operations create. Without an established Improvement Time Policy, however, there is a danger that needed improvement will never happen. Improvement can never turn into a workplace habit if we simply leave it to the willing who see the vision burning brightly before them and eke out small pockets of time to make magic happen. In their determination to find a way, these quiet heroes do themselves and the rest of us some bit of harm.

When they succeed in the absence of a clearly-defined improvement time policy, they unintentionally send the message that separate time is not needed. It is the wise executive who sees through this double think and takes steps to establish an official improvement time policy. The lack of an established improvement time policy is one of the greatest company roadblocks to making continuous improvement a way of life. Here are three key points:

- Improvement time is separate from operations time and clocked as such.
- Improvement time is not associated with meetings or general house cleaning.
- Your improvement time policy is piloted for a few months and tweaked as needed until it works for its three stakeholders: the enterprise, operations, and continuous improvement.

But a written improvement time policy is only an intent. After the policy is written, it must be operationalized, tested, and tracked. For that we collect raw data (the actual hours used/not used) on a tracking sheet which value-add employees complete, I-driven. This tracking sheet is either posted on the area bulletin board or, if the work culture is troubled, handed out and handed in privately. (See samples in Figure Series 3.4.)

In over thirty-five years of implementations, I have never found a more finely-tuned yet robust tool for diagnosing the true health and resiliency of a company's work culture than a written improvement time policy that has been operationalized.

This ends our overview of the six leadership tools that executives and managers need to utilize in order to resource, support, and drive the enterprise to a fully-functioning visual work environment. For more, listen to my many podcasts on these topics and all topics in this book. Visit our website *(www.visualworkplace.com)*, iTunes, and Voice America.

Figure Series 3.4 Samples of Improvement Time Tools.

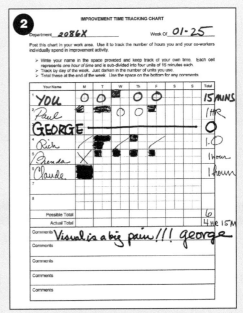

2. Improvement Time Tracking Sheet. This form is handed out to associates so they can track their time directly on it—each in their own hand, as shown here. No pleading. If associates do not submit their info, you have a valuable measure of your existing work culture.

① IMPROVEMENT TIME POLICY
ACME COMPANY
• AUGUST 14 •

The management of Acme Home Repair in Fresno, California is pleased to announce we have been chosen by headquarters in New York as a demonstration site for implementing *The Visual Workplace*.

The Visual Workplace

The Visual Workplace is a systematic improvement method, designed to build the key work information directly into the physical work environment—so that the right information is available to everyone and anyone who needs it, when they need it. The goal is to help us provide excellent service and satisfy—even delight—our customers.

By working together with you to learn and apply visual workplace principles, tools and methods, we firmly believe our on-time, quality, and cost performance will improve—in many cases, greatly. We ask you to join in.

Our first cycle of Visual Workplace training (classroom and hands-on) begins the second week in September and continues, once a month, through the winter.

Targeted areas for the first training cycle are: Customer Service, Audit Department, Truck Stock Specialists, and Human Resources. Dock and Sales personnel, as well as Truck Technicians, are scheduled for the second training cycle that begins in October.

Improvement Time Policy

Acme Management in New York recognizes, as we do, the outstanding care each of you puts forth every day to attend to and care for our customers. We also recognize that, as things now stand, you and your colleagues are busy with daily tasks from the moment you arrive until you go home. There's very little time for improvement.

For that reason, we ask employees, beginning with those in the first training cycle, to dedicate one hour per week for Visual Workplace improvement activity. We call this our *Improvement Time Policy*. As part of it, we ask that you:

• Use this improvement time during normal business hours.
• Keep *Improvement Time* separate from *Work Time* and log it as such.
• Not combine Improvement Time with preparation time, meetings, daily clean-up, breaks or lunch.
• Track your Improvement Time on the forms provided—*even if you don't get a chance to use any*.
• Hand in your completed *Improvement Time* form at the end of every week to your supervisor or to Antonia Caldwell, our Visual Workplace Coordinator.

We will keep this policy under review for several months to give it a good test—and revise it as needed.

As ever, our success in this and all endeavors depends, squarely, on the participation, cooperation and enthusiasm of everyone—YOU! My entire management staff stands ready to support you and do whatever is needed to ensure a dynamic and successful visual workplace implementation.

Please do not hesitate to come see me, Antonia or your supervisor if you have any questions—or just want to talk about this important undertaking. Thank You.

Angela Arsenio
District Manager
Fresno, California

SUPERVISORS & MANAGERS/FRESNO

J. Tomson _____	K. Pruett _____
C. Quasy _____	B. Townsend _____
A. Caldwell _____	W. Hurtz _____
R. Renault _____	P. DellaBuono _____

1. Written Improvement Time Policy. This policy was signed by the ranking site executive plus her direct reports. Notice that the policy calls for a distinct separation of improvement time from any other time use, including actual work and meetings. This policy gets written first.

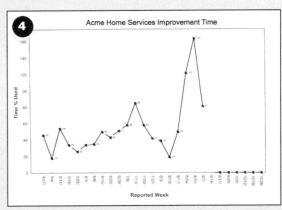

4. Improvement Time Trend Chart. The Coordinator prepares this trend chart for the champion weekly—a valuable way for her to assess the extent to which the policy is working.

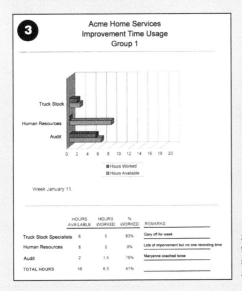

3. Improvement Time Usage Chart. The Visual Workplace Coordinator collects people's usage data, area by area, and creates a chart such as this one to compare the hours which the policy makes available to the hours actually used. Another excellent diagnostic.

3. Your Hit List (a tool to help you target)

The laminated map shows you how to target specific locations in your work area for visual improvement. Now it is time to define the exact improvement tasks and projects that will visually transform those locations—and keep you focused until you are done. This is the job of the third implementation tool: your *Visual Workplace Hit List* ("hit list" for short).

Your hit list is an inventory or log of tasks and projects that you and other associates in your area want to undertake—alone or with a buddy—in order to visually improve the department and take more struggle out of the work that goes on there. The hit list helps you target where to begin and how to keep going by telling you if and when you completed what you set out to do. In this way, you stay focused on your plan and use limited resources—including your own time—productively.

Here are four things to know about these hit lists:

- Your hit list is I-driven. You and your colleagues choose the tasks that get posted there.
- Just because you thought of an improvement task does not mean you have to do it.
- Just because no one else wants to undertake a given task does not mean it should not get done.
- You can work alone. But if you decide to work with others, limit it to no more than two others.

Figure 3.5 shows a standard visual workplace hit list, reflecting a simple six-step procedure. Before I walk you through it, notice the headings: *Your Visual Workplace Project • Point Person • Start Date • Target Date • Status • Comments/Problems/Special Needs*. Since it is important to make your hit list work for you, use these headings as guides, not requirements. Change the language as you wish. It is also perfectly fine to start your own personal hit list. The steps are the same; just post it so everyone knows.

Step 1. Name the Task. Think about the motion challenges you face in your work area, and the information deficits that trigger them. Choose one such challenge and name it in the first hit list column ("Your Visual Improvement Project"). If more words are needed so others understand, add some under the project name.

Step 2. Name the Point Person. Next, decide if you want to undertake this task yourself. If you do not, leave the point-person cell empty; another area associate will pick up the task or your supervisor will help to find one. If you do want to undertake the task, decide if you want to do it solo—or with a buddy. If with a buddy, find that person or ask your supervisor to help find someone. Once found, you and that person decide who takes the lead (the point person) and who assists.

Visual Workplace Action Hit List							
Department: Mag Test and Clinic		Supervisor: Donald x426		Visual Coach: Maryanne x444			Date: June 16
Your Visual Workplace Project — Describe it in a few words. ↓	Point Person — Buddy	Start Date ↓	Target Date ↓	Traffic Light Status			Comments Problems Special Needs
				Red X (started)	Yellow X (half-way)	Green X (done)	
1. We are missing real time feedback on our defect tracking— huge info deficits.	Sue — Dave	5-14	5-25	●	○	○	We need 1/2" drill bits for plastic.
2. Incoming and Outgoing keep getting mixed up—by us and forklift drivers.	Gary — Henk	May 14	May 30	●	X	○	Please get us some more blue and green Floor-Mark.
3. The Stamper SOPs are too hard to get to, especially for newcomers.	Geo	05/18	05/25	X	○		What can stick to the Stamper sides?
4. We need a match between parts and blueprints. Will do.	Mary — Dan	May 21	June 3	●			Who's color-blind in our area?
5. All shipping stations are disorganized in different ways. We need to develop at least three prototype benches.							
6. We want to develop a way to store + track test samples while in our area.	Dan — Joe	May 21	~~May 30~~ June 20	●	○		We need a white board by the door.
7. Our consumable supply area is a mess, no order, no visuality, lots of mix ups. We will fix.	Mary Pat — Nate	6-4	6-14	●	○	●	Can we work with purchasing, please?
8.							
9.							
10.							
11.							
12.							
13.							
14.							

Figure 3.5 Standard Visual Workplace Hit List.

- Again: Just because you thought of a project (AN already important contribution), does not mean you have to do it. And just because no one else wants to do it, does not mean it shouldn't get done.
- Consider working with a second person so you have a back-up—another brain and an added pair of hands and eyes, especially if it is a big project. Or invite the new person in your area (or to the company) to join you and help. Or invite a colleague who you know wants to participate but has not yet thought of an improvement project of his own. Reach out. Improvement projects can be challenging, fun, and satisfying—so spread it around.
- If the project is a big one, break it down into two or three sub-projects or tasks. Post these as separate hit list tasks. Tackling and completing smaller tasks make for early victories and keep the momentum going and interest high. Lots of base hits win ball games as surely as home runs.
- Supervisors start hit lists of their own for related tasks you cannot handle (see *Leadership Task 4*).

Step 3. Set the Dates. Fill in the *Start Date* (the day you actually start the project, not when you post the task). Next, figure out the *Target Date*—when you (and, as applies, your buddy) think the project should be completed. The clock starts ticking when you start working on the project—and when you do, put a red dot in the first cell of your Project Status section. (Don't have the right color dot? Just mark an *X*.)

- Reserve one column on your hit list for comments, worries, and/or special needs—for example, special materials or technical support from engineering.

Step 4. Tackle the Project and Track Your Progress. As you get more of the project done, the color shifts, like a traffic light. At the halfway point, put a yellow dot or an X in the yellow column.

- The yellow level is not exact but simply your fair opinion that the task has reached a mid-point.
- If your Target Date arrives and there is still more to do, reset the date. That is the law.
- Capture comments, problems, and special needs. If you need more room, create it.

Step 5. Complete Your Project. At some point, your improvement solution is in place and you know it. Check off the final box and make sure to take a photo of your result.

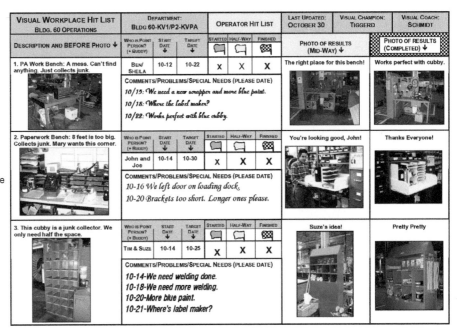

Figure 3.6 Photo Hit List. In this type of visual hit list, you use photos to track your progress—capturing the *Before*, the *Midway*, and the *After*. Notice the use of Nascar Flags, instead of color dots or Xs.

Step 6. Choose a New Project. Keep going. Name another visual improvement project. Tackle another information deficit. Your hit list is a powerful targeting device you can and should use repeatedly. Make it a permanent tool in your implementation tool box.

- Feel free to expand your use of the hit list to suit your needs. If a computer is not handy, ask your supervisor for access or to make the changes for you.
- Add photographs of your project to your hit list—before, during, and after (Figure 3.6).

Leadership Task 4: Hit Lists and Punch Lists for Supervisors & Managers

No matter how experienced and skilled, associates often discover that some or many problems in their area caused by information deficits are beyond their scope to address—sluggish machine repairs, murky quality measures, upstream ordering errors, and the like. Because the causes (and therefore often the solutions) of these problems lay outside the control of area associates, managers and supervisors must take them on. To that end, they start their own hit lists (sometimes called "punch lists")—with tasks that only management are in a position to tackle.

Higher-level challenges can also be handled through a Visual-*Macro Team* (Doorway 9/Chapter 1), a small group of ace visual thinkers who analyze and troubleshoot the overall implementation and often create higher-level visual solutions—for example, visual linkages between departments and across the organization. Managers and supervisors also bring other issues and concerns to this team. All get posted on a *Macro-Visual Team Hit List*, following the same format associates use—but with members of that team leading the charge.

4. Your Supplies (tools to help you invent)

Here's a short story about Dave.

It's the Saturday morning Dave has been waiting for—enough free time to tackle the garage and create a nifty visual wall system for the new tools he got for his birthday. As long as he is done by 10:30—in time to take his kids to practice—he'll be all set. At 8:15 on the dot, Dave opens the garage door, with the sheet of paper he has mapped everything out on. Brilliant! Dave is ready to make magic happen....

But wait a minute, where's that cardboard he needs? What about the paint and that blue tape he was counting on—and those metal drawer dividers? Where are Dave's supplies? "Oh darn, I'm gonna have to make a run to the hardware store—but I'll never get there and back on time. Darn! I'll have to wait for another Saturday I guess... but when? Darn."

Sad postponements of exciting improvement happen all too often—"I have this great idea but I don't have the supplies to make it happen!" The same can occur with the improvement projects on your hit list if you do not do your part. Your part is to:

- First, help your supervisor identify a list of basic supplies you need. (Make sure to include cleaning supplies. You need sparkling surfaces if your visual devices are going to stick, especially those borders, addresses, and ID labels discussed in Chapters 7 and 8); and then
- Make sure to tell him/her if you need any special supplies.
- Help managers think of easy ways to keep basic supplies well stocked and to add new supply items as needed—because as your knowledge of visuality grows, your improvement supplies will need to grow too.

Leadership Tasks 5 and 6 give more detail on getting this done. Photo Series 3.7 shows pictures of great supply storage solutions.

Photo Series 3.7
Visual Supply Stations and Carts: many choices.

Leadership Task 5: Create Visual Workplace Supply Stations

Managers and supervisors, you are responsible for identifying, ordering, stocking, and replenishing visual improvement supplies for your department.

You also need to identify a place to store them—a cabinet, rack, or shelf. Make it some place handy so associates can get supplies quickly. Use a cart, and they can pull supplies directly to point-of-use when needed and remove them when done. If the department is large, several carts will be needed. No one wants to be a "Dave."

Make sure every supply station you set up is highly visual. Borders, addresses and ID labels are requirements. Also think about:

  · A *Table of Contents* on or near the supply station (preferably with min/max levels indicated).
  · A simple pull/kanban system to keep supplies well-stocked.

5. Your Visual Workplace Blitz (a tool to help you drive)

A Visual Blitz is time set aside for a small team (or the entire department) to stop production activities and focus instead on improvement—by applying visual workplace principles and practices (Photo 3.8).

There are three kinds of visual blitzes:

• Visual Macro-Blitz: The entire department shuts down for two to three hours to work on hit list projects.
• Visual Mini-Blitz: Two to three people (or teams, if your area is large) stop work for a few hours to work on hit list projects.
• Visual Micro-Blitz: One or two people stop work for an hour or so to work on their hit list projects.

Photo 3.8 Associates at Denison Hydraulics work together during a Visual Blitz.

Leadership Task 6: Provide Spending Money

Some companies supplement basic improvement supplies by providing each area with a "brown bag of

money"—$50 or $100 that associates can use at will to buy small things that make their job easier (Photo 3.9). When the money is spent, the bag is turned in with receipts and replenished with another round of cash. Consider this option for your company.

Are associates trustworthy? Most of us are not surprised to learn that area associates are not only trustworthy but also meticulously careful about spending and tracking these funds—to the penny. There has certainly never been

Photo 3.9 Renewable funding.

an ROI issue. This level of trust and respect feeds on itself, producing bottom-line benefits far beyond the dollars spent. If you are hesitant, then just pilot the concept. I feel certain you will continue.

Throughout, a visual blitz remains I-driven; you and other area associates decide which improvement projects to undertake, with whom, and how. Your area's hit list forms the backbone. This means that the kinds of things that get improved during a blitz are driven by your ideas and inventions—your need-to-know and, later, your need-to-share.

At first, your WTMS trainer supports you and the blitzes in your area, keeping an eye on hit list projects, helping people buddy up, ensuring supplies are on hand, and coaching as needed. Gradually, your supervisor takes over. The following details begin at that point.

The Visual Blitz: Partnering with Your Supervisor. When your supervisor takes over, he/she helps you prepare for and participate in blitzes in your area, just as your trainer did. Your supervisor will:

- Help you find and hold your improvement focus through the use of the area hit list.
- Check in with you before each blitz to make sure you have any special supplies you need; be sure to tell him/her.
- Help you build your improvement vision, think ahead, and see a successful outcome in your mind's eye.
- Coach you to keep building the power of your visual solutions until they trigger the exact behavior you are looking for—in yourself and in others.
- Show you photos of other people's visual solutions and point out specific visual principles to keep you thinking and inventing.
- Respond to your questions with questions—because your supervisor wants to build your strengths, she is likely to answer most of your questions with another question. Something like this….

> - You ask: Hey, boss, how would you handle this type of motion?
> - Your boss responds: Why do you think?
>
> - You ask: Hey boss, why do you think this device doesn't work?
> - Your boss responds: Why do you think it doesn't work?

You may find this a little annoying ... but sometimes it is the best way for your supervisor to get to know *your* thinking. She already knows her own!

- Help you follow the visual steps you learn in this book, reminding you to do first things first so you follow a systematic approach. (For example, when you start laying down floor borders, the floor surface must be squeaky clean. If you rush past that step, all the effort that follows can come to nothing.)

- Take lots of photos (including *Befores* so you don't forget the past), photos of visual solutions—and solutions-in-the-making—and of people (Photo Series 3.10). People thrive on attention, appreciation, and recognition. Taking photos of them and their ideas is a powerful way of expressing that. Tell your supervisor if you don't want your picture taken. He will respect that—no questions asked.

Photo Series 3.10 Videographer and the Talent.

- Meet with you after the blitz to say "thanks" and, if there is time, to share photos/video and next steps.
- Check in a day or so later to admire what was achieved and find out if anything else is needed. (The company CEO may even stop by. Time for more photos!)

See Photo Series 3.11 for the blitz in action. For more on what supervisors do during a visual blitz, see *Leadership Task 7*.

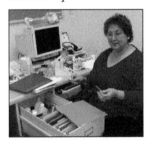

Photo Series 3.11 Visual Blitz in action.

Leadership Task 7: What to Do During a Blitz

Here is a rundown of the finer points of the supervisory role during a blitz.
- Stay visible during the blitz.
- Where given a chance, work shoulder-to-shoulder with area associates, lending a hand, and modeling the behavior you want others to adopt. (Please do not walk around with coffee cup in hand—I think you know why.)
- Share photos on the area bulletin board, on the web, in newsletters, and/or passed on to blitz participants to take home and show their families. Make a video, a visual blitz documentary.
- And remember, as supervisor, you are in charge of time from the outset. You decide what time can be spared for a blitz, realizing that making time for continuous improvement is part of your job. If your operations schedule is tight, a full visual blitz may be unlikely. Look for ways to free up a few people and schedule micro-blitzes instead.

So that is the what, the why, and the how of a visual workplace blitz, the final tool in your Implementation Tool Box. Regular blitzes will help you turn your improvement ideas into practical outcomes that take the struggle out of work. You are going to love what a blitz can do for your area and for you!

With the three outcomes (achieve a showcase, achieve bottom-line results, and adopt an attitude of learning) firmly in mind and the five implementation tools purposefully in hand, you are ready to launch a systematic WTMS conversion of your area. Oh boy!

Leadership Task 8: Avoid Standardizing Too Soon

Starting with the next section in this book, the journey to visuality begins. As you go through the coming pages, you will encounter hundreds of remarkable visual devices, created by value-add associates in other companies. A word of caution at the start: Avoid standardizing too soon.

Standards are the bedrock of operations. Standard work is the bedrock of pull, which in turn, is at the heart of lean conversions. Because of these and other reasons, managers tend to rush to standardization—in this case, standardizing on visual improvements—as an unalloyed, automatic good. "Make it all uniform. Make it all the same," they declare. When they do, they "make it all vanilla." Where the visual workplace is concerned, Cherry Garcia rules, side by side with Coffee Heathbar Crunch.

All visual workplace methods are *repetitive processes, including WTMS.* That means operators keep going until they develop visual solutions that really work. They keep going until each visual device triggers a precise result and the associated improvement in behavior. Rarely does this happen the first time. The first attempt is only a beginning, a draft. That draft gets tested and, if found wanting, strengthened. Is the motion minimized—or only reduced? Is this good enough or is it splendid?

If you, as manager or supervisor, seek to standardize on the first go-round, you will not only rob value-add associates of becoming scientists of their own work as they observe, explore, and experiment, you will rob the company of ripping good visual solutions, with all the attendant benefits.

Instead of standardizing on early efforts, wait for an outcome worthy of the term V*isual Best Practice.* Standardize on that and announce that this new practice will serve as a base for further improvement. Model this and instill it in others. Better makes us best.

This was one of Lockheed Martin's smartest moves during its visual conversion when the company was challenging for the government contract on the Joint Strike Fighter (which it won). Not standardizing too quickly turned the entire enterprise into a laboratory and the employees into a workforce of visual thinkers.

Learn from the mistakes of others.
You can't live long enough
to make them all yourself.

Eleanor Roosevelt

Smart Placement

Where things are located matters—a lot. It matters so much that we are about to spend three chapters learning how to improve the location of things in order to improve the flow of work, people, and information into and through your work area. You are about to learn and apply the logic of *Smart Placement*.

In Chapter 4 you learn the logic's fundamental formula: *Function + Location = Flow.* Hand-in-hand, you learn two powerful mapping procedures. The first map helps you identify motion that is triggered by un-smart placement. The second map you make shows you exactly how to remove that struggle by applying the *14 Principles of Smart Placement*—a set of powerful, insightful tools for change.

Chapter 5 presents the first seven principles. These start you re-thinking the placement of things (of function) in your area. As you will see for yourself, they are far more than simply common sense. They are a fresh, systematic plunge into the tactical logic of location, performance, risk, and flow.

The second set of seven principles are explained in Chapter 6. They focus on larger, more strategic concepts such as design efficiency, the utilization of vertical space, and innovation.

All fourteen principles are made to be applied. When this section concludes, you prepared to undertake the smart improvements you have identified and validated on your maps. The actual increase in the flow, safety, and speed of materials, people, and information in and through your area begins.

Chapter | Four

Smart Placement: The Logic, Meaning, and Mapping

The Logic: Function + Location = Flow
Smart Placement Begins with Thinking
Two Powerful Maps
Ideas, People, and Minority Reports
Your What-Is Map: Step-by-Step

All of us know the value-mantra in the real estate industry: Location, location, location! Location is critical in the workplace, too. This is not just because you need to know where things are—but because, to begin with, those things must be in the right place.

By *right place*, we do not just mean in a designated home location—as in "a place for everything and everything in its place." While that is important, it comes later; and it is secondary to the process this chapter describes.

Instead, by *right place*, we mean the *smart place* for an item—the right location for it in relationship to every other item in the work area (and eventually in the company). We call this conscious and conscientious location of things—*Smart Placement*.

When all the items in the workplace are smartly placed in relationship to each other, the entire landscape of work becomes connected, letting material, information, and people flow into and through work areas with a minimum of struggle—a minimum of motion. Smart placement makes it possible to generate a flow of work that can accelerate (and de-accelerate) at will. Whose will? The will of your customer—and therefore yours.

When smart placement is not applied, the opposite is all too often true. When you and the objects in your work area—tools, parts, materials, information, consumables, benches, cabinets, shelves, chairs, and even trash cans—are physically placed without careful thought and intention, the result can be a tangled muddle that feeds motion instead of supporting a smooth and elegant flow of work.

Let's take a trip to Cycle Hub, a motorcycle shop in Portland, Oregon. The front of the store is filled with Triumphs, Nortons, BSAs, and other English motorcycles (Photos 4.1 and 4.2).

Behind the counter stand Mr. and Mrs. John Mahjor, shop owners and expert motorcyclists in their own right (Photo 4.3; see yellow circles).

Photo 4.1 Cycle Hub.

Photo 4.2 The showroom.

Photo 4.3 The Mahjors, store owners/cycle experts.

In the store's back rooms are mountains of astonishing clutter—monuments to motion (Photos 4.4 and 4.5). Smack in the middle of that clutter, on the side wall (just where the red arrow is pointing) is an oasis of order: the tool board (Photo 4.6). All of the tools needed to keep a bike in good repair are on that board—and orderly.

Photo 4.4 Just behind counter.

Photo 4.5 Chaos in the back room.

Photo 4.6 Smart Placement on the Cycle Hub tool board.

The tools are in smart placement (though, as you will discover, they are not yet *visual*), reflecting the importance Mr. and Mrs. Mahjor assign to the function those tools provide: to keep their cycles running. Yes, the location of function at work matters—a lot. Improve the location of function and you automatically improve the flow of material, information, and people into and through the area. The result? Motion takes a nose dive.

In this chapter, we learn about the logic of smart placement. The two chapters that follow this one then present the fourteen principles of smart placement and show you how to use them to build smart location into the physical landscape of work. No matter where you work—in a bank, factory, medical center, military depot, office, or open-pit mine—when you apply this logic, you create powerful improvements in the design of your work area that pave the way to excellent visuality and superior performance.

The Logic: Function + Location = Flow

The smart placement process begins when you evaluate the current location of the items (things) in your work area—or as we say it: the current location of function.

In a manufacturing cell, for example, this means we look at the individual location of each machine, bench, tool set, incoming raw material, outgoing WIP, dies rack, commodity part storage, desk, and so on. In a hospital, this means the location of charts, medicines, consumable supplies, beds, desks, cabinets, racks, and so on.

In all cases, we recognize that each work item (thing) represents a *specific function*—a specific and particular use or purpose. A desk, for example, represents the paperwork function whereas a machine represents the conversion function—the conversion of material into product specifications, thereby adding value.

The concept of function plays a big role in smart placement. Only when you recognize the true function of an object can you place it correctly—smartly—in your work area. In understanding an item's true function, you also understand its relationship to other nearby functions (items). As a result, you position or locate each of those accordingly. By so doing, you surface and strengthen that network of relationships.

This is the central question in smart placement: What is the best location of function in your area—the smart location of things—so that the flow increases and becomes safer, more aligned, and less costly? The answer is: the "best" location for a given function is always *in relationship* to other functions (things) in that same area. All the things in a work area must function together in support of important outcomes—the product, process, or service for which your department is responsible. Each item in your work area is (or should be) designed to contribute to that outcome—and it must do so safely and conveniently. If it doesn't, then change the item's location so it does—or get rid of the item because it is an intruder. If workplace items are not smartly placed, their location triggers struggle, the footprint of the enemy: motion/moving without working.

Here is the formula that captures that thinking: *Function + Location = Flow*.

And here in a sentence is the perfect logic of smart placement: When you improve the flow of material, people, and information into, in, and through the physical work environment, you automatically reduce motion. You automatically reduce struggle in its many forms: searching, wandering, wondering, risk, handling/handling again, counting/counting again, re-doing, re-working, stopping, asking/answering questions, waiting, and on and on.

Let's look at the case study on the next page that shows us the impact of the unintentional, un-smart placement of things.

Smart Placement Case Study

Here's a smart placement case study of Greene Rubber, a Boston stamping company (Photo Series 4.1).

Figure Series 4.1

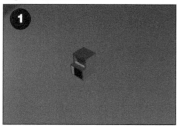

Here is the stamping cell with only its primary value field or function in place: a blue press for stamping small rubber parts.

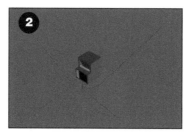

Right now, accessing that function (the blue press) from any angle is safe, straight, and easy.

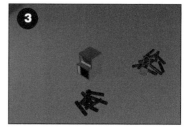

But the blue press needs material to stamp—rolls of rubber plus a sturdy red hand cart for moving the rolls.

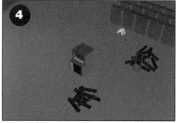

It also needs dies. With hundreds of models, we need hundreds of dies, stored on the tall brown racks, with a nifty yellow step stool so we can reach the top shelves.

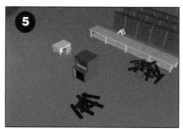

We're almost ready to start stamping —as soon as we have a long table where we can cut rubber into sheets and a desk and chair for our paper work.

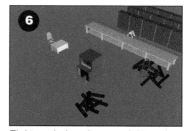

Eight workplace items—eight workplace functions. But accessing them (including the blue stamping press) is no longer straight and easy. Look at the red flow lines.

Now let's look at the impact of those eight simple functions on the direction, volume, and complexity of the flow of materials, people, and information in and through the area—over three hours of lapsed time.

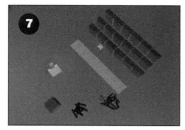

Here's a bird's eye view, a snapshot of the existing layout of function in the area.

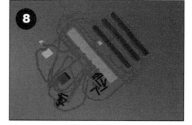

Same view, with motion revealed over a three-hour period. Dinner is served— it's spaghetti, a plate full of motion!

Time to eat the spaghetti and get rid of the motion—caused by the unconscious location of function. Time for smart placement!

On the next page are the first four changes that happened when the Greene Rubber team applied the logic of smart placement (Figure Series 4.2).

Figure Series 4.2

The first re-location of function: Turn the desk and chair around, making it easier to slip in and out while doing paperwork.

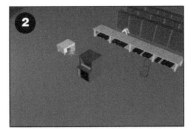

Now put the rolls of rubber under the long table (that shelf was always there—we just never thought of using it). Now materials are at point-of-use.

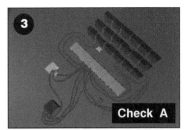

Let's check: Did those two simple changes make a difference? Yes! A huge reduction in motion. And we did it ourselves. Can we do more?

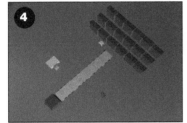

Wow, we can turn the table, moving it closer to the blue machine, closer to point-of-use. It also clears access to the tall shelves. Great smart placement thinking. Can we do more?

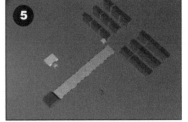

Why not open the tall shelves, making twelve points of access instead of only six. Great idea. But we can't do it alone. We need management approval for outside help. And we got it!

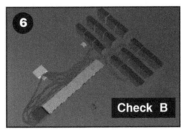

Did these two moves help? Let's check. Yes, look at this three-hour period: The flow is smooth, easy, direct, with a huge reduction in motion.

Greene Rubber's smart placement thinking paid off (Figure Series 4.3). They moved from a ton of motion (*Before*) to an easier flow (*After-1*)—and then to a safe, fast, smooth, and accelerated flow (*After-2*).

Figure Series 4.3

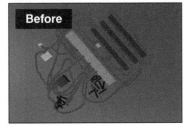

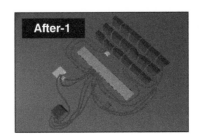

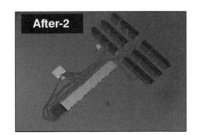

Smart Placement Begins with Thinking

The smart placement process we just walked through in the Greene Rubber case study began just as yours will—with thinking.

What is that thinking? First you identify the functions in your area. Then you name the specific forms of motion caused by the current location of those functions—often an unconscious, unplanned layout. Then you develop ways to change and improve that layout in order to minimize (or even eliminate) motion. You think through ways to improve the location of area functions.

But note: Nothing has changed up to now but your thinking.

Only after that thinking is clear and complete—discussed, vetted, and agreed upon—do you turn to concrete actions. Only then do you move functions to match your new thinking. Then after that, you get *visual* and lay down borders and addresses—the *visual where* that you learn about later in this book.

I'll say that again: Before you move a single trash can or lay down your first border, you need to understand the current layout of your area: what functions exist and where, and how material, information, and people flow into and through your work area in the course of a single day. You do this by a systematic study of a map with your area's current layout. Next, on a second map, you study and apply the fourteen smart placement principles, considering improvement changes on that map alone. Only after those changes are validated and finalized do you make actual physical changes. *The thinking comes first.*

Two Powerful Maps

There is no better way to cultivate smart placement thinking than to develop those two powerful maps I just mentioned. Step-by-step details on developing and using both maps are at the end of this chapter. Here is an overview.

Both maps use different colored sticky-notes to represent different kinds of functions: yellow for hard-to-move functions, blue for easy-to-move functions, pink for work-in-process, green for consumables, and orange for your primary value field.

The first map is called the *What-Is Map*. You and your colleagues develop this map so you can see the true extent of motion, as it is, in your area—motion triggered by the current location of function. The second is called the *Could-Be Map* (or *Dream Map*). At first, this map is identical to your What-Is Map. Then you change it (often radically) as you think through and apply the fourteen smart placement principles you will soon learn.

These two maps give you a concrete way to see, probe, think, imagine, and experiment with the logic of smart placement. You find and discuss many improvement possibilities. One idea type is easy-to-handle changes you can safely undertake on your own; they are *in your control.* A second idea type holds great promise, but you need serious outside help and/or management approval; they are *not in your control.* These are *Big Ideas,* written on yellow post-its. These two types of ideas are handled differently.

Big Ideas: Changes Outside Your Control

As you travel deep into the logic of your area's current layout, you may discover compelling opportunities for improvement *outside* of your direct control (yellow post-its). Maybe these ideas require heavy lifting or are linked to functions that are bolted or wired in. Maybe they are too expensive or too dangerous to undertake without outside help. One way or the other, management has to approve *Big Ideas.*

Ideas, People, and Minority Reports

Sometimes, some of your *Big Ideas* will not get approved. Usually, your management explains why (see *Leadership Task 9*). But you may not be satisfied with the decision. Getting cranky will not change the fact that the decision was never yours to make; it was outside of your control. Let me advise you to concentrate instead on things you can change safely, easily, and quickly yourself. They may be significant or small. But they are yours and can quickly add up to a big difference. Let that momentum work its magic.

Leadership Task 9: Handling the *Big Ideas*

Most of us have active imaginations and, invited or not, love to envision possibilities. The smart placement section of the Work That Makes Sense process may seem to be an open invitation to do so—but it is not. You as a manager are responsible for setting limits on safety and cost.

I make the same point to associates many times in these smart placement chapters: "Just because you think of a great improvement idea does not mean it is going to get done. It may not be in your control." We call this a "hard-to-move" or yellow idea—also known as a "Big Idea."

When managers do not handle *Big Ideas* correctly, smart placement efforts can crash and burn. You as a manager/supervisor must not confuse "I-driven" with open-handed permission. If you do, associates may develop inappropriate expectations. As just stated, they could think that because they thought of an improvement idea, it is as good as done—even though it is a yellow/hard-to-move. Again, this is both not so and cannot be so. Safety, costs, and plain old timing are important decision-making factors. If you promote other expectations, associates will rightly become discouraged, even angry, when their *Big Ideas* are not approved.

Management can if it can—and can't if it can't. Stay open, listen to the improvement ideas of associates, and resist the temptation to over-promise, especially if an idea is out of your control as well. Be realistic. Be honest. Build trust. If it is a no, get back to area associates promptly and respectfully share what you know. That means sharing the real reason/reasons the idea did not get approved. This also means saying when you cannot share the reason because it is confidential. Yes, that is a tough response. Use it sparingly, and when you do, speak with genuine care.

Therefore, when we apply smart placement, we put a premium on collecting ideas, all ideas—ideas from everyone—because smart placement is, first and foremost, a thinking step. Ideas will be triggered simply by making the first map. Then more ideas will come as you apply the fourteen smart placement principles. Some ideas will target the detailed placement of specific items; others will focus on the layout of a cluster of functions or even on your entire area.

The point is this: At the thinking stage of smart placement, there is room for everyone's ideas.

I want to go even further with this. I want you to stand by your ideas as well, even if they are not well received by other people, appear to be unpopular, or are simply different from what your colleagues think. When this happens, instead of retracting your idea or bowing to the popular will, go in the opposite direction: Develop your idea further, explore it, play with it. See where it takes you. Ask your trainer for time when you can present a *Minority Report*—your concept of how smart placement principles could or should work in your area. This so-called "report" is your chance to publicly describe and demonstrate to everyone your unique perspective, peculiar though others may think it is.

At this stage in the process, you and your colleagues do not need to agree on a final set of ideas or changes. It is perfectly usual and acceptable for different people in the same area to see different solutions to the same challenges. This is especially true for common spaces—where people work closely in the same sub-area, for example, and/or share the same bench—either because of cross-manning or different shifts. In such circumstances, focus on staying open; adopt an attitude of learning; and listen carefully. That is what everyone else is supposed to be doing as well.

Getting people to agree on improvements related to shared areas is not out of reach. But it will require patience and tolerance—sometimes a lot of each—before you and your buddies can actually get to the point of moving forward together. This process is called *consensus*, and it is one of the four people tools you will learn about now.

Four People Process Tools

To make sure all ideas are encouraged and collected, the following *Four People Process Tools* are an important part of the smart placement approach.

These four tools share a double purpose: (1) to help you and others find lots of different ideas about smart placement and put them on the table; and (2) to safeguard and even bolster tolerance, respect, and collaboration between people so all ideas get shared. The result? Our thinking gets clearer, stronger, and more complete—and we and others make better decisions with longer-lasting benefits.

People Tool-1. Brainstorm. If you want other people to share their ideas, better make it safe for them to do so. Here are the six absolutes of brainstorming; I encourage you to adopt them:

- All ideas are acceptable and accepted.
- There is no such thing as a dumb idea.
- Ideas are collected first and evaluated later.
- Piggy-back on other people's ideas.
- Keep your non-verbal comments to a minimum—no squirming, sighing, muttering.
- Stay open.

People Tool-2. Appoint a Gate Keeper. If the group gets too rowdy or certain personalities dominate, let a group member take on the role of shutting the gate (temporarily) on energetic, sometimes overbearing characters—while opening the gate for those who have not had much of a chance to speak.

People Tool-3. Use the Talking Stick. A Native American friend of mine told me about the talking stick and how his people use it in community pow-wows.

- Sit in a circle, around a table, for example, with a stick in the center (Photo 4.7).
- If you wish to speak, pick up the stick and speak. Everyone else in the group listens, without interrupting you, not even for questions—no comments, grunts, groans or squirms. When you are done, put the stick back into the center of the table.

Photo 4.7 A talking stick.

- Someone else then picks up the stick and speaks.

- The person with the stick speaks as long or as briefly as he or she likes. Some people simply hold the stick in silence—a long, calming silence. Good idea!

- Keep doing this until no one picks up the stick.
- If you happen not to have a stick handy, use something else—an eraser, a shoe, a book.

People Tool-4. Carry out Consensus. *Consensus* is the most involved of the four process tools. Indeed, you can use the other three tools as part of your consensus process.

There is a lot of misunderstanding about consensus. Here is what consensus is not: It is not about getting your own way by getting other people to say yes. It is also not about caving in and going along with others against your better judgment. That is not consensus. That is just politics as usual.

True consensus requires two things. First, it requires an *active search* for disagreement. That means, we make a special effort to find out what other people are thinking and exactly what their objections are. We dig out the differences and surface the opposition in detail.

Second, when the details of the opposition are known, understood, and appreciated, consensus requires looking for areas where we *can* agree until there is enough agreement for everyone to move forward together. We look for common ground.

In a sentence, true consensus is this: *The active search for disagreement until enough agreement is reached for us to move forward together.*

True consensus takes time, care, and commitment. It deserves a worthy focus. For example, it would be overkill (to say the least) to use the consensus process to get your team to agree on the type of pizza to order (at least it would be for most teams). But it may be just the ticket as you develop smart placement ideas.

So make sure to use these four tools as you share your smart placement thinking with others and they share theirs with you.

Minority Reports are Welcomed (a repeat)

Even with the best people process skills, though, there will be times when it is hard to convince other people about ideas that are different from theirs, especially if those ideas are a bit edgy. As stated before, I want you to share those ideas anyway—by showing them, not defending them: Create a Minority Report (Photo 4.8).

A Minority Report gives you a chance to put your ideas into form—on your own Could-Be Map—so these get a fair hearing. People can listen to something they see better than they can hear something they are told. Please keep this in mind if you run up against push-back when your area does smart placement.

Photo 4.8 Tom had unique ideas for an improved layout in the retail department where he and five others worked. His co-workers pushed back so he asked to make a Minority Report. Granted! Tom made his own Could-Be Map and presented it, on his own, after the rest of his team shared their smart placement thinking. When he was done, everyone was impressed by his clear, practical, innovative ideas, especially his co-workers. But that was icing on the cake. The most important part was that Tom had a formal opportunity to share his ideas, and people listened. (Sears Home Repair/California)

Consensus Mini-Case Study: Three Layouts

The Cables Department at the Harris plant in Quincy, Illinois is responsible for assembling electrical wire harnesses for large radio communication systems. Only a few weeks before the visual conversion began, three cabling areas were merged into a single new department. The seventeen women from those three areas were suddenly faced with a far more complex product flow than they were used to (Photo 4.9)—with the added challenge of never having worked together before.

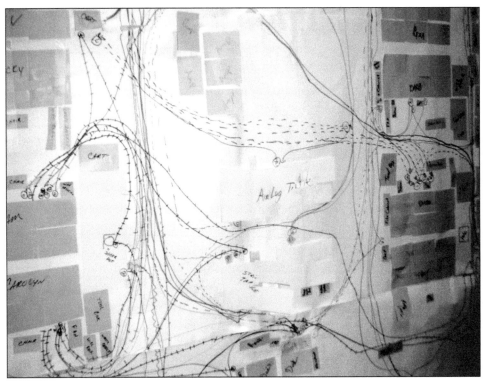

Photo 4.9 Each dashed or colored line represents a different product made in the area.

When the smart placement process began, these women—who didn't really know each other all that well—found themselves sitting around a very large table, mapping out the current layout of function (the What-Is Map). That went pretty well.

Then it was time to map out ideas about improving that layout (the Could-Be or Dream Map). Everyone expected the discussion to get pretty lively. But it didn't. The women simply sat in silence. They appeared to listen, but one couldn't be sure because no one said anything. Not one word.

Behind the scenes, however, the group broke into three factions, each organized around a different layout preference. This evolved into three distinct Minority Reports which people talked about informally, making quiet efforts to persuade others to their respective point of view. (Photo 4.10).

Then the process stalled again. People stopped talking completely.

Photo 4.10 Three layouts/three choices (each on a heavy plastic backing).

Photo Series 4.11 Smart Placement discussions in the Cables Department.

Happily their supervisor, Deanna Butler, was attracted to the description of true consensus that her WTMS trainer had shared a few weeks before (defined above). She launched the process, officially, with the complete department. She put a premium on sharing publicly (Photo Series 4.11).

It worked, taking several weeks for everyone to work through the details. As a result, the people in new Cables Department not only developed a fine new layout, they also got to know each other.

Mental walls left over from the old thinking came down and a new level of respect, cooperation, and departmental performance emerged. The seeds of trust were planted because each group had a chance—through the Minority Report format—to air its differences and preferences to an audience of their respectful peers. (And yes, the talking stick was used more than once.) The final new area layout contained elements from everyone's map for a flow that was safe, sound, precise, and accelerated. It made more sense.

Think about this if you and your colleagues get stalled during the smart placement process—or anytime. The Four People Process Tools are there to help. They really work!

Now let's walk through the steps for developing your own What-Is Map—and for starting your Could-Be Map.

Your What-Is Map
Step-by-Step

Purpose

To discover the cause of motion and risk, embedded in the current layout of function in the area

Time

2.5 to 3.5 hours + 1.5 hours to present findings to group, often with managers (can be split in two sessions)

Supplies Per Team/Table

- 4-6 large blank sheets of chart paper (if possible, with faint pre-printed grid lines)
- Plenty of pencils with erasers
- Plenty of rulers
- Plenty of pairs of scissors
- Several rolls of plain beige masking tape
- Plenty of black, red, green, and blue markers (bullet point)
- Plenty of yellow, blue, pink, green color paper/sticky notes in assorted sizes (a sheet of orange for later)
- Several rolls of clear removable tape
- 3-4 sheets of 0.75 transparent, red, removable dots
- One large see-thru plastic bag

Creating Your What-Is Map

Work together and share tasks across the following 14 steps as you develop your What-Is Map. Remember to give everyone a chance to share. Welcome all ideas. Use the *Four People Process Tools*!

Step 1. Take a large sheet of chart paper. Decide which way to position the layout of your area—portrait or landscape.

Step 2. Turn the chart paper that way. On the left top, write the words "What-Is Map" and your area name. On the top right, write today's date and names of the people working with you today.

Photo 4.12 Sketching out boundaries.

Step 3. With a pencil (not a marker or pen), sketch out the boundaries of your work area. Leave an outside margin of 1.5 to 2 inches around the edge of the paper (Photo 4.12).

- Use a solid pencil line—for walls/other non-moveable structures. Use a dashed pencil line - - - for invisible/non-structural boundaries, such as aisle ways that touch your area.

- Pencil-in brackets "[   ]" for doors (or leave a space). Use a wiggly pencil line for windows. Pencil-in any I-beams with a big **I**.

- **Again:** Start with pencil—not markers! I have never seen a group not make a mistake in sketching out their work area. Use pencils first. Save yourself the trouble of having to correct a marker mistake. (But if you do make a marker mistake, use masking tape to correct it.)

Step 4. When you complete these tasks in pencil, retrace your pencil lines in a bullet-point black marker (flat-tipped markers are too wide).

Step 5: ENCORE. When you complete Step 4, prepare a second sheet of chart paper, identical to the first—only name it the "Could-Be Map" and, as before, add your area's name, date, and team members. Then duplicate the layout you just created on your What-Is Map.

Shortcut (Photo 4.13)

- Tape your What-Is Map to the table.
- Put the new sheet of chart paper over that map.
- In pencil, trace the outline (boundaries) of the map underneath—plus other structural features.
- When you have it right on the second map, re-trace those pencil lines in black marker.
- Remember: Give everyone a chance to partici-pate. Use the *Four People Process Tools*!

Photo 4.13 Shortcut: Lay fresh paper on your What-Is Map.

Step 6. Make paper cut-outs for all items in your area—anything with a floor print or wall print. Color-match your cut-outs to one of the four categories of items. (The use of orange paper comes later.)

Hard-to-Move	**Yellow = Hard-To-Move:** For items that are bolted down, recessed in floor, wired in or the like—or too costly, heavy, or dangerous to move. *Management authorization required.*
Easy-to-Move	**Blue = Easy-To-Move:** For items that you and a buddy can handle yourselves. Don't forget those wastebaskets, chairs, and pallets. (If you work in a union company, follow labor rules and procedures.)
WIP	**Pink = WIP (Work-In-Process):** For WIP in the area—raw material, parts, orders, assemblies, sub-assemblies, finished goods, and so forth.
Consumables	**Green = Consumables:** For packing supplies, drill bits, lubricants, rags, grease-off, and any other item you regularly consume.

Note-1: Cut paper to shape. Use double tape on back to fix each shape on the paper. ***Do not use glue.*** Make items as close to scale as you can. If using sticky notes, combine for larger items; cut for smaller ones.

Note-2: Write the name of each item on its paper. Be specific.

CNC Machine	**Tool Cabinet**	**J-190 Parts**	**Brown Boxes**

(continues next page)

Note-3: Your map layout does not need to be "engineering exact." Instead, focus on getting things roughly correct: the size of the item, space between items, and position of one item to other items.

Note-4: Get creative. Construct 3-D items. Make your paper items look like what they represent: a) Put PINK on BLUE for WIP on pallets, b) Mark circles on items for wheels, c) Fold the cutout to mimic shelving, etc.

Note-5: Let everyone participate. Share scissors, rulers, pencils, markers—everything!

Photo 4.14 3D layout.

Photo 4.15 3D: Green on blue plus wheels.

Step 7: ENCORE. Now make a duplicate set of sticky notes for your Could-Be Map. Place them on that map exactly as they are on your What-Is Map. Include your orange primary value field/s. Do not include the red-risk dots. Work as a team (Photo Series 4.16). See Step 5 for handy reminders.

Photo Series 4.16 Teams working on their maps.

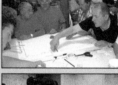

Step 8. Place each cut-out/note on your What-Is Map exactly where the item is in your area today.

Step 9. Find places in your area that are risk or safety concerns for you and your colleagues. Put a red risk dot on your What-Is Map for each such location (Photo 4.17). DO NOT put the red-risk dots on your Could-Be Map.

Photo 4.17 Place red-risk dots.

Step 10. Place an orange square on your *primary value field.* If you work in sub-assembly, there is probably more than one primary value field (Photos 4.18 and 4.19). Place your orange square/s on Could-Be Map.

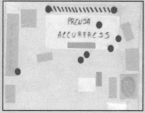

Photo 4.18 Single value field.

Photo 4.19 Many value fields.

Inset 4.1. Mapping: Why not use CAD? (Computer-Aided Design)

I am often asked why I do not let people get/use CAD maps instead of asking them to draw their What-Is and Could-Be Maps by hand. "Think of all the time and bother they would save...." There are two main reasons for asking you to draw by hand.

1. Deeper Insights. I have found no better way for people to connect to micro and macro levels of motion in their current location of functions than to sketch out—using pencil and paper—the work area by hand. And then to populate it, by hand, with sticky notes, cut (by hand) to the size and shape of the things in that area. Because your own muscles are engaged, deeper levels of insight are triggered—and discoveries are more deeply understood and owned.

If I let you use CAD maps, I would rob you of your own thinking and your own engagement. You can be sure the technician who created those maps got to know the area very well, intimately. There a difference between using a CAD drawing and creating one. A deeper level of insight is triggered when creating these maps by hand and from scratch.

2. Smoother Working Relationships. Relationships between people often become smoother and more aligned when they join with others in the simple task of creating these maps from scratch. In the training field, this is called a normalizing activity—a way for everyone to contribute equally, with a high promise of success. The focus is outward—and not directly on each other. If the culture in a given work area is a bit touchy, doing these maps together can clear the way for better teaming (though you may need to use the talking stick for a while as well). It is also often a lot of fun.

Note: Some trainers like to keep CAD blueprints handy for people to refer to as they create their maps by hand. But I don't. I like the depth of understanding that comes from people recalling the area, without prompts. I believe that when they do, they notice a lot more about the location of function in their area. Later in Step 8, they will go to the floor to verify and see what they missed.

Step 11. When you think you are done, go to your work area to check for accuracy of your What-Is Map. See if you missed any item that casts a shadow (Photo 4.20).

- Take your What-Is Map with you, folded in on itself.

- First secure all sticky notes/paper bits with non-stick removable tape. Lay the tape down in long strips, row-by-row, across all loose items. (It's removable so you can pull it off later.)

- Put supplies into a large see-thru baggie: sticky notes, color paper, tape, rulers, pencils, scissors, etc.

- When you finish, return to the training room and finalize your What-Is Map.

- Adjust your Could-Be Map accordingly. Then set it aside on a nearby wall or table. You will use it later.

- Remember: Everyone contributes and lends a hand.

Photo 4.20 Smart placement team from Hitchcock Industries (Minnesota) goes to the floor to check their What-Is Map. They found some things missing.

(continues next page)

Step 12. Trace the material flow in pencil on your What-Is Map. That is, trace out where material first enters your area and then where it stops—and each time it stops—as it flows in, through, and then out of your work area (Photo 4.21).

Number each place the flow stops (pencil first, then marker).

- Mark a #1 for where the material enters your area.
- Mark a #2 for where it stops next. (Photo 4.21)
- Mark a #3 for the next flow stop, and the next, etc.
- Mark the final number where material leaves the area.

Note: You may not have time to also trace the flow of people and then of information into, through, and out of your area. Don't worry.

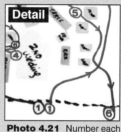

Photo 4.21 Number each step of the flow from when the material first enters your area until it leaves— and every stop in between.

Tracing material often provides plenty of insight into both these other types of motion. Still, if you know people and info flows are motion-critical, make time to add them.

When you have the flows just about right, re-trace them with markers. Show different models or products by using different colors, double lines, dashed lines, and the like (see Photo 4.22 and again Photo 4.21).

If you make a mistake after you started using markers, use masking tape to correct it.

Photo 4.22 Harris team traces many flows.

Step 13. Estimate the motion on your What-Is Map in terms of distance traveled and the time that travel takes. This calculation includes waiting time—the duration of each stop.

Mark these numbers on a card or big sticky note in one of the corners of your What-Is Map so it is easy to spot (Photos 4.23 and 4.24) It is the evidence of why we say: *Function + Location = Flow.*

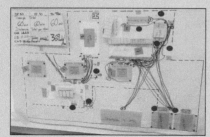

Photo 4.23 A completed What-Is Map, with time and distance motion noted.

Photo 4.24 Close-up of the motion note: time and distance on a completed What-Is Map.

Step 14. Organize your thinking and prepare to present to the group and managers. Share the insights you gained from your What-Is Map about risk and motion caused by the current location of function (Photo 4.25). These are called your *findings*.

Photo 4.25 Operator team presents What-Is Map findings.

Photo 4.26 shows a complex multi-flow What-Is Map (Royal Nooteboom Trailers/Netherlands).

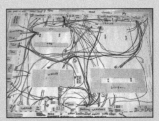

Photo 4.26 Mega multi-flow map.

Note: Each shift can do its own What-Is Map. This works even better if supervisors organize joint shift sessions so important insights and discoveries are made together and thoroughly discussed.

This concludes the 14 Steps for preparing and applying your What-Is Map. I hope you thoroughly enjoyed this discovery experience.

In the next chapter, you focus on the second smart placement map: the Could-Be Map. First you follow the steps for completing the set up of this second map. Then you learn and immediately apply the first seven of the 14 smart placement principles.

You can look forward to a lot of great smart placement thinking and discussion between you and your colleagues as you engage this splendid process.

> You can do anything
> but not everything.
> David Allen

Chapter | Five

Smart Placement Principles (1-7)

Your Could-Be Map: Step-by-Step
Principle 1: Locate Function at/near Point-of-Use
Principle 2: Nothing on the Floor/Nothing on Top
Principle 3: Capture the Full Range of Function
Principle 4: No Doors/No Drawers
Principle 5: Put It on Wheels
Principle 6: Make It Safe and Ergonomically Sound
Principle 7: Make Function Appear/Disappear at Will
Next Steps

In smart placement you look for ways to reduce or even eliminate the *motion* caused by the un-smart location of function—of things—in your area. When you do, you automatically improve the flow of materials, people, and information in and through your area. The key to these improvements are the *14 Smart Placement Principles* you will learn in this chapter and the next (Figure 5.1).

This chapter discusses the first seven principles. They target practical, easy-to-make changes (yellow box). Your success in applying all smart placement principles is tied directly to the understanding of motion you already developed when you developed your What-Is Map. That is the foundation of smart placement's logic: *Function + Location = Flow.*

Developing and using a second map—the Could-Be Map—you imagine specific ways to improve the existing flow by testing out each principle, one at a time.

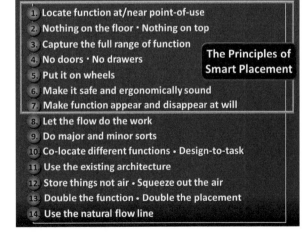

1. Locate function at/near point-of-use
2. Nothing on the floor · Nothing on top
3. Capture the full range of function
4. No doors · No drawers
5. Put it on wheels
6. Make it safe and ergonomically sound
7. Make function appear and disappear at will
8. Let the flow do the work
9. Do major and minor sorts
10. Co-locate different functions · Design-to-task
11. Use the existing architecture
12. Store things not air · Squeeze out the air
13. Double the function · Double the placement
14. Use the natural flow line

The Principles of Smart Placement

Figure 5.1 Principles of Smart Placement.

We will begin that process in a moment. First, let's make sure your second map is ready to go. It may need some finishing touches. Then we will walk through the Could-Be Map steps.

Your Could-Be Map: Applying Smart Placement Principles

Purpose

To apply the 14 smart placement principles in order to develop ways to improve the level of safety, current layout of function, and flow of material, people, and information into, through, and out of your work area.

Time

2.5-3.5 hours (often across two sessions) + 1.5 hours to present findings to group and often managers.

Supplies Per Team/Table

As before (Note: Both maps are already done; supplies are needed for edits, add-ons, and the like.)

Step 1. Double check Your Could-Be Map. Put it on a table. Tape your What-Is Map to a flip chart, chair back, or on a nearby wall (Photo 5.1). Check your Could-Be Map.

a. Make sure that the size, shape, and position of each paper item on your Could-Be Map is exactly the same as on your What-Is Map.

b. Make sure the paper color and name you marked on each item match your What-Is Map.

c. Make sure each primary value field is noted with orange square.

d. Do not trace any material flow lines. Do not add red-risks dots.

Photo 5.1 What-Is Map nearby.

Step 2. Prepare a Smart Placement Change Chart. You need to keep track of the improvement ideas you will develop related to the 14 smart placement principles. Here is one way. (See others on page 97.)

- Draw a grid on a large sheet of with 15 columns. Make the first column on the far left triple-width. Title that column "IDEAS."

- Make the remaining 14 columns equal in width. Number them "1 through 14, one narrow column for each principle (Photo 5.2).

- Post your Change Chart on a flip chart or nearby wall.

- Write each of your IDEAS on a single sticky note in the item's color category (blue, pink, green). Post the IDEA in the far left column.

- Put a check in the column with of the principle associated with each posted IDEA. There may be more than one.

Photo 5.2 Smart Placement Change Chart.

Step 3. Consider each smart placement principle. Study examples of how others have applied it.

a. Look for ways to apply each principle to the blue, pink, and green items on your Could-Be Map. *Special Note: Leave the yellow/hard-to-move items alone until Chapter 6.*

b. Test out each idea directly on your map. Move paper items around to see how your ideas work.

c. If an IDEA looks promising, write it on a sticky note in the correct color. Post it on your Change Chart.
   - Put a check under the principle to which the IDEA applies. There may be several.
   - Posting an IDEA does not mean you commit to do it. You will have time to re-consider it later.

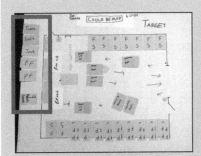

Photo 5.3 Put items you plan to remove in margin of your map (red box).

Note-1: Do not hesitate to remove an item from your work area if you don't need it or it's in the way. Remove the item from your map. Place it in the margin of your map (Photo 5.3).

Note-2: Add items in order to reduce motion and improve the flow. Make a sticky note for each (in associated color). Mark its name on it, the word "NEW," and a dashed border so you can spot it at-a-glance (Figure 5.2).

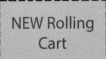

Figure 5.2 Put a dashed border on NEW items.

Respectful Discussion

Let everyone try out his/her ideas. That is, let people show you what they envision by picking up sticky notes and moving them around. That is how ideas get shared (Photo 5.4).

Engage in respectful discussion. Use the *Four People Process Tools*: brainstorm, gatekeep, talking stick, and consensus. If your ideas don't really interest other people, develop your own Could-Be Map (create a Minority Report). Your instructor will help you set up.

Photo 5.4 Respectful discussion.

Photo 5.5 Check off each principle.

Many Ideas Reflect More Than One Principle

As you learn about each smart placement principle, review your previous improvement ideas to see if that principle could apply to one of your earlier ideas. If so, add a check to that row on your Change Chart (Photo 5.5).

Leadership Task 10: Leaders Walk the Talk

Make sure enough training and improvement time is allotted so your employees can build their maps, work through the smart placement principles, and implement the improvements they discover there. As a manager, you'll get a better understanding of the time needed by mapping your own value field—desk or office.

This is exactly what Harris Corp. plant manager, Sue Osier, did in Quincy, Illinois. She not only put many improvements in place in her own work area, she also realized that the 15 minutes of improvement time she had allotted per person/per week were not nearly enough. So she upped the allotment to one hour. Operator-led improvements soared in all the work areas undergoing WTMS training.

Nothing motivates as powerfully as leaders who "walk the talk" and lead by example. There is no better way for you, as a supervisor or manager, to appreciate the value of Work That Makes Sense than to apply it to your own work environment. Remember, waste in front office functions can account for 70%-80% of overall lead time. Be a leader of improvement on all levels of your organization.

Photo 5.6. Sue Osier, plant manager, develops her Map.

Study, Consider, Experiment

With your What-Is Map on a nearby wall as a motion reminder, study and apply the first seven smart placement principles, one by one. Have your Could-Be Map on the table in front of you. Experiment directly on it. That is, unless you are working solo, you and your co-workers consider each principle and look for ways to apply it to the existing layout. Move sticky notes around on the map itself. Remember: Smart placement begins with thinking. After you study all 14 principles, you/your team review that thinking and decide which specific changes to implement (managers weigh in on the yellows). Then, when smart placement is implemented, you'll learn how to "get visual."

Principle 1: Locate Function at/near Point-of-Use

Look at the things in your work area and think about how often you use each: Daily? Weekly? Monthly? Yearly? Based on your answer, determine how near to—or far from—its point-of-use that item (that function) should be located. In other words, how close to—or far from—your primary value field.

Daily or Hourly Use. Keep items you use daily or even hourly close—very close. It is called: *at point-of-use* (POU). The work light in Photo 5.7 is used all the time in this assembly area; it is situated on the assembly fixture itself.

Photo 5.7 POU work light.   **Photo 5.8** POU air hose.   **Photo 5.9** Air hose and outlet at POU.

Same with the air hose in Photo 5.8. It is located just under the fixture, at point-of-use and within easy reach. In Photo 5.9 the operator cleverly embedded the air hose into the floor of the assembly mezzanine (under the metal plate), along with the electrical outlet. Perfect point-of-use thinking. The closer to the point-of-use we can position items that are used daily, the more safely and easily they can be used.

Look at Photo Series 5.10 for examples of weekly, monthly, and less-than-monthly use.

Photo Series 5.10 Other POU Applications.

◄ Weekly Use. Certain items may be needed, but only once a week. When that is so, keep them in the work area (in a cabinet, for example) so they are handy but not cluttering up your value field.

◄ Monthly Use. Items needed at least once a month get stored in a central location, close to but not in your immediate work area. The specialty dies you see here are used for products only periodically ordered.

◄ Less Than Monthly. Move items not used in the past month out of the immediate area and into temporary storage. In this company, such items are put on a red pallet. Then the supervisor decides if the item should be permanently removed.

Photo 5.11 shows another daily point-of-use function, installed directly into the value field: machine changeover tools on the face of the machine itself.

Take a moment right now and think: "Can I use this principle in my area?" If so, make a note of it. If you are working with a Could-Be Map, then target the blue, pink, or green sticky notes—changes under your control that you can make on your own or with a colleague. Leave the yellow notes alone (for now).

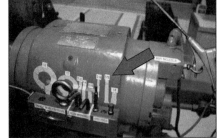

Photo 5.11 POU changeover tools on the machine.

Principle 2: Nothing on the Floor/ Nothing on Top

When you improve the flow of function in your area, you automatically improve safety. That's why smart placement always puts safety first. We see that as well in this next principle: *Nothing on the Floor/Nothing on Top.*

The Floor as Real Estate

Far too often, we can fail to see the actual floor as an asset. Instead, floors are taken for granted and simply used to hold stuff. Viewed differently, floors can be elevated in importance to become partners of our work. In fact, in my experience, a company's floor is the single most valuable operational real estate a company has.

When I say "nothing on the floor," I do not mean to vacate the floor. I mean the floor must be properly and intentionally used—designed for use, designed to task. One of the first steps in getting maximum use out of the floor is to avoid putting items directly on it (Photo 5.12).

Doing this has four immediate pay backs. First, you can use the floor for actual work and work support. Second, when you do not put things directly on the floor, you automatically make moving them easier. Third, with no items directly on the floor, floor surfaces become much easier to clean and maintain. Fourth, when you target *nothing on the floor as a principle,* stumbling, stubbed toes, and other accidents are minimized.

Photo 5.12 "Something" on the floor.

Here are four of *nothing on the floor* ways to "get it off the floor."

Photo 5.13 The problem and its solution are side by side in photo: problem/boxes of parts under the metal rack, sitting directly on the floor; and solution/boxes of parts on pallets in front of rack.

1. Put it on a pallet or in a bin. Instead of putting an item directly on the floor, put it on a pallet or in a bin (see Photo 5.13 for the before *and* after). This is especially helpful for multiple items and heavy items—or both. Do this and you can also then change their location by simply moving that pallet or bin, instead of having to move "things" one by one (Photo 5.14). Minimum motion, minimum time.

Photo 5.14 These large plastic containers protect what is inside while making the contents easy to access and move. Now put the containers on a pallet.

Photo 5.15 Airborne fan.

2. Make it airborne. Get the item off the floor completely and permanently when doing so does not impair its function.

A fan currently standing on the floor (or on your bench) functions just as well hanging from a bracket—with the added benefit of not taking up valuable surface area (Photo 5.15). Now you can use the space you liberated for something else—or leave it free for the unobstructed flow of other functions.

Photo Series 5.16 shows a sequence that began with making yellow part bins airborne and then led to the same for allen wrenches.

Photo Series 5.16 Make it Airborne.

The simple decision to move small yellow bins off the bench surface and onto the backboard is Principle 2 in action. The result? The value field is widened, cleared it for its true purpose: work.

These allen wrenches are smartly placed at point-of-use and anchored in the value field with a border and address. But can we go further?

Yes: Clear the value field and make the wrenches even handier by making them airborne, positioned on the backboard. (See next segment on "Use the Wall.")

3. Use the wall. Dave Martin, head of Maintenance at Seton Name Plate (Connecticut), removed tools, coils, pulleys, and wiring from the floor and put them on the only available space in his shop—the wall (Photo 5.17). Next he added addresses (Photo 5.18) and then borders (Photo 5.19). See Chapters 8 and 9 for more on borders and addresses.

 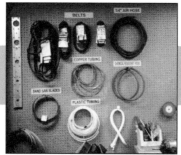 

Photo 5.17 After Smart Placement.

Photo 5.18 Addresses are added first instead of borders.

Photo 5.19 Borders came next and, with them, the visual where.

4. Build a Wall. No spare wall space? Build one. That is, find or create a partition or backboard. Then invent ways to get things on it. Photo Series 5.20 shows five applications.

Photo Series 5.20 Build a Wall.

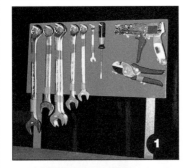
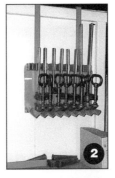

1. A small steel back plate is welded to a work bench so hand tools can be kept close to their point-of-use, yet off the bench surface.

2. This blue hanging fixture for fixtures hooks onto the partition and keeps the surface of the work bench clear and available. Now there's room for the actual work.

3. A metal peg board, fastened onto a wooden partition, smartly places many fixtures, tools, and consumables at—or very near—their point-of-use. (Red borders and addresses were added later.)

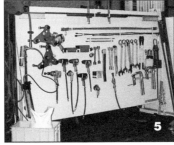

4. Reels of wire could have eaten up valuable floor space. Instead, a white partition with a blue fixture was built so that the reels could be stored airborne.

5. Building this plain white partition was the answer to getting many tools and fixtures off work surfaces and off the floor.

Nothing on Top

The second part of Principle 2 tells us to put *nothing on top*. Have you noticed? The tops of cabinets and high shelves are like junk magnets (Photo 5.21). At some early point, that junked-up space had been vacant—and should have stayed that way.

When we store things up high, we usually forget they are there simply because we cannot see them—because we stored them out of sight. When we need them again, we can spend a lot of time searching before we remember to look up. That's motion enough!

But then when we reach for them, we learn yet another unfortunate result of "putting things on top"—the darn stuff comes crashing down on our heads. More motion. Ouch!

Photo 5.21 Everything on top.

The lesson is plain: Using remote out-of-reach/out-of-sight locations for storage is not smart. What to do? Here's one way: make that impossible (see next page).

The top of the shelving unit in Photo 5.22 was a junk magnet. So Anne, a night-shift operator at this Kansas facility, built a peaked roof out of scrap metal, secured it on top, and painted it all a pretty blue (Photo 5.23).

The result? No one had the slightest chance of storing anything on top! The principle of *nothing on top* got built into the real estate. Good visual thinking.

Photo 5.22 Junk magnet.

Photo 5.23 The solution.

Principle 3: Capture the Full Range of Function

Ensure that you and your work flows smoothly through your work area by stepping to see how the location on one function impacts others nearby. Don't build obstructions. For example, look at Photo 5.24. Even though this corner looks orderly, those handsome yellow borders are not smartly placed.

As a result, we cannot access the cabinet without having to first move the cart—motion! (The borders are not the problem. The problem is the thinking that allowed them to be put there in the first place. When the thinking improves, your borders improve.)

In Principle 3: *Capture the Full Range of Function*, we look for ways to improve the flow of material and work by looking for unintentional blocks to that flow. The key is to capture each item's full range of function.

Photo 5.24 Obstructed access.

Look at the cabinet in Photo 5.25. Its range of function goes beyond its flat front. It extends through the full swing of the two doors, captured in the red curved borders. Smart placement thinking came first. Without that thinking, vital access can get blocked and the flow halted. With it, we see the full range of this item's function. Can you use this principle in your area?

Photo 5.25 Access insurance.

Principle 4: No Doors/No Drawers

Adding value is a physical action—it requires our bodies. In smart placement, we constantly think about what our physical bodies have to do in order to access function—arms, legs, hands. Anything you can do to minimize body movement is a step in the right direction.

One of the more hidden forms of motion—something we do so often it hardly seems like we are "doing" anything at all—is opening a door or drawer to retrieve something (Photos 5.26 and 5.27).

Photos 5.26 and 5.27 Hmmm, wonder what is in there? Guess I will have to open those doors to find out....

The motion meter creeps up if, after we open that door or drawer, we discover that what we are looking for is *not* there and have to shut it and walk away empty-handed.

That's just the start. We still haven't found what we set out to find. Information deficits abound, with lots of other drawers and doors banging open and shut in the aftermath. That's why we say that drawers and doors trigger the first moment of motion—and lots of other motion moments can follow.

In Chapter 8 (addresses), we talk about putting a table of contents on the face of every drawer and door so you don't need to open them to find out, all too often, that what you are looking for is *not* there. But there is another issue to moan about first. This smart placement principle questions the existence of doors and drawers in the first place: *no doors/no drawers.* This is surgery, not a band-aid: Get rid of doors and get rid of drawers. Here are two ways to do that.

Open-Air Storage

The first way is to store things out in the open. Günter at a Rolls-Royce machining site (Germany) removed his changeover tools from nearby drawers and cabinets and put them within easy reach on both sides of a foam-control A-frame panel (Photo 5.28). Next, he plans to put the frame on a daisy wheel (smart placement principle 4: put-in-on-wheels). When he does, he can access tools from either side, at will. (Yes, he will have to make some other adjustments first ... and he will.) Good smart placement thinking.

Photo 5.28 Open access to tools.

See-Thru Doors When Doors are Required

When you must have a door for security reasons or to protect contents against contamination, consider using see-thru material such as screening or acrylic, instead of opaque material, so you can see "through." You still get the protection—and you also get information sharing (Photo Series 5.29).

1. Use Screening.
Expensive tools on the inside required a door on the outside. Screening lets you see you've come to the right place.

2. Use Acrylic Doors.
See-thru doors protect items inside the cabinet and allow us to know at-a-glance, without opening the doors, if what we need is/is not there.

3. Use Acrylic Lids.
These bins hold many small look-alike parts, with acrylic lids that prevent us from dropping them into other bins.

That's a Good One! Look at Photo 5.30. No, your eyes are not deceiving you. The panels on these two cabinet doors have been cut out—no see-thru acrylic panes, just air.

The guys in Final Assembly at Royal Nooteboom Trailers (Holland) proudly announced to me that they had finally found a way to eliminate the first moment of motion on this steel cabinet. I was excited. Then they showed me what you see.

I laughed and laughed. They got me!

Photo 5.30 A *no-door* door.

Principle 5: Put It on Wheels

The wheel is one of the first tools invented by primitive man—and we can still get excited about its revolutionary capability. Here's why:

- Wheels make it easy to move just about anything.
- Wheels make it possible to turn heavy objects.
- Wheels make it easy to bring things closer to the point-of-use quickly and safely—and then get them out of the way just as fast.
- Wheels allow us to maneuver around corners.
- Wheels make it handy to get what we want when we want it—the perfect smart placement partner!

Principle 5 tells us to *put wheels to work* in the name of smart placement.

70% Less Material Handling Because of Wheels

Fleet Engineers (Michigan) manufactures steel, spring-loaded mud flap holders for the trucking industry (Photo 5.31). At the time of this account, a single forklift driver serviced this non-union plant of some 110 employees.

With heavy bins of cast steel work-in-process (WIP), that single driver was very busy. All shift long, he moved WIP between departments and from station to station within departments. Despite the forklift driver's best efforts, some person or operations was always waiting for material, even with a mere ten feet of travel between stations. Motion—and the habit of motion—was so deeply embedded in the landscape of work that most Fleet employees simply accepted long waits as part of their work day—managers, supervisors, and associates alike. At the time of this story, the company had not yet embraced lean; it was, however, about *to get visual.*

Photo 5.31 A steel, spring-loaded mud flap holder.

Photo 5.32 Piles of WIP.

The company's WTMS conversion began in the FB-27 Welding Cell, where steel parts for mud flap models got welded into their initial form. Photo 5.32 shows the *before*: stacks of excess and out-of-date WIP. Area associates began by cleaning up the area, inventing many dirt-prevention devices, and attending to safety issues. Then they tackled smart placement.

Photo 5.33 FB-27 cell after first cycle of improvement.

Photo 5.34 What a difference wheels made.

Using their What-Is and Could-Be Maps, FB-27 operators mapped out a smooth flow of work, later captured in the crisp white borders you see in Photo 5.33. Productivity within the cell immediately improved despite the fact that material handling delays continued whenever a bin of WIP had to be moved—which was many times a day.

It was during one of those long delays (after the white borders were in place) that a light bulb went off: "Hey, why wait? Let's put the bins on wheels and move them from station to station ourselves!" That is just what associates did.

The FB-27 guys constructed metal pallet frames (an easy task for a welding cell), painted them a pretty blue, and fastened on wheels (red arrow, Photo 5.34). WIP-on-Wheels came to Fleet!

The invention spread like wildfire through this hard-working plant. Material handling in the FB-27 was instantly reduced to zero inside the cell and to 70% for deliveries to the cell (because bins still had to be moved by forklift between departments). But with wheels in place inside cells, associates could easily move them on their own. No one was happier about this than the forklift driver.

Wheels for the Fixture for Fixtures

The heavy steel fixtures mounted on the black frame in Photo 5.35 used to lie in a heap on the machining cell floor where Rick Ell, master machinist and ace visual thinker worked (Denison Hydraulics/Ohio). Rick would have to spend a lot of time and muscle heaving those tools around before he found the one he needed. Then he would have to lug it to his machine.

When he learned about smart placement, Rick decided to build a fixture for his fixtures and put the whole thing on wheels. Now Rick rolls the dolly to the machine, replaces the old fixture with the new one, and rolls it back out of his way until the next machine changeover—safe, elegant, and inspiring.

Photo 5.35 A fixture for fixtures.

Photo 5.36 Orange box on wheels.

Box at Point-of-Use

The small orange box in Photo 5.36 contains specific tools and plastic clips needed to secure electrical wiring harnesses onto trailer frames that span 50-60 feet or more. "Why not put it on wheels?" thought the three inventors, "since what is in the box gets used along the length of a trailer chassis?" (See the three inventors on the next page, Photo 5.37.)

Wheels allowed assemblers to make their way around the chassis with a kit of materials and tools always at the point-of-use.

Notice the work instruction folder on the lid of the kit (white circle, Photo 5.38)—a great example of *use the existing architecture*, a smart placement principle you learn about in the next chapter. (Royal Nooteboom Trailer/Holland)

Photo 5.37 The three Dutch inventors: Berry Vogt, Sven van Maanen, and Willie de Swart.

Photo 5.38 Work instructions on the lid.

Lazy Susan/Daisy Wheel

Lazy Susan-1. Yes, the humble lazy susan is also an example of *put it on wheels*—or, at least, on bearings—and can become a very smart part of your smart placement process.

In Photo 5.39, a lazy susan for binders is mounted on the broad top of an old computer monitor, minimizing the clutter around the area and keeping this information within easy reach. (This is also an example of the smart placement principle *store things not air*, discussed in Chapter 6.)

Yes, we know: Fat monitors are obsolete, thrown on the trash heap. But don't throw this great idea away. Use it in principle—and send us a photo!

Photo 5.39 Binders on a daisy wheel.

Lazy Susan-2. The group of small dies (specialized machine tools) shown in Photo 5.40 used to be stored flat on this same deep shelf. But the dies in the back often got damaged when lifted over those in the front. What to do?

The brilliant Bob Comeau (United Electric Controls/Massachusetts) made a lazy susan to store them on, making it easier and safer to access the dies he needed simply with the turn of the wheel.

Reels-on-Wheels. In much the same way, the Cables Department at Lockheed Martin (Texas) mounted wire reels on a pipe rack and fixed the rack to a base also on wheels—

Photo 5.40 Dies on a lazy susan.

Photo 5.41 Reels on wheels.

reels-on-wheels (Photo 5.41). As a result, an assembler simply pulls the whole rack into his/her value field (the assembly bench itself), takes what is required, and then rolls the rack out of the way.

More Reels on Wheels

Many of our "teaching examples" in this book, including the next one, come from United Electric Controls (UE), a manufacturer of electrical switches and controls that won the Shingo Prize in 1989. UE has always had a strong improvement work culture. For example, they made it a point, early on, to involve associates in book study (see *Leadership Task 11*). This before/after story takes place in the department where Bob Comeau works. Bob is a long-time UE employee and, as you have already seen, a master visual thinker (his solutions are throughout this book).

Before. Each time Bob had to cut wire (which was often), he had to search through the spools, lifting and moving many until he finally located the right one (Photo 5.42). Next he would haul that spool over to his bench and cut it to measure. Then, of course, he would haul it back— only to repeat the procedure the next time he needed wire.

Then Bob got smart about placement. He decided to put the entire system on wheels—and took it to the limit. Here's how.

Photo 5.42 Before: Lots of spools of electrical wire.

After. Bob assembled a metal frame and, instead of shelves, installed a series of cross pipes. Then he loaded his wire spools on the pipes, taking advantage of the fact that spools are already "wheels." Look at the details in Photo 5.43.

Notice that Bob decided to organize the spools by color—an industry approach to separate wire specifications by gauge, voltage, open/closed/common, and so on.

Once the spools were loaded on the racks, Bob never had to lift them again except for restocking—a very easy, safe, and smart system.

Photo 5.44 After: Everything is on wheels.

Photo 5.43 Bob Comeau, ace visual thinker!

But wait! Bob went further. Instead of having to carry a spool to his bench for cutting, he got rid of his bench completely. In its place, he installed his cutting machine on the small rolling cart you see in Photos 5.43 and 5.44. The result? Bob simply rolls his portable bench along the length of the shelving, stops at the required spool, cuts the wire lengths on the spot, and rolls away. Genius!

Leadership Task 11: Book Study

This book is an implementation manual. Put it to work for you and your company through regular book study groups. Everyone has a book. Then invite area associates to meet to discuss this book chapter by chapter, usually once a week, possibly during a paid-lunch (rules permitting). Provide a quiet place and allow the group to discuss a chapter, share insights and questions, learn from other perspectives and experiences, and find opportunities of possible application.

I recommend a group facilitator at first in order to gate-keep, focus discussion, keep the reading schedule, and so on. Typically, a supervisor, manager, or WTMS trainer initially takes on this role. Over time, invite area associates to take the lead, usually on a rotating basis. This approach is also excellent for encouraging personal development. Many associates eagerly participate because of their own interest in learning and in seeing improvement happen in their areas—for their benefit and the benefit of the company.

As a manager, please consider book study as a powerful, low-cost option for capitalizing on your investment in continuous improvement and in this book.

Principle 6: Make It Ergonomically Sound

The sixth principle of smart placement is to make the area and everything in it ergonomically sound. Make it fit for us humans. That means we consider the body, its parts, and their range of function.

In Photos 5.45 and 5.46, principle 6 is in action with the addition of a small shelf to this workbench, raising the packing function high enough that we do not have to bend down to fill the box. This small but useful addition can make all the difference in the world for repetitive work. Plus the small, knee-high shelf swivels out of the way when not in use (Photo 5.47)—which also demonstrates the next smart placement principle you will read about next in Principle 7: *Make function appear or disappear at will.*

Photo 5.45 Retractable shelf.　　　**Photo 5.46** At just the right height.　　　**Photo 5.47** Now out of the way.

You see the same flexibility and attention to ergonomic detail in the assembly cell shown in Photo 5.48 (United Electric Controls, Massachusetts). First look at the slanted positioning of the wooden box

in the foreground (arrow 1) to keep hand tools within easy and comfortable reach. The same principle is applied to the long, slanted, gravity-feed shelf above the bench for component parts (arrow 2). They simply slide towards you as needed. Ditto for the drills; they are suspended from the bench on yellow cords (green box 3). You don't even have to pick up a drill; it is already in the air and ready to use.

The bottom shelf on the bench (arrow 4) reflects the same placement intelligence. It is constructed 10 inches off the ground, making it just a bit easier to reach the items on it. "Just a bit easier" is the difference between a reach and a stretch.

Photo 5.48 Ergonomically well-designed assembly cell.

Even the stools in this cell are ergonomically designed—flexible, with a small floor print, as easy to move as a briefcase, and yet they allow the body to be at ease and relaxed, even when active.

Photo 5.49 shows more gravity-feed positioning in the same cell—FIFO, a first in/first out process. This puts sub-assemblies ready for packing within easy, comfortable reach (top slanted red arrow). Notice that the same shelf keeps demand levels visible as well. Reverse gravity-feed on the lower shelf (lower slanted red arrow) helps others retrieve empty boxes.

This cell is an excellent demonstration of many smart placement principles. Now it is ready to get visual—the next step in the WTMS conversion process.

Photo 5.49 Upper and lower gravity-feed shelves.

Principle 7: Make Function Appear/ Disappear at Will

By now you know that a big part of smart placement is getting maximum flexibility out of your location choices. Principle 7: *Make Function Appear or Disappear at Will* asks us to figure out how to get function front and center when we need it—and make it invisible when we do not. Here are some examples, again from United Electric Controls.

United Electric Controls: Three Examples

Example 1. The 8-foot bench shown in Photo 5.50 was in the UE Machine Shop. This was where John

Pacheco, master machinist and ace visual thinker, used to do paperwork. When he began to get visual, he got rid of all the things on that bench not related to paperwork. Only a few items were left—the logbook, some binders, masking tape. They took up so little room that John decided to get rid of the bench entirely—and with that, its 8-foot footprint.

In its place, he installed the 30-inch wide shelf you see in Photo 5.51—just room enough for the items John needed for the paperwork function. Notice his use of vertical space—that small paper rack. But it is the fact that the whole function slides in and out, as needed, that makes this innovation especially noteworthy.

Thanks to the sliding brackets on each side of the shelf, John can now draw his paperwork to him when he needs to do it—and push it out of the way when he does not. The "in-and-out" action of this shelf

puts function at his fingertips and saves space that John can now use for something else. It also lets him clear the other value field of obstructions when he is done—allowing easy access to the metal parts rack that existed long before John situated his paperwork function on it. After he built this excellent application, he spruced it up with paint and a host of helpful visual devices (Photo 5.52).

Two other smart placement principles are seen here and in the next two examples: *Use the existing architecture* and *Store things not air*; both are discussed in Chapter 6.

Example 2. In Photo 5.53, we see the same "appear/disappear" principle used on this sliding shelf for a small punch press. Why buy another workbench when all you have to do is remove a spare shelf from an already-existing rack and turn it into mini-value field?

Photo 5.53 Pull-out machine.

Photo 5.54 Pull-out coils.

Example 3. In another department at United Electric (Photo 5.54), the vacant space under a work bench was converted so it could also contribute to the company's bottom line. This sliding drawer holds coils of steel ribbon used in switch assemblies. Operators simply pull the drawer out to access the coils, and when done, push it back and out of the way.

Scania

Scania manufactures what many consider the best truck engines and cabs on the planet (Photo 5.53). We visit the Scania facility (Holland) and find an excellent application of the appear/disappear principle.

On its *takt-time* driven assembly line, Scania operators need some of their tools some of the time—but not all of their tools all of the time.

Because of that, sets of tools are located at specific points along Scania's indexed assembly line. But operators do not go to their tool boxes or a bench to get them. The tools are mounted on extendable metal arms so operators can pull tool sets to them, at will—and, at will, clear them out of the way (See white boxes in Photos 5.55 and 5.56). This is precisely Principle 7 in action.

Photo 5.55 A Scania-built engine in a Scania-built cab.

Photos 5.56 and 5.57 Exactly the right tools on this Scania assembly line are instantly available at every station along the way.

Next Steps

As we walked through this first set of smart placement principles, I hope lots of possibilities occurred to you. "Gee, I could use this. Gee, I think I might try that out too." This is exactly what is supposed to happen—the realization that there are things you can do by yourself (or with a buddy) to improve the flow of materials, information, and people in and through your area.

Through the examples, you saw that you can accelerate the flow in ways that are simple and yet also powerful.

If you are also using the mapping process described in the last chapter, then you've been moving sticky notes around as well and seeing the changes both on the Could-Be Map and in your mind's eye. That is an excellent place to start.

Your Change Chart

Before we move on to the second set of principles in the next chapter, take a moment and take stock. Review the ideas on the Change Chart you developed—either like the chart on page 82 or something like the chart formats in Photo Series 5.58. Combine elements if it helps your process. Whichever chart format you use, make sure your thinking is clear before you move on.

If a change affects only your own work, you can probably undertake it right away. But you may not change *anything* that is in a common or shared area unless and until everyone who works there accepts that change or welcomes an experiment. (Remember: There is no such thing as an improvement that is unsafe.)

Photo Series 5.58

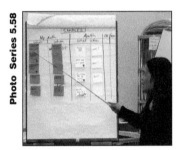

This chart separates ideas needing approval from those that do not.

This chart uses the four colors of sticky notes as an organizer.

This chart separates items based on cost/no cost.

If you are working in a group and the discussion warms up, this may be an ideal time to apply the *Four People Process Tools* you learned in the last chapter: brainstorming, appoint a gatekeeper, talking stick, and consensus making. All thinking is valuable. Keep you mind open and receptive as you listen, share, and learn.

In keeping with our definition of consensus (Figure 5.3), you want to surface areas of enduring differences as well as areas of easy agreement. If that process stalls, do not hesitate to create a *minority* list—one that satisfies you but perhaps no one else. Then, when you are ready, move on to Chapter 6 and the second set of smart placement principles.

Consensus

The active search for disagreement . . .

Until enough agreement is reached for us to move forward together.

Figure 5.3 Definition of true consensus.

Whether you think you can or think you can't, you are right.

Henry Ford

Chapter | Six

Smart Placement Principles (8-14)

In the last chapter, you studied and applied the first seven of smart placement's fourteen principles—and discovered ways to accelerate the flow of material, information, and people in and through the work area by improving the location of function. You reduced motion caused by the unintentional layout of func-tion. In this chapter, you consider and apply the second set, principles 8 through 14 (Figure 6.1).

There is an important difference between the two sets. Principles 1 through 7 target improvements on a micro—or detailed—level related to safety, comfort, and ease of access. You studied: 1) locat-ing function at point-of-use, 2) clearing the floor and the tops of things, 3) showing the full range of function, 4) minimizing motion caused by doors and drawers, 5) putting functions on wheels, 6) using gravity-feed and other ergonomic elements to ease handling and retrieval, and 7) making function appear/disappear at will.

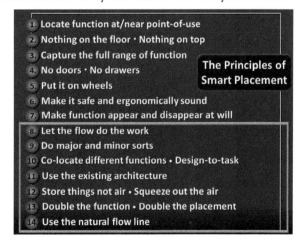

1. Locate function at/near point-of-use
2. Nothing on the floor · Nothing on top
3. Capture the full range of function
4. No doors · No drawers
5. Put it on wheels
6. Make it safe and ergonomically sound
7. Make function appear and disappear at will

The Principles of Smart Placement

8. Let the flow do the work
9. Do major and minor sorts
10. Co-locate different functions · Design-to-task
11. Use the existing architecture
12. Store things not air · Squeeze out the air
13. Double the function · Double the placement
14. Use the natural flow line

Figure 6.1 Second set of smart placement principles (yellow box).

Principles 8 through 14 look at larger conceptual matters related to the overall design and use of the space in your work area. While you will consider several detailed applications for each new principle, I also ask you to search for the wider opportunities of each to streamline and accelerate the entire flow into and through your department.

As you walk through these principles, consider where you might apply each—actually, really, physically. If you are keeping your Could-Be Map close at hand (I sincerely hope you are), experiment directly on that map. Move your sticky notes around, developing ideas into real possibilities. Track your ideas on your Change Chart. Remember to create your own separate map if you have a burning vision and others do not quite get or support it: Create a Minority Report.

Principle 8: Let Flow Do the Work

As mentioned, we addressed many micro applications in the previous chapter. Now we widen our focus and consider the bigger picture: Principle 8: *Let Flow Do the Work*.

That single word—*flow*—captures the big picture of what we want and get from smart placement: a flow of value that moves through the area with a minimum of obstructions or surprises (motion), one that lets us move through our work day not just without struggle but with ease, safety, precision, and completeness. Think about this in terms of your own individual work as well as the work undertaken by your entire department. Think about *flow* (Photo 6.1).

How would you describe that flow? To help do this, step back and look at the overall layout. Look at the path—the flow line—that material, people, and information follow as each makes its way through your department. What do you see? What happens? Do material, people, and information flow smoothly in, through, and then out of the area? Or do things pool and puddle, getting stalled in the nooks and crannies of your department?

How would you describe the flow in your area? Do this now and, if you are working with others, share your impressions and insights.

Photo 6.1 The flow in action.

If you have your Could-Be Map at hand, survey its surface and the sticky notes that populate it and consider the flow you see there. (You can get even more insights by re-examining your What-Is Map.) As ideas occur, talk about them with your colleagues, moving around post-its to show what you mean.

If you are not using a map, go directly to your area and study the flow there, just as it is.

Flow, Pull, and the Yellows

Here is something else to consider: Flow paves the way for pull; flow is pull's foundation. They are allies. Pull is flow under demand. Pull is flow driven by time. And time is driven by your customer. That makes pull—and the flow that comes first—an indispensable part of enterprise excellence. Think about this and discuss it with others.

As you study the flow in this way, you are now allowed to consider moving the *yellow sticky notes*, representing those items that are hard or impossible to move by yourself or without authorization. The "don't touch the yellow" restriction has been lifted—as long as you recognize and accept that: a) Just because you thought of it does not mean it will happen, and b) Just because it does not happen does not mean your idea was dismissed or not considered worthy. Remember that yellow sticky notes are, by definition, under management's control, not yours. Before committing to changing any yellows, company managers need to consider a range of factors (some public, some private)—one or more of which may prevent your idea from getting implemented.

Rest easy with that. Your job is to show up, tell the truth, and stay open. After that, let the cards fall where they must and keep going forward.

Two Mini-Case Studies in Yellow. Here are two mini-studies when area associates, such as yourself, developed smart placement *Big (yellow) Idea* solutions that got approved and implemented.

Study 1: Drop Line Ceiling Grid. Parker Hannifin, a company in Irvine, California, specializes in engine overhaul and repair in the aerospace industry. At the time of this case study, it had been on its visual-lean journey for nearly a decade. Continuous improvement had long become a habit, eagerly exercised by associates, supervisors, and managers alike. The enterprise fairly hummed with innovative thinking.

Over the years, models changed often, requiring many bench moves. Parker Hannifin managers were always a bit reluctant to make these moves because re-installing drop lines (electrical wiring and pneumatic tool air lines) was time-consuming and expensive. They craved ways to improve installments. One day a group of associates offered a different angle. Instead of trying to improve drop line installation, why not improve the *change itself.* Yes, you read that right. Since the cost of re-installing drop lines slowed down layout changeover time, why not flip the equation and leave the drop lines alone and move the benches instead. After all, most benches were already fully-loaded and on wheels (smart placement principle 5).

Photo 6.2 Ceiling Grid.

Photo 6.3 Close up of drop lines.

That is just what happened. Management had a permanent grid of quick-set drop lines installed at ten-foot square intervals across the production floor. When a model change required a new bench layout, the benches were moved based on the drop line grid. Connect the drop lines and you were ready to go.

Hurray for the shrewd pursuit of a *Big (yellow) Idea*, led by value-add associates who were clearly already ace visual thinkers—just as you will be soon.

Study 2: Test Clinic Transformation. Hitchcock Industries (Minnesota) provides precision aluminum and magnesium castings for the aerospace industry. HI's demanding final inspection, which takes place in the Test Clinic, triggers piles of rework. With Could-Be Map in hand, the Clinic team found many

small smart placement opportunities—plus a *Big (yellow) Idea* way to improve the flow of rework surrounding the main test booth. That booth sat at the end of a narrow passage, crammed with units waiting for test. It was a major bottleneck (Photo 6.4).

Photo 6.5 (next page) is the Test Clinic's What-Is Map. See the yellow box on the lower left; it indicates the location of the main test booth. The blue box that surrounds it shows the waiting WIP.

After the Clinic team presented improvement ideas within their control to GM Ronn Page, they shared their *Big (yellow) Idea*: Move the main test booth out into the open area to the far right,

Photo 6.4 Before: Test Booth, blocked by WIP.

and add a second test booth (Photo 6.6). The red box marks area where the two booths are now; the red arrow points to where the single test booth used to be. The icing on the cake was to replace the back wall of the two new test booths with heavy plastic curtains. Similar to a grocery store check-out counter, units then flowed into the two booths from the left, got tested, and flowed out on the right (again red box in Photo 6.6). It was the perfect solution for speed, quality, ease, and convenience.

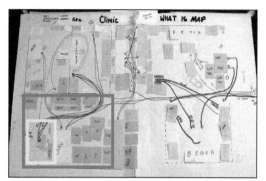

Photo 6.5 Clinic's What-Is Map shows test booth (yellow box), surrounded by pink WIP (blue box).

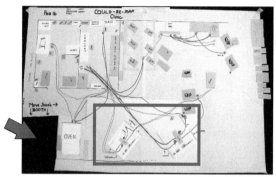

Photo 6.6 Clinic Could-Be Map, with main test booth moved into the open area and split into two test booths (red box).

This change was so well thought out and made so much sense that Ronn Page approved it on the spot. With all the wiring, air hosing, and partitioning, the change took nearly five weeks. Area associates used that time to implement their many small smart placement improvement—the ones in their control.

You may discover similar opportunities with your yellow sticky notes. Just remember: No matter how elegant and worthy an idea may be, other factors can impact management's response—safety, cost, timing, organizational structure, misalignment with future changes not yet announced, and so on. The result? Your idea may not get approved. No matter, you still have blues, pinks, and greens in your control.

Principle 8: *Let Flow Do the Work* is a powerful organizing concept in smart placement. Its successful application benefits everyone—your area, your company, up and down the supply chain, and across the company's customer base. That is why it is important for you to continue to keep *the flow* in the forefront of your smart placement thinking. Notice the flow, study the flow, assess the flow—improve the flow.

Principle 9: Do Major and Minor Sorts

"Piles of things" is a classic trigger of massive motion. Just because a bunch of things pass the first point-of-use test (you are certain you need them on a daily or weekly basis) does not mean it will be easy for you to access the exact "thing" you need when you need it. This is especially true of things that come in many sizes, like drill bits, inserts, packaging materials, fasteners, needles, material types, grades, shapes, and on and on.

Photo 6.7 Nesting Bowls: Sorting the universe. (Courtesy of www.chefs-resource.com)

A simple and powerful way to handle "lots of things" is to determine their sub-sets or categories. I have several names for this: doing major and minor sorts, sorting the universe, and finding the buckets (Photos 6.7 and 6.8). They mean the same thing: Find the sub-sets so you can see the differences in things that appear to be identical but are not. Once you see that, you will be better able to figure out how to locate them smartly.

Sorting the universe is particularly important when we feel overwhelmed by the amount of "stuff"—the universe. "How can I get my arms round all this? How can I handle it?" There is simply too much of whatever "it" is.

Photo 6.8 Sorting the universe: Finding the buckets.

How to Sort

Begin your sorting by noticing what is different about that "stuff" (that universe) and what is the same. For example, what is standard and regular *versus* what is special and occasional?

- That will give you your first two categories or chunks.
- Now look at those two chunks and see if you can make them into four chunks (or categories).
- Then see if you can sub-set those four into eight and, after that, into sixteen. Find the buckets.

Start with a major category and then sort down into minor ones. That is the logic behind the many colors and sizes of the nested kitchen bowls shown in Photo 6.7. All the bowls have the same overall function but noticing their sub-categories helps us locate—and use—them more effectively. We notice the differences.

Photo 6.9 Inserts in family groups.

Inserts Example. The same principle applies to the rack of machine inserts in Photo 6.9. Instead of having all the inserts in a single huge tray, they are grouped in so-called families and smartly placed in separate trays. More precise locations means faster retrieval. You have sorted the universe.

International Example. Another brilliant application of the sorting principle is found at Seton Name Plate, a Connecticut catalogue company that sells and ships thousands of ID products every day to locations around the world. But a category called "shipments" was too broad for the Pack & Ship Team to handle with precision. So the Team sorted the universe into two major buckets: domestic shipments and international shipments. Yet a still finer focus was required. The team sorted the international category into countries—Germany, Australia, Canada—as shown in Photo 6.10. Later, this very smart placement was captured by the splendid color-coded borders and crystal clear addresses you see here. But the smart placement thinking came first.

Photo 6.10 International vs. domestic sorting.

Scania Example. To picture the *Do Major and Minor Sorts* principle on a large scale, we go back to Scania and its facility in Zwolle, Holland where engines and cabs are manufactured (Photo 6.11).

Photo 6.11 Scania-built engine.

Scania is a master at driving out costs through modularization—standardizing as many vehicle components as possible and then making sub-assemblies that are interchangeable between models. Yet the company also had a strong market for custom-made vehicles.

Before, standard and customized vehicles were made on the same assembly line. But business at the Zwolle site was growing. Scania knew it needed 30% more capacity and contemplated the construction of a second plant.

Instead, it applied the principle of sorting (finding the buckets) and separated its operations into two assembly lines—one for standard, highly repetitive vehicles and the other for specialty orders.

The result was the brilliant nested layout you see in Figure 6.2 (Scania dubbed this design *Castor & Pollux*, the famous twins in Greek mythology). The green U-shaped assembly line on the outside is for standard models (notice it is longer) and the red inside U-line is for specialty models.

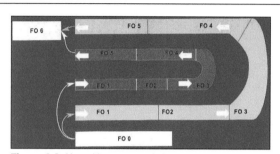

Figure 6.2 Nested layout: green is for standard models and red is for customized models.

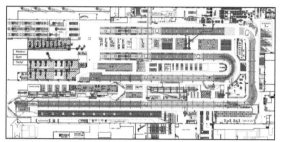

Figure 6.3 Castor & Pollux: architectural detail of the same nested layout.

Scania achieved the needed 30% increase in capacity by nesting the custom line within the standard line and enjoyed the added benefit of enabling the same supervisors to oversee both lines in parallel. Figure 6.3 provides a detailed layout drawing. *Think: Where can you use this principle?* (Inset 6.1).

Inset 6.1 Time to Take Time To Think, Discover, and Use

Make sure to explore each principle as you learn about it. Where could you apply it in your area? How many places? Walk this through directly on your Could-Be Map. Move around the paper cutouts. Try out ideas. Experiment. Change the layout on paper. Activate the logic of Smart Placement: *Function+Location=Flow*. Do not wait! Do it now.

Photos 6.12 and 6.13

Principle 10: Co-locate Different Functions/Design-to-Task

At first glance, Principle 10/*Co-locate Different Functions/Design-to-Task* may look similar to the Principle 9/Sort the Universe. Look closer and you will see that it is not. Here is why.

Principle 10 is about putting *different* functions in the *same* place. We co-locate different items, not to organize them into families as we did in Principle 9 with inserts and parts. We co-locate them because we need different functions in the same location in order to accomplish a specific task.

Design-to-Task: Type 1

This co-location principle is called *design-to-task* because we place items (functions) for a common purpose or outcome. The focus is on linking functions.

You saw the orange box in Photo 6.14 before when we discussed *Put it on Wheels* (Principle 5). This time we look beyond the *wheels* to inside the box. Here associates pre-gathered in a box the tools and clips they need to secure electrical wiring harnesses onto trailer frames. The box is designed for that specific task—and no other. Every item in the box shares the same purpose: some aspect of fastening harnesses onto the trailer chassis (Royal Nooteboom Trailers/Holland).

Photo 6.14 Design-to-task assembly box.

Lockheed Martin Aerospace (LM-Aero) set the pace in its use of the *design-to-task* principle when the Fort Worth Logistics Team wanted a better way to deliver assembly parts. Until then, sets of parts were stuffed—or kitted—into plastic bags; but those bags were often missing parts, or the parts got damaged in transport. So the team devised a series of stiff-foam delivery boxes (Photo 6.15). Each box held all the components for a specific sub-assembly. Here is more on how this intelligent delivery approach works.

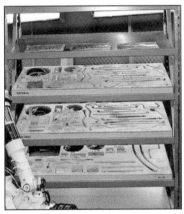

Photo 6.15 Design-to-Task delivery box for parts and special tools (LM-Aero).

• The approach has four elements: a) the assembly parts, b) a carrying box, c) a stiff white foam insert the size of the box, and d) heavy stencil paper, cut to fit the top surface of the box.

• First, lay the parts out on the stencil paper for a snug fit. Second, trace the outline of each part. Next tape down the ends of the stencil paper onto the stiff foam. Then, with a sharp knife, cut out the shape of each part from the foam. Now insert each assembly part into its corresponding foam cut-out. The box is ready for delivery.

Later, an LM-Aero operator had the bright idea of enlarging the box to include special tools. The result? All the parts for a specific assembly—plus any special assembly tools—got delivered at the same time in a single box. Fantastic! This design-to-task delivery approach became a Visual Best Practice across all seven LM-Aero sites. It gained further importance in areas where foreign object damage (FOD) was a concern (Photo 6.16). For an important design-to-task material innovation for anti-FOD and clean rooms see Inset 6.2 on the next page.

Photo 6.16 Happy anti-FOD customer.

A variation on this is a design-to-task box for tools only, shown in Photo 6.17. Here you see the exact set of tools needed to assemble (or disassemble) a specific product in this overhaul and repair facility. The stiff foam cut-outs act as borders to the tools and also control their positioning. The yellow lining makes it easy to see, at-a-glance, when a tool is not there.

Photo 6.17 Design-to-task tool boxes.

Take a moment and study both blue boxes. Does anything catch your eye? Yes, each box has its own mallet—but they differ in weight because of the specific task each box supports. Anything else? Yes, each box contains identical needle-nose pliers. Yet these boxes sit side by side. *Isn't that tool duplication costly?* No. This company, which employs highly-skilled assemblers, discovered that it is more cost-effective and productive to provide each skilled employee with complete tool sets in design-to-task boxes than to chance that someone will have to search for or share a tool. As with a missing part, if you can not find the tool you need when you need it, work stops.

Inset 6.2 HDPE Material for Design-To-Task Kits in Clean and Anti-FOD Areas

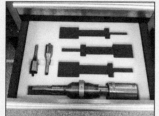

The Design-to-Task principle was deployed for nearly a decade before companies noticed that the high-density foam used in these customized boxes broke down (particulated), leaving many tiny contaminants.

At first, aerospace, anti-FOD assembly areas, and clean rooms had to avoid these applications due to the deteriorating foam. Then technology caught up with the problem. Long-lasting, highly durable HDPE (high-density polyethylene) plastic is now available in a foam-like format for these applications. Contact your supplier for more information.

HDPE plastic in action.

Design-to-Task: Type 2

In Photo 6.18, we see an ingenious application of the *Design-to-Task* principle, created again by the LM-Aero workforce—a motion-buster of the first order, thanks to the brilliant location of function. Called

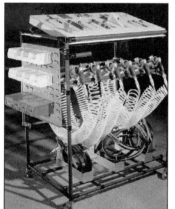

the *Six-Pack* because of the six pre-set pneumatic drills it holds, this lightweight assembly bench is specifically designed for assembling the parts in the foam cut-out box sitting on the top of the Creform bench. The top of the bench is actually the parts box itself, ergonomically positioned for ease of use.

At hip-level are six pneumatic drills, identical except for their bits. Each bit is set for a specific assembly task related to the same parts box—another example of the design-to-task principle.

The bench's bottom tier holds three identical air hoses, each pre-set with a different PSI value (pounds per square inch)—again to reduce the motion called "adjustments."

Photo 6.18 Six-pack assembly bench.

Principle 11: Use the Existing Architecture

Buying stuff for a company is not unlike buying items for your home. "Things" cost money and buying one thing usually means the purchase of some other thing has to wait. That is why making one item serve two (or several) functions means you save money on two fronts: (1) You do not have to buy the second thing, and (2) You do not need to find additional space/real estate or use up the existing real estate to accommodate something new.

Use the Existing Architecture is one of several doubling-up smart placement principles. It simply means this: Attach one function to another. That is, locate the second function onto an existing function. When you do, you double up on that structure so new space (or a new item) does not need to be acquired.

This powerful principle has a wide range of uses, perhaps many already in place before you learned that it was part of smart placement thinking. Now you can exploit this principle on purpose.

Applications

A. I-Beam Application. A plain application of this smart placement principle is shown in Photo 6.19. The primary purpose of the I-beam is to bear weight—keeping the ceiling up and the building intact. We get more mileage out of that I-beam by fastening an air hose reel onto it. This does not subtract from the beam's first function. Plus, the reel is airborne. It does not eat up valuable floor real estate (*Principle 5: Nothing on the Floor*).

Photo 6.19 Let's maximize the use of this I-beam.

Photo 6.20 The end of this shelving unit now holds three additional functions—a thrifty use of space.

B. End Cap Application. Tall shelves like those shown in Photo 6.20 are used to store inventory. That is their primary purpose/function. Yet their usefulness is increased when a notice board—a second function—is added to the shelving unit. Though the primary purpose of these shelves is storage, posting that notice board gets double-duty out of them. That also saves us from having to find (or buy) a new way to post announcements.

We used the existing architecture for multiple purposes. In fact, in this example, two more functions were added: a place for outgoing mail (on the low blue shelf to the right) and a place to hang hard hats (the red one is for visitors).

C. Forklift Innovation. Frank Mulder, a material handler at Royal Nooteboom Trailers (Holland), is well-trained in workplace visuality and an innovative visual thinker in his own right (Photo 6.21). He cleverly and safely applied the existing architecture principle to his forklift in four ways (Photo Series 6.22). He: (1) fastened his red paperwork bin to the forklift door, (2) kept his schedule in a plastic sheet he taped to the door, (3) wrote notes and reminders directly on his side window, and (4) marked his route on the upper windshield, without obstructing his driving view.

Photo 6.21 Frank Mulder and his smart forklift.

Photo Series 6.22 Use the Existing Forklift Architecture

D. Tool Cabinet Application. Look at the doors of the tool cabinet in Photos 6.23 and 6.24. Before, they served one purpose—to enclose and protect the tools inside. Now they have a second purpose, a double function. The inside of one door holds a set of metric wrenches. The inside of the other door holds allen wrenches, an adjustable wrench, and an oil gun. Very compact!

Photos 6.23-6.24 Even the doors of this tool cabinet are put to use.

Photo 6.25 Belt storage on back of bench.

E. Backboard Application. In Photo 6.25, the back of this assembly bench doubles as a storage location for crane belts at point-of-use (the yellow crane column is to the right). This is a clever and handy way to maximize your real estate.

F. Tool Box Application. Photo Series 6.26 presents a little masterpiece of *Use the Existing Architecture*, created by a Boston operator. He started with a common red toolbox (on wheels), added a slab of wood to extend the top surface, fastened a white board and cork board to the back, hung two wire bins for paperwork plus a hook for hoses, fixed his drill bits to the top, and added a chair to rest his weary bones on. Since the entire unit is organized around a specific set of tasks, this is also an example of the *Design-to-Task* principle.

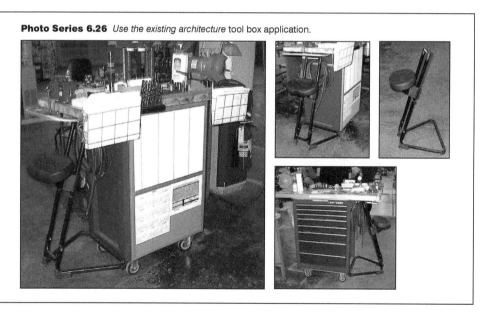

Photo Series 6.26 *Use the existing architecture* tool box application.

Principle 12: Store Things Not Air/Squeeze Out the Air

What maintenance department ever has enough room? Not many. But if we look closer, we might notice unused space in some unexpected places.

When the visual thinkers in maintenance at Denison Hydraulics (Ohio) noticed a wide-open white wall above the entry way, they thought: "Why not use that space for something—instead of for nothing? Why not apply the *Store Things Not Air* principle of smart placement?" So they gathered the pulleys and coils piled up here, there, and in corners—and made a designated home for them on that wall (Photo 6.27).

The result was excellent on every level. The empty space above the entrance way use to cost the company money and never gave anything back. It was under-used. I call that "negative" space. Afterwards, when it became home to all those coils and pulleys, the same wall area made a positive contribution to the company's bottom line. I call that "positive space." The company pays for that wall whether or not it is used. Now there is a return on that investment. The red arrow points to a clipboard with location numbers.

Photo 6.27 This wall now pays for itself.

Photo Series 6.28 shows a wide variety of applications for the *store things not air* principle. Please read.

Photo Series 6.28
Store Things Not Air

1. Not only does this cabinet not have doors, the inside space is maximized by replacing deep, horizontal shelves with metal peg board panels at a slant, positioning tools for easy access.

2. Pallets, stored high off the warehouse floor, make excellent use of the usually un-used and un-noticed real estate called "air."

3. A modest application of store things not air shows a white rag bucket that fits perfectly under a small blue stool; the company saves money that few accountants realized got spent.

Applying this principle requires a form of reverse thinking: You have to see what is *not* there to spot the opportunity that unused air provides as you seek to maximize the use of space through smart placement.

A second form of the *Store Things Not Air* principle is: *Squeeze Out the Air*. Both are in action in the next example of a HazMat (hazardous materials) cabinet at Delphi Deltronicos (Mexico).

A. Store Things Not Air. In Photo 6.29, notice the use of vertical space on the upper left where the two yellow tubs of grease-off are stacked on two shelves (see red arrows). If you are not thinking about "air" as an asset, you might use all that space to store one tub, only.

This is out-of-the box thinking that can lead to many first-rate smart placement improvements. Develop an appetite for it.

Photo 6.29 Turning negative space into positive space.

B. Squeeze Out the Air (1). You can see the *squeeze out the air* dimension of this principle on the bottom shelf of the same Hazmat cabinet (red arrow 1, Photo 6.30). The air has been squeezed out so only the three containers that are supposed to sit on that shelf can fit.

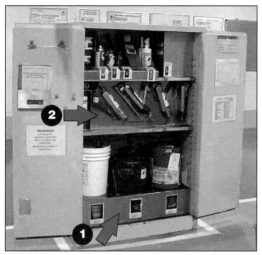

Photo 6.30 Behind the yellow doors of this HazMat cabinet is an expert level of smart placement—and the visual where.

How was that done? Maintenance operators raised the base of the cabinet by welding in a 12-inch metal L-shape plate that squeezed out the excess air. Now the shelf can be used exclusively for the purpose for which it was designed. Nothing else can fit.

The middle shelf for grease guns shows the same principle in action (red arrow 2). We could have just laid the grease guns down on the shelf. But the extra space around the guns might have invited the arrival of more stuff, with the shelf getting so cluttered we might have failed to see the grease guns at all.

Instead, that middle shelf was tilted up and pushed forward. The result? The air got squeezed out. Then the grease guns were affixed to what had become a back plate. In doing this, not only did the air "disappear," but the shelf itself was designed for a single task (Principle 10)—and the grease guns were situated ergonomically for easy, safe retrieval (Principle 6). Three smart placement principles in one application. Fantastic smart placement thinking.

C. Squeeze Out the Air (2). Susan Heater and Lucy Manley, assembly experts at Vibco Vibrators (Rhode Island), wanted to go further in their 5S efforts so they added smart placement principles. Photos 6.31 and 6.32 show one of their many innovations. Lucy and Susan could have: a) filled the three ten-inch shelves with a ton of supplies that were bound to fall over, or b) left the shelves mostly empty, with the now-few items falling over and out of sight. They did neither. Instead, they backfilled each shelf with empty white packing boxes, squeezing out the air so only the wanted quantity could fit and stay upright and visible. Great visual thinking. See Inset 6.2 for more on smart placement and 5S, perfect partners (page 114).

Photo 6.32 Smart placement plus a great use of borders, addresses, and arrows.

Photo 6.31. Vibco Innovators Lucy (left) and Susan (right).

D. Squeeze Out the Air Out (3). If you can not physically reduce the air footage, then at least look for ways to prevent air from acting as a "junk magnet."

The blue shelving unit in Photo 6.33 is a case in point (next page). You saw this unit before in Chapter 5 when we discussed *Nothing on Top*. Remember? Ann, the operator, made a metal cap and welded it on the top of the shelving to prevent stuff from landing there.

When Ann began to identify the use for each of the unit's 25 cubbies, she realized that she did not need them all. She only needed nine: two rows of four and one long top shelf. Instead of risking the other cubbies would get filled with "junk," she squeezed out the air. Ann welded on a metal junk barrier that blocked off 16 other cubbies and left her with the nine she wanted (Photo 6.34). She created a junk barrier. Later, a colleague welded a pipe on the side for yellow bungee cords (Photo 6.35). He added another smart placement principle. Can you name which one? (Yes, Principle 11: *Use the Existing Architecture*.)

Photo 6.33 Twenty five chances to collect junk.

Photo 6.34 Since only nine cubbies are needed, barricade the rest.

Photo 6.35 The pipe that holds the yellow bungies swings out for easy access.

Principle 13: Double the Function/Double the Placement

Question: What is to stop us from using the same "thing" for two purposes, for two functions—the same real estate or same device?

Answer: Nothing but our imagination!

In smart placement, we call this: *double the function*. Let's study three examples for starters. There are many more throughout this book.

Application 1: The Original Double-the-Function Application

Photo 6.36 Double-function borders (with the addresses removed to make you think).

It was the first year of the visual conversion at Fleet Engineers (discussed in *Put it on Wheels* in Chapter 5). The journey began in the FB-27 Cell where mud flaps were welded by a smart, determined and—as you will see yet again—remarkably innovative team. I stopped by the area and saw the floor device in Photo 6.36: Two borders that seemed to overlap, plus a bin of mud flaps, sitting purposefully in one of them. Huh? What was that?

Why have two borders in the same location? My mind flashed on the law of physics we all learn in school: "Two physical objects cannot occupy the same location." What could this thing mean? I had no clue. *Time for a Pop Quiz.*

Pop Quiz! What do you think it means? Why do you think there are two overlapping borders with a bin of WIP on them? Speculate, guess, imagine. HINT: Think about pairs of reasons—like *good WIP* versus *bad WIP* (which, by the way, is not the correct answer). See if you can find three or four other pairs of possibilities. I bet you hit upon the correct answer.

Take some educated guesses and come up with the possibilities, as many as you and your imagination can conjure. At last count, people just like you named eleven. See how many you can name. Just be assured that: a) This double placement means *something* because it came out of smart placement thinking, and b) The borders came second, after the thinking.

The actual answer is: *Model A vs. Model B* (Photo 6.37). Here is more. This double device was situated at the top of the FB-27 cell (see the green X in Photo 6.38), put there by Gary, who worked at the far end of the cell, red arrow).

Gary wanted a way to know which mud flap model was coming through the line next so he could get the right tool set ready (he wanted to be prepared). He wanted to know that at-a-distance, without motion—without questions and without walking over to the work order. Getting that answer began with doubling the function through smart placement. (Note: Gary's own need to know—his "I"— drove this solution.)

Photo 6.37 Answer revealed.

Are there places where doubling the function would help you in your work? Would the principle of *Double the Function* also help the overall flow in your work area—and its safety? Think. Use your Could-Be Map directly, hands-on, and think.

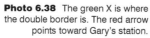

Photo 6.38 The green X is where the double border is. The red arrow points toward Gary's station.

Application 2. A Lot and a Little in the Same Spot

Since I first saw FB-27 cell's application of double function in 1995 (with its visual translation into borders), I have shared it with thousands of people all over the world, including at Royal Nooteboom Trailers (Holland) where it triggered lots of new thinking. Here are two examples.

See the large solid orange outside border in Photo 6.39? See the smaller dashed orange inside border? Both mark out real estate but for two separate sets of materials. Right now, a delivery of bogies (wheel/axle sub-assemblies) is in the small dashed border. The larger bordered location is not in use.

Photo 6.39 Same space, two uses.

That's the point. Sometimes operators in this area need a lot of space for materials. Sometimes they need a little space. But they never need a lot and a little at the same time. So they can use the same floor location for both. Because that use is dictated by the sequence of work, there is never a conflict in using the same physical location for each.

This is splendid smart placement thinking (the visual borders came second). Here is why: This application uses the same real estate for stacked purposes—not for just one thing. Why is that important? Think of the impact of this principle on scarce floor space. Why rent or buy, borrow or steal more space if just thinking differently means you already have enough? That is exactly what you see here. "Sometimes we have a lot. Sometimes we have a little. But we never have a lot and a little at the same time." Wonderful!

Application 3. Work Sequence Borders

The group in Final Assembly at Royal Nooteboom Trailers used the double-up principle in yet another

way (Photo 6.40). They mapped out smart locations for the sequence of operations in each trailer work bay. At the moment of this photograph, the work utilizing the area bordered in orange had already been completed. The next operation is now underway, covering the space previously utilized.

Smart placement thinking came first, followed by the actual smart location of function. Then they made it visual through borders. The floor became a true partner in the important work done in this area.

Photo 6.40 Sequence-related borders.

Principle 14: Use the Natural Flow Line

We opened this chapter stating that *flow* rules smart placement. Our final principle, 14, echoes that theme: *Use the Natural Flow Line.*

You and I both know that very little in life happens at right angles. In the same way, right angles are not a requirement of a sound layout design at work. Right angles are certainly not required for smart placement. The truth is: Right angles can often cause motion instead of removing it. Instead, we use and follow the natural flow line.

The positioning shown in Photo 6.41 is a good example of the natural angle of the relationship between parts-in-process on the left and completed parts on the right. The white borders reflect that. But those borders came second—only after the visual thinkers in this area made the correct link between those two functions—that is, only after smart placement had been determined.

Photo 6.41 Natural positioning.

Here is a mini-case study that tells you more about this powerful final smart placement principle.

Mini-Case Study

Denison Hydraulics (DH) in Ohio is a union-based manufacturer of high-precision hydraulic pumps. When DH began its improvement journey, piles of WIP covered the production floor (Photo 6.42). Since the company had not yet begun to implement lean practices, those piles did not go away. Instead people learned how to make them visible by implementing floor borders. Suddenly they could see the WIP and the categories of WIP.

Photo 6.42 Piles of WIP everywhere.

You see the first generation of floor borders in Photos 6.43 and 6.44. Pallets of work-in-process are organized into grids, neat, straight, and orderly—everything at right angles.

Photo 6.43 This grid looks neat and orderly —but it masks a big problem.

Photo 6.44 More of the same.

Though these grids looked crisp and beautiful, they held a surprise problem—they triggered motion. Can you see why?

Frankly, none of us saw it at first—not operators, managers, supervisors or engineers. And not I.

▲ **Photo 6.45** Bill Podolski.

▲ **Photo 6.46** Another right-angle grid.

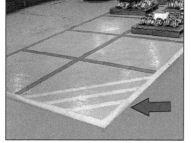

▲ **Photo 6.47** The brilliant solution.

It was Bill Podolski (Photo 6.45), the first shift forklift driver, who opened our eyes—though he did not call it a *problem*. He simply asked for a favor about a bit of struggle he was having.

Bill's Struggle. Bill is a man who puts a high premium on civility. He is by nature polite and respectful. About a month after beautiful, crisp grids were implemented in the CNC cell (Photo 6.46), Bill visited Dorothy and Sheila who worked there. He asked if they would mind if he cut across the grid when he turned that corner in his forklift.

"No, we wouldn't mind," they said. "But, Bill, why would you want to do that?" Dorothy and Sheila had tremendous respect for Bill but were curious about his request. "Well," said Bill, "It's pretty hard for me to make that 90° right angle turn in my forklift. I have to back up quite a few times to do it. It just seems like a lot of motion .... If I could just cut the corner a little, I'd be OK. Would you mind?"

"Oh sure, Bill," they replied, "No problem. Just go ahead and cut the corner. We'll make sure not to put any pallets in that square."

Bill hesitated. "What's wrong?" Dorothy asked. "Well," replied Bill, "Errrr, if people see me cutting across your beautiful grid, they might not understand. They might think I am disrespecting you. I wouldn't want to do it in that case."

Dorothy and Michael understood. The three of them thought about how to handle this. They and came up with a brilliant solution—a visual solution: Implement a cross-cut on the border to indicate that Bill (and the other forklift drivers) were supposed to cut the corner (red arrow, Photo 6.47). Bill felt good about that and the motion caused by that particular right-angle turn disappeared.

And there is more to this story. Read on ....

When the DH Visual-Macro Team (Doorway 9) heard about Bill's worry and saw the solution, they investigated further and realized that a lot of motion was caused by the other right angles across the facility. They observed that each time a driver picked up or delivered a pallet, it took three or four maneuvers to get a 12-foot forklift in and out of position. Those right angles were crisp and neat—but they were frustrating the forklift drivers and slowing down material movement throughout the plant. The solution? Another DH innovation: slanted borders—and they soon became a Visual Best Practice.

Slanted Borders. Slanted borders are simply borders at an angle that permit forklift drivers to make easy in/easy out deliveries. Photo Series 6.48 shows what happened next. And remember, this brilliant solution resulted from smart placement thinking first; the borders came second.

1. Operator, Mel Foreman and engineer, Paul Baker, measure out slanted borders.

2. Bill Podolski (bent over) joins them, tape measure in hand.

Photo Series 6.48 Slated Borders Help Us Follow the Natural Flow Line.

Having discovered the immense positive impact of an angled pick&put approach, the Denison team applied the flow principle throughout the facility. Remember, at the time, Denison was a high WIP site. Inventory was everywhere. Smart placement allowed the company to optimize its traditional/non-lean manufacturing approach.

All levels of management actively supported this and many other operator-led visual innovations. Look through this series to get a better understanding.

3. The result was splendid to look at and very effective!

4. This new system of slanted borders spread—yes, you guessed it—like wildfire through the facility.

5. That small triangle of space closest to you is lost due to slanted borders, but made up for in speed, time, safety, and efficiency.

Next Steps

In the past three chapters, you learned a great deal about smart placement and its fourteen principles. You now know for certain that the location of function matters—a lot. (If your company uses 5S, ask to make smart placement part of that process as well. It can help a lot; see Inset 6.3.)

You have discovered so many ways to improve through smart placement thinking. Many of these are easy to do (the blues, pinks, and greens). Others (the yellows) require management review and, at its option, approval.

Let's look at the several next steps needed to deliver on the smart placement promise.

1. If you have developed a Could-Be Map and time permits, trace and number the improved flows (in pencil first, then in color marker). Then calculate the new flow distance and flow time and your savings. Mark these in an upper corner of your map.

2. Add your improvement proposals to the smart placement change chart you started in Chapter 5. See Photo Series 6.49.

Photo Series 6.49

Then it is time for you and your team to get ready to present your ideas, big and small. If you and your colleagues have developed the two maps, use them to show and share your thinking as you present. If you created a Minority Report, you'll present that right after the rest of your team presents.

Inset 6.3 Smart Placement and 5S

Here's something I haven't talked about that may be very important for you and your company. Smart placement is a process that can help every 5S team before a single border ("line") is put in place. In fact, that is exactly why I first developed the smart placement process. The early companies I worked with on 5S were not getting enough benefit from their efforts. For one thing, borders were thought of as nothing more than "lines." As a result, the company never expected those "lines" to do anything more than frame items.

That is why smart placement was added to my version of 5S. I called it: *5S+1: Visual Order*. Here are the steps:

    S1: Sort Through/Sort Out (remember, the first *S* is for Spirit)
    S2: Scrub the Workplace (focus on dirt prevention)
    S3: Secure Safety (reduce risk in your area)
    S4: Select Locations (apply smart placement)
    S5: Set Locations (install borders and addresses for everything that casts a shadow)
    +1: Sustain (make visual order a way of life in the company)

Keep this in mind if you are about to implement 5S or have it well under way. For more, see my book, *Visual Systems: Harnessing the Power of a Visual Workplace*.

Your Presentation

If at all possible, the presentation session directly follows the completion of your change chart and/or Could-Be Map, after a break. Your supervisor, trainer, and/or coordinator facilitates the session. They help you get ready, and then welcome and introduce the managers invited to sit in (including, I hope, the ranking site executive, members of your maintenance department, and, as applies, representatives of your union leadership). Your facilitators will help set up a flip chart with team names and the order of presentations.

These presentations are an important opportunity for you and your colleagues to share your thinking with senior management. But remember, you do not need permission to make improvements based on the blues, pinks, and greens. These are "Just-Do-Its." Only the yellows require authorization and approval. As we have discussed many times, present these with an attitude of openness. Expect appreciation for your thinking and your efforts to innovate. Expect nothing beyond that—though it may indeed come. And if it does, smile and say "thank you."

When it's your team's turn to present, I like to see all members stand (or sit) up front together, taking turns at presenting, two or three minutes each. It's that simple and people will definitely love your ideas. See Photo Series 6.50.

· If you are certain that you do not want to present, just tell the facilitators. They will probably still invite you to "stand" with your team. I hope you say *yes*.

Photo Series 6.50
Hitchcock Teams present their smart placement thinking to COO Ronn Page (also the WTMS Management Champion).

More Presentation Detail. Here's how presentations usually run when maps have been developed.

1. Walk us through your What-Is Map, sharing insights and understandings about the causes and the extent of motion. If you are with a team, make sure everyone has a chance to present: Pass the baton.

2. Your facilitator asks the audience for clarifying questions—questions about your ideas, thinking, and assessment. This is not the time for the audience to share their ideas. Questions only.

3. Then walk us through your Could-Be Map, sharing insights, understandings, and improvement ideas about reducing the causes and extent of motion through smart placement. Show us what you want to move (or remove) and why. Step us through your Change Chart.

4. Once again, your facilitator asks for clarifying questions from the audience. Then he/she asks the audience to name what they really liked about your thinking and recommendations (collectively, a minimum of three things and a maximum of five).

5. You/your co-presenters respond to everything either with "Thank you," or with "Wow, that's so interesting. Thank you." Do not defend your ideas, but you can ask clarifying questions back.

6. Then your facilitator asks for constructive feedback—ways that audience members think you could strengthen your improvement ideas or adjust them in some way. Once again, respond to everything with a *thank you* unless you need something cleared up. Sometimes an open exchange with the whole group happens at this point. Your facilitator will continue to facilitate—and then ask for things to wrap up when time runs out.

7. And finally, everyone gets their photos taken. Well done! (No problem if you don't want your photo taken. Just make sure to say so.)

Adding to Your Hit List

After the formal presentations, the tasks you are going to tackle get posted on your Area Hit List. Because there are almost always things that people outside your group must undertake, your supervisor and maintenance group also develop a hit list with those tasks on it. I call this the *punch list* or Management Hit List (Figure 6.4). Some groups use a special two-color Smart Placement Hit List, similar to the one in Figure 6.5—blue for associate tasks and yellow for management tasks.

Lead Team Punch List: Smart Placement   090804

Sequence	Associate Name	Lead Team Name	Action Item	Date	Due Date	Estimated Time to Complete in Hours	Associate Assistance Required Yes or No	Lead Team Member Required Yes or No	Maintenance Person Required Yes or No
1	TOM / JOE	Wes	ONE HOSE SYSTEM OF AIR TOOLS	27-Aug				No	No
2	TOM / JOE	Wes	AIR FEED DRILLS	27-Aug			Joe Saracono	No	Yes
3	TOM / JOE	Wes	AIR HOSE REELS ON WALL	27-Aug			No	No	No
4	TOM / JOE	Wes	DOOR LOCK CHANGED.	27-Aug			Yes	Yes	No
5	TOM / JOE	Wes	063 / 1306 FIXTURES NEED NEW WHEELS	27-Aug			Yes	No	No
6	TOM / JOE	Wes	804 FIXTURE NEEDS NEW BASE	27-Aug			Yes	No	No
7	TOM / JOE	Wes	COMPUTER IN ROOM	27-Aug			Yes	No	No
8	Dave/Chuck/Mr. Harpo	Melanie	Clean Ceiling	27-Aug			Yes	Yes/No	No
9	Dave/Chuck/Mr. Harpo	Melanie	Clean Walls	27-Aug			Yes	Yes/No	No
10	Dave/Chuck/Mr. Harpo	Melanie	Repair cracks in floor	27-Aug			Yes	Yes/No	Yes
11	Dave/Chuck/Mr. Harpo	Melanie	Paint floor	27-Aug			Yes	Yes/No	No
12	Dave/Chuck/Mr. Harpo	Melanie	Clean shelves - excess alloys	27-Aug			Yes	Yes	No
13	Chuck	Melanie	Build Chucks Workbench	27-Aug			Yes	No	No
14	Dave	Melanie	Build Dave's Workbench	27-Aug			Yes	No	No
15	Dave/Chuck/Mr. Harpo	Melanie	Build Shelving for Pressure and Milling Fixtures	27-Aug			Yes	Yes	Yes
16	Dave/Chuck/Mr. Harpo	Melanie	Build Pressure Tank Lid.	27-Aug			Yes	Yes	No
17	Dave/Chuck/Mr. Harpo	Melanie	Remove Dust Collector	27-Aug			Yes	Yes	No
18	Dave/Chuck/Mr. Harpo	Melanie	Clean Lights	27-Aug			Yes	Yes	No
19	Dave/Chuck/Mr. Harpo	Melanie	Clean Air Vent	27-Aug			Yes	Yes	No
20	Dave	Melanie	Fixture Rack (workorder submitted)	27-Aug			Yes	Yes	Yes
21	Dave	Melanie	Dirt Prevention - Hand Saw Area	27-Aug			Yes	Yes	No
22	Dave	Melanie	Make decision on need for table at hand saw.	27-Aug			Yes	Yes	No
23	Mike / Tim	Ken	Remove crucible pot cleaning Cabinet	8/27/2004	9/9/2004	4.00	Yes	No	Yes
24	Mike / Tim	Ken	New Lights Mixer Room	8/27/2004	9/9/2004	2.00	Yes	No	Yes
25	Mike / Tim	Ken	Remove gas reel from ceiling	8/27/2004	9/9/2004	0.50	Yes	No	Yes
26	Mike / Tim	Ken	Remove Swing Arm	8/27/2004	9/9/2004	0.50	Yes	No	Yes
27	Mike / Tim	Ken	Remove Flood Light	8/27/2004	9/9/2004	0.50	Yes	No	Yes
28	Mike / Tim	Ken	Build New Pegger	8/27/2004	9/9/2004	36.00	Yes	No	Yes
29	Mike / Tim	Ken	Run Computer lines to office	8/27/2004	9/3/2004	2.00	Yes	No	Yes

Figure 6.4 An actual *smart placement management punch list* from Hitchcock Industries (Minnesota).

Smart Placement Hit List

	SMART PLACEMENT HIT LIST	DEPARTMENT: NORTH WAREHOUSE	EASY-TO-MOVE / NEEDS EXTRA HELP OR AUTHORIZATION		START DATE: NOVEMBER 1, 2009	VISUAL COACH: KENNY + DAVE
	SMART PLACEMENT TASK DESCRIBE IT IN A FEW WORDS ↓	WHO IS POINT PERSON? (= BUDDY)	START DATE ↓	TARGET DATE ↓	STARTED / HALF-WAY / FINISHED	COMMENTS/PROBLEMS/SPECIAL NEEDS
Operator-Led Tasks	1. Locate filters at each work station.	Bob	11-1	11-9	X	Wrong filters were ordered again.
	2. Install new lines from west hall.	Vern / Jo	11-1	11-11	X X	
	3. Locate gap board at each tank till tank.	Vern / Les	11-5	11-25	X X	We need more wood and green paint.
	4. Connect high pressure water on Tote Line.	Mary	11-3	11-12	X X X	That works great.
	5. Move Flow Aid closer to point-of-use.					
	6.					
	7.					
	8.					
Management-Led Tasks	1. Move manifold 1 to left corner.	Bud / Frank	11-8	11-8	X X X	That was easy. Let us know how it works.
	2. Rotate manifold 2.	Cindy / Merle	11-8	11-20	X	This has to wait til next week. Compliance issues.
	3. Move Test Booth to the Docking Line.	Frank / Cindy	11-3	11-19	X X	We need another three days for the wiring. Almost there!
	4. Build new entrance at XH Rover.	Merle / Bud	11-9	11-12	X	We're in for a long wait. Harry had a baby.
	5.					
	6.					
	7.					

Figure 6.5 This special two-color hit list separates associate tasks (blue top section) from management task (yellow bottom section).

These special hit lists get posted—along with your What-Is and Could-Be Maps—on or near your area's visual workplace bulletin board. In that way, everyone continues to think about the changes that are on the way and keeps his or her eye on what is or isn't happening. This is critically important when you have multiple shifts the way many organizations do (having five to eight shifts is not unusual anymore).

What to Expect

What should you expect from all this great smart placement thinking? If you and your colleagues came up with a lot of ideas, count on it taking two or three weeks to get them in place. Maybe longer. This is not just a question of management follow-through (see *Leadership Task 12*). It is often also a matter of time availability. In organizations that adopt improvement time as a measure, that will mean how much time your supervisor can afford to release for improvement activity.

One further point. Some companies committed to continuous improvement can nevertheless go through a period where things seem to get a bit rocky. That is usually because people are learning to balance improvement goals with production demands. It can take extra time before improvement gets steady and the production schedule does not suffer. With patience and a strong resolve, the tide usually turns and good progress is made.

One More Thing: The Paper Doll Layout

If you have big plans for changing the current area layout, you and your group may want to do a *Paper Doll Layout*. First make full-size cardboard cutouts of all floor items (benches, machines, WIP, cabinets, chairs, etc.) in as close to their actual size and shape as possible. Then lay out the cardboard pieces in a large, vacated space, such as the parking lot (weather permitting), a warehouse area, or the cafeteria when not in use.

In that way, you can check out your thinking for real. You may discover, for example, that you over-estimated or under-estimated the distance between value fields and the direction and complexity of the flow. The paper doll layout allows you to validate your "dream" and to edit it. Your supervisor will help.

Leadership Task 12: Smart Placement Follow Up and Follow Through

Leaders, there is no way to over-emphasize the importance of your responding to people's smart placement improvement ideas with clear, speedy support. (Do this for all improvement ideas.)

For easy-to-move items (blue, pinks, and greens) that means: a) releasing improvement time so associates can get those tasks done, b) making sure they have the required supplies and use the hit list to focus and target, c) schedule blitzes as time permits, d) stay positive, e) give lots of positive feedback (*specific praise* is better than general thanks), f) check in through open-ended questions, and g) before, during, and after, ensure that lots of photos of things and people are taken (as permitted).

Your active involvement and support are key to ensuring that your company reaps the many benefits and rewards that smart placement can produce.

Of equal importance is your follow-through on the tasks on your Management Punch List—the yellows. Walk the talk. Nothing dampens the excitement and commitment that smart placement can trigger more than lukewarm or non-existent follow-through on your own commitments and those of your peers. As a rule, this is a three-week window. If something doesn't happen during that time, associates start dropping out, first in their minds and then in their hearts. You may never get them back.

By the same token, if a management task gets legitimately stuck, you need to communicate that. "I know we planned to move on your idea by this Friday—but Jerry is out ill. We will pick this up as soon as he gets back. Sorry, guys." The "guys" will usually understand—because they have something to understand. I know this may sound overly simplistic. But in fact I cannot over-estimate the importance of communicating, communicating, communicating. There is truth in the adage: "The biggest mistake in communication is thinking that it has happened." Don't let that happen to you.

So follow-up and follow-through. Reap all the benefits of the splendid smart placement thinking your value-add associates develop. And remember, the 14 principles are strongly applicable in office and support settings too.

> What lies behind us and what lies before us are tiny matters compared to what lies within us.
> Oliver Wendell Homes

The Visual Where

Once you have applied the principles of smart placement and made the related physical changes, you are ready to nail down these new locations—to anchor them—in your work area through the *visual where*.

The visual where consists of three types of visual devices: borders, addresses, and ID labels. Chapter 7, the first of the two chapters in this section, teaches you all about borders, the indispensable first step in installing the visual where. We'll study more than 70 border examples so you can come to appreciate the breadth and depth of the border function and the inventive ways it can be used to reduce information deficits, and the motion that they trigger.

Chapter 8 is all about addresses and ID Labels. Together, they make what lives in your borders crystal clear. More than 60 examples of those support your new learning.

Get informed. Get inspired. By the time you finish this section, you will understand the power of the visual where and how to implement it in your area.

Chapter | Seven

Visual Where: Borders

Now that you have improved the current location of function in your area through the principles of smart placement, you are ready to "nail" those locations in place through visual location information—visual devices that embed the visual where.

The Visual Where

Among its many important purposes, the visual where provides many work items with the ability to find their own way back home—to their proper and designated locations—based solely on the visual location information in their borders, addresses, and ID labels (see Photo 7.1).

The visual where is applied to *everything* in the work area that casts a shadow. Said another way, everything that casts a shadow in your work area gets a border, address, and, if possible, an ID label. That means *everything*.

As you soon will discover, this "everything" requirement is a powerful driver of the level of visual excellence that in many companies results in a 15% to 30% improvement in productivity.

Remember Cycle Hub in Portland, Oregon? The back room was mayhem—except for one spot that was carefully laid out: a panel of tools (next page: Photos 7.2 and 7.3). That makes sense, doesn't it?

Photo 7.1 The three elements of the visual where: border + address + ID label.

The owners (Mr. & Mrs. Majhor) use their tools many times a day. Because these tools are so important, the Majhors took steps to ensure they were always handy. Yes, they made sure the tools were *smartly placed*. But there are no borders—no visual where. That means, when the Majhors finish using their tools, they have to *think about* where the tools

Photo 7.2 Cycle Hub back room.

go on the board. Information deficits and a ton of motion stand between them and a simple return process, simply because "where" is not built into the board itself—visually.

Photo 7.3 Tools are smartly placed but there's no automatic recoil.

The same thing applies to the stamping cell at Greene Rubber where area associates applied smart placement principles in the case study in Chapter 4. They moved work items into the physical locations they had chosen, and motion (the spaghetti) was hugely reduced (Figures 7.1 and 7.2). Then they nailed those locations in place through a border, address, and, where possible, an ID label. They implemented the visual where, the topic of this chapter and the next (Figure 7.3).

Figures 7.1 and 7.2 Smart placement at Greene Rubber meant a lot less spaghetti.

Figure 7.3 Borders are next logical step.

Begin with Borders

The visual where begins with borders—starting from the floor up. Borders are the foundation. Floor and wall borders are implemented for every item that has a foot print or wall print (that casts a shadow on the floor or the wall). That applies to items that are moveable, like the buckets in Photo 7.4—and items that are *not* moveable, such as the large CNC machine in Photo 7.5.

Photo 7.4 Buckets, easy to move.

Photo 7.5 CNC, not easy to move.

Borders for the Floor

When we commit to borders as a regular and required part of our visual conversion, they become like words in a book—an operational vocabulary. The more specific the application, the more borders become a language for us—a visual language. Photos 7.6 to 7.8 show three classic examples.

Photo 7.6 The simple placement of two trash cans on red squares and the trim yellow border that surrounds the blue cabinet create a geometry that defines the pattern of work. You feel it in your brain.

Photo 7.7 The pattern of work is well defined in this machining cell—for everything that casts a shadow. From the rolling fixture for fixtures to the blue machine behind it and WIP locations in front of it, the pattern is completed by person-width borders.

Photo 7.8 This double orange/white border allows operators to precisely position large cable reels for feeding into the machine so when the first reel (top right) is emptied, the second reel can get threaded in fast, and production resumes.

Borders on Benches

Just as borders help us understand work by capturing its pattern on floors, borders are equally useful on work surfaces—on top, underneath, and inside. On work surfaces, borders help a lot with little things. It can be as simple as bordering the location of workplace items, as you see in Photo 7.9 (left), in a sup-

Photo 7.9

porting value field for the electron microscope at the top of that photo. (This is an anti-static area; red was the only anti-static tape color available at the time.) The bench top is covered with blue paper that is then covered with Plexiglas, keeping dust to a minimum and borders from fraying. (Alpha Industries/Massachusetts).

Photo 7.10

Photo 7.10 (right) is yet another window on the remarkable visual mastery of Rick Ell at Denison Hydraulics (you see his visual solutions throughout this book). Here is the backboard to a side bench, home to assorted gauges, with borders cut to shape from yellow contact paper.

Borders on the Inside

Some people think of borders only for the outside—on floors, walls, and work surfaces. But borders are useful everywhere, including when they are hidden behind doors and drawers. Look at three examples in Photos 7.11 to 7.13 on the next page—rare because few companies can be convinced to install borders on the inside too.

Borders on the Inside

Photo 7.11

Photo 7.12

Photo 7.13

Borders in the Office

We already said it: Borders on work surfaces help a lot with little things. Here are two good examples in office settings—and a third for a laugh. Photo 7.14 shows a paperwork station, with borders for a paper cutter and a small office machine. The hatched area permanently claims a space where we temporarily lay paper we want to hole punch (hole puncher on left). Photo 7.15 show us a computer station with a blue square for the work that is being done now. Photo 7.16 shows the same boundary concept but with a twist (see red arrow). Can you guess what it says? "Rich, keep your stuff on your side!" (As if that would help!)

Photo 7.14

Photo 7.15

Photo 7.16

Border Worries

Laying down borders can trigger strong and logical opinions in favor of borders but also some hesitation. Those sound like this:

> *"Isn't it better not to lay down floor borders in the first place—if we are just going to change our minds about where they go? If we skip borders, we won't ever have to change them!"*

This is a faulty perspective based on the faulty belief that borders take so much time to apply and remove. They are not worth putting down in the first place, the logic goes. Based on more than 35 years of helping companies implement borders, I have three responses:

1. Borders and the time needed to implement them are well worth it because of their positive and significant impact on safety, quality, productivity, and on-time delivery—often on a micro level.

2. Borders do not take any longer to implement than any other safety, quality, productivity, or cost-saving improvement.

3. Changing your borders can become a routine and fluid part of your improvement process—when you have a procedure already in place for pulling them up overnight and laying them down to last a year. When you do, you'll want your borders to get smarter as you get smarter so they improve as your thinking improves. (For more on laying down borders, see page 139.)

The Logic of Borders: Six Reasons

Yes, there are many reasons why borders make sense. To date, I have collected a list of twelve—and counting. We will examine the first six in some detail. (See Inset 7.1 for all twelve reasons.)

Reason 1: Meaning to the word "empty." Without borders, the real estate called the workplace (floor/desk/bench) remains un-designated—not selected. As a result, when an item is elsewhere, the space it is supposed to occupy looks unclaimed, available, and "up for grabs." Walk through the barrel sequence in Figure 7.4 for the impeccable logic of borders.

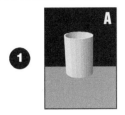   

Figure 7.4 The Impeccable Logic of Borders. Frame A shows a barrel sitting in its spot. But when it is not sitting in its spot (when it is elsewhere), we do not know that this spot is its home (Frame B). The spot has no meaning; it simply looks unclaimed. Put a border around the barrel as it sits in its spot (Frame C) and, suddenly, the floor has meaning. It sends the message: "This is an item's home—even when (especially when) that item is elsewhere" (Frame D). Add an address (discussed in the next chapter) and you make this border even more powerful.

Photo 7.17

Reason 2: Out-of-place. With borders in place, you can tell at-a-glance when an item is out-of place and simply shift it back. If always out-of-place, we may learn it is in the way of something else, a nearly impossible discovery in a non-bordered work area (Photo 7.17).

Photo 7.18

Reason 3: Something Missing. With borders in place, you can tell at-a-glance when something is missing. Combine that border with an address and you can also tell exactly what is missing—at-a-glance (Photo 7.18).

Photo 7.19

Reason 4: Intruders. With borders in place, you can spot intruders at-a-glance—items that do not belong in your area. The cart in Photo 7.19 does not belong in this work area—and anyone can plainly tell, thanks to borders. (If it had an ID label, you could send it right back home.)

Reason 5: Room-No Room. With borders in place, you can tell at-a-glance what part of the real estate is currently not available and what part still is. In the case of the machining cell in Photo 7.20, there is zero available real estate. You know this at-a-glance—thanks to the excellent system of borders that capture the floor print of everything that occupies the cell (everything that casts a shadow).

Photo 7.20 Jimmy's machining cell —every inch is making money for the company.

Reason 6: Seeing the Flow. We apply borders from the bottom/floor up for a specific purpose. That purpose is to make the flow or pattern of work plain and obvious—the course or pathway that materials, people, and information follow into and through your work area (and your company). That pathway (also called the "critical path") is extremely important; you want to be able to know it at-a-glance. Without borders, that pathway is hidden beneath the surface of things.

Many of us have worked in departments like that—where the flow of work is anybody's guess because it is not made plain. It is not visual. No borders, no nothing. In such an area, we still manage to manage. But we pay a price in motion, morale, and performance. And so does the company. Over time, we may memorize the flow and the sequence of work it contains. But many telling details remain beyond our reach. The absence of those reference points wears on us. We get irritated and feel unsafe. Our true work—adding value—suffers.

What do I mean by the flow of work? You already know that too. It is the flow of function (materials, people, and information) in and through your work area—the smart placement formula: *Function + Location = Flow*. Work gets done—one way or the other, flow or no flow. It is also true that work flows better, faster, and safer when smart placement and that flow are anchored in borders. In fact, that is one of the hidden powers of borders: to reveal the pattern of work.

> **Inset 7.1. Twelve Reasons for Borders**
>
> 1. Borders reveal the pattern of work
> 2. Borders give meaning to the word *empty*
>
> ***Borders also allow us instantly to see:***
>
> 3. When an item is out-of-place
> 4. When an item is missing
> 5. Intruders
> 6. What space is available
> 7. What space is not available
> 8. Where we are supposed to walk
> 9. Where we are not supposed to walk
> 10. The extent (or range) of function
> 11. Where we are supposed to work
> 12. Where we are not supposed to work

The Mind and the Pattern of Work

I first discovered the hidden power of borders when I began helping Denison Hydraulics (Ohio) implement *Work That Makes Sense*. Incoming Inspection was one of the five targeted areas in the first training cycle. The four men from that area were tough and pretty gloomy. They kept complaining about the two day-shift forklift drivers (Bill and Donny) who kept dropping pallets of boxes in any unoccupied space if the proper lanes were full (Photo 7.21). I assured the men that visuality could be a big help in changing behaviors. They were skeptical. Nonetheless, they attended the WTMS training, along with 30 other DH associates, learning about information deficits, motion, I-driven, smart placement—and now borders.

When it was time to implement, the Incoming Team installed a beautiful set of crisp color-coded borders for the Incoming lanes: red for on hold; orange for just arrived (with a blue inset for the tow-motor); and, at the top, green for ready-to-go. I was happy and told them so. The Incoming Team was not.

They told me I had promised them a behavior change if they laid down borders—and it didn't happen. "Whose behavior?" I asked. "Donny and Bill's!" they exclaimed. Gosh, I didn't know what to say in that situation: "Look, it's my job to teach you visual concepts, principles, and practices. It's your job to figure out how to apply them until you get the change you want—including a change in other people's behavior. You are great visual thinkers-in-the-making," I said. "Keep going!" And they did.

Photo 7.21 *Before*: Incoming Inspection.

They added a big yellow **X** in each aisle in their effort to communicate that this space is "Off Limits!!" (Photo 7.23) It did not work. Bill and Donny simply took boxes off the pallets and placed them in the four vacant spaces within the **X**. Clever humans, Denison's forklift drivers found a way to do the wrong thing despite the best improvement efforts of the Incoming Team.

Fuming by now, the guys in Incoming reminded me of my promise of behavior change and again asked me what to do. I told them to keep thinking, and keep going. (The truth was, I was also surprised by the "craftiness" of the material handlers. But I could not have thought of a better solution than the **X**'s—which clearly were not powerful enough to change the drivers' behavior. I was as challenged as they.)

Photo 7.22 *After-1*: Color-coded borders were handsome but did not help.

For its third attempt, the Incoming Team painted the entire width of each aisle a bright solid yellow (Photo Series 7.24). The behavior stopped. *Instantly*. No material handler (or anyone else) put overflow parts in the aisles again. Why? How? That, visual thinker, is the question: What made them stop? (I did not, in that moment, know the answer.)

Photo 7.23 *After-2*: The clever addition of **X** did nothing to change the behavior.

The drivers had not undergone any new training. Nor had they suddenly decided to "obey" the request of the Incoming Team to "deliver pallets to the proper lanes only!" Their behavior simply changed from wrong to right overnight. Could it have been the power of bright yellow paint? Perhaps. But I sensed there was something else to this. Then I remembered!

Photo Series 7.24 New person-width borders in the Incoming area captured the pattern of work, visually.

The Mind is a Pattern-Seeking Mechanism

I remembered an incident that had happened 25 years earlier when I lived in New York City in a fifth-floor walk-up on the Lower East Side, holding down four jobs to make ends meet and basically going nuts from the pressure. I was tense. I was unhappy. A friend noticed and said I should learn to meditate. "What's that?" I asked. My friend handed me an address. Miserable and ready to try anything, I went. It was a meditation center and the teacher told me to close my eyes and not think of anything. I closed my eyes—and thought of everything. The drive-in movies came on! In fact, I could not stop thinking. I went back to the teacher with my complaint. He then said something I suppose he thought would help. He said: "Don't you understand, Gwendolyn, the mind is a pattern seeking mechanism." Huh?!

Twenty-five years later, staring at those intensely yellow person-width borders, I remembered his words, "the mind is a pattern-seeking mechanism." BINGO! I suddenly realized that the Bill and Donny had simply recognized the pattern of that layout—now that it was undeniably visible—and accepted it. As a result, their behavior changed literally overnight. This was a staggering insight for me. In a flash, it led me to a whole new set of understandings. I will share these now so you understand as I did why borders are so important to you—and to the full, reliable, predictable, and excellent functioning of your work area as well as to your company's journey to excellence.

Seeking the Pattern. When we say the mind is a pattern-seeking mechanism, we mean that our mind—when faced with a puzzle, mystery, or challenge—will seek to make sense of it. It will seek to find the pattern. Why? Because that is what the mind does: It seeks patterns. That is its nature.

All of us have had the experience of our mind not letting go. It latches on to a thought and churns. This can happen at work when we are trying to puzzle out a new procedure. It can happen at school when we are tangling with a new concept. It can happen in personal relationships when we are trying to figure out what the heck our spouse/girl friend/boy friend is trying to communicate as the cause of her/his unhappiness. In all three cases, we are trying to make sense of them, trying to—understand. We won't let go until we succeed!

> ### Inset 7.2. Human Brain Function & Visuality
>
> Did you know: 50% of our brain function is dedicated to finding and interpreting visual information—information that the eye sees? That part of our brain is automatic, involuntary, like our heart beat or our breathing. We have no control over it. Did you also know that the human eye sends visual inputs to the brain at roughly 10 million bits per second? These "inputs" are what the brain interprets in order to make sense of what it sees. It first needs to determine if we are safe—then it wants to figure out what we are supposed to do.
>
> When we learn how the eye and brain work together, it becomes easy for us to understand why a visual workplace is important to our work success—starting with borders.
>
>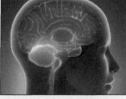
> **The connection between our brain and eye is automatic.**

That is our mind, determined to complete its function: Find the pattern. And it usually succeeds. Our minds are very bright. When our mind does "get it," it can be very satisfying. But then what happens? What happens after the mind finds the pattern it was seeking? It seeks the next level of pattern. And the next and the next and the next. Cats chase mice. Minds seek patterns.

The focus of this reaches far beyond borders—and includes them. Here is what I mean.

Continuous Improvement Naturally. If our mind is a pattern-seeking mechanism, what happens if we do not find the pattern? Our mind continues searching for it. And if we still do not find the pattern after, say, a couple of weeks? The search simply moves to a back burner, but it does not leave the stove. Our mind keeps at it but in the background now. We experience this as noise, a small dose of stress.

When this happens a lot, when there are lots of unresolved searches, then we hold on to lots of small doses of stress. The pressure builds. But the mind does not stop because that is not its nature. The mind continues to search even if we are not aware of it. If this goes on for an extended period, the mind can simply check out from the effort (go numb)—or go ballistic.

What happens in the reverse? What happens when your mind seeks the pattern and finds it? The mind pauses a moment to absorb and savor its victory. Then it seeks the next level of pattern. There is a term for this recurrent, relentless seeking and finding, seeking and finding, seeking and finding. The term is important for our discussion, for this book, and for your company. The term is: *continuous improvement.*

Do you see? That means continuous improvement is a natural condition of our mind. We were made to seek improvement, level by level—to improve our surroundings and ourselves, our work and our lives, our work area and our company. It is our nature, the nature of our mind.

Finally, I understood what that meditation teacher had told me 25 years before. I also understood why those yellow person-width borders at Denison worked so superbly well! I understood this: When the Incoming Team laid down person-width borders, they unknowingly put a powerful pattern in place that the forklift drivers simply recognized and accepted. With that in place, they could continue layering in more and more advanced pattern levels as they visually transformed their area. That brought me to another big realization: Borders support a fundamental need of the mind—its need for pattern, and with it, for harmony, balance, and a sense of unity (Photo 7.25).

Photo 7.25 When you see borders, see function.

Smarter Borders: Adding Dimensions of Meaning

The more we understand our work and the motion that keeps us from it, the more fully we recognize how borders can help us create work that makes sense. That means the borders change as our understanding of the work flow and work content changes. Our visual intelligence grows. If you adopt that mindset, then as we get smarter, our borders will get smarter too. We will require that.

Think about it: When you improve the flow of your work (your value stream), your borders must change in response—because borders engrave that flow into the physical landscape of work. A simple application of the concept that borders evolve is shown in Photos 7.26 and 7.27—for safety's sake.

Photo 7.26 This yellow border marks a busy forklift lane (called an "aisle border.") One day, a forklift operator was driving by when, suddenly, the door opened. Wham! Later, he admitted he had never even noticed that door existed. Vital visual information was missing.

Photo 7.27 Then people got smarter and made that aisle border "smarter." See the yellow notch? It visually reminds forklift drivers that there is a door and therefore the possibility of a human. You can see the trace of the previous aisle border at the red arrow.

Because visuality is a form of language, we can use visual devices to communicate very specific information and convey detailed messages. We can add *dimensions of meaning*. Borders can do more than merely mark aisles (called "aisle borders") or frame an item (called "framing borders"). We can make them *smart*—and then *smarter*. In this section, we add eight new border types to the two named above:

1. Range-of-Function Borders
2. Borders as Visual Controls
3. Commas and Dots
4. Person-width Borders

5. Dashed Borders
6. Photo-copied Borders
7. Slanted Borders
8. Double Borders

Have your updated Could-Be Map close at hand and look for applications of each new border type on your map as you learn them.

1. Range-of-Function Borders. As you learned in smart placement, we need to locate workplace items so they can perform/function completely. Once an item is situated, we do more than merely put a line around its physical edges; we visually capture the item's complete function through borders.

See the yellow border around the blue CNC machine in Photo 7.28 (discussed earlier in this chapter). Notice the edge of that border at the far right of that machine (red arrow 1). Notice that that edge does not hug the machine base. Instead, it stands some three feet from it. Why? Because the yellow border marks the extent of the machine's full range-of-function, defined by the shadow cast by that narrow aluminum conveyor (red arrow 2). This is smart placement principle 3 in action. That is why we call this a "range-of-function border"—because it makes the item's full function visible.

Photo 7.28 Borders and range of function.

You see the same logic with the rolling rack in the Screen Department at Seton Name Plate (Photo 7.29). First-shift operators prepare silk screens for the second shift to process, stored in this rack. The rack's true function is not restricted to the frame. If we border only the rack, we miss what the rack is really for: storing silk screens. That is why the white-dot border extends more than a foot beyond the physical rack, enclosing both the rack and the screens stored there. The border encompasses the rack's full range-of-function.

Note: At Seton, white dots are used to border items that are moveable or portable—carts, trash bins, racks like this, and so on.

Photo 7.29 Silk screen rack.

2. Borders as Visual Controls. A colleague once said to me: "Borders are just fences that have not yet reached their full potential." He said it as a joke, but I thought he made a good point. By building size, number, or volume into our borders, we can use them to direct, limit, or even control behavior—our own behavior or the behavior of others. In this way, borders do double-duty as visual controls (a visual control limits or restricts our choices). Here is a series of visual control border solutions.

Solution 1 (Photo 7.30): With the orderliness of borders and the precision of controls, this storage corner does its own counting. Boxes of vinyl are stacked one high, three deep, and, if you could see the entire section, five across: fifteen boxes at-a-glance, minus any that are not there. Counting has never been easier.

Photo 7.30

Photo 7.31

Solution 2 (Photo 7.31): The lower shelf of this bench is another case of combining the border and control functions: fastener boxes two rows deep by five rows long—only and just enough room for ten boxes. We are in control of the details.

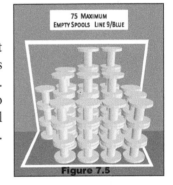

Figure 7.5

Solution 3 (Figure 7.5): The same control principle is at work in this spool storage image. Exactly 75 empty spools are held in this bordered location (5 wide/5 high/3 deep). When that quantity is reached, the spools are sent back to the supplier. That standard is built directly into the physical environment so we can tell merely by looking. No counting.

Foam/HDPE Control Materials. There are ways other than tape or paint to achieve the combined border and control function—for example, stiff foam (Photo 7.32). Stiff foam (and more recently HDPE/high-density polyethylene) are used extensively in the aerospace and medical industries for parts delivery (discussed in Chapter 6), owing to their powerful control capability. Your supervisor can contract out this work; but, regulations permitting, you can also do it yourself. The steps are easy:

1. Cut a piece of stiff foam to the size of the box, drawer, or cart.
2. Cut a piece of brown paper to the same size.
3. Lay your tools on the paper (remember to squeeze out the "air").
4. Trace around each tool with a dark marker.
5. Lay the paper on the stiff foam and, very carefully, cut your shapes into the foam through the paper.

(I described this same process in Chapter 6, related to LM-Aero's design-to-task foam-based parts delivery approach.)

Photo 7.32 Foam serving as both borders and visual control.

Presto Chango! The visual where, plus—thanks to foam/foam-like material—we also get visual control. Photos 7.33 to 7.35 show three levels of foam solutions.

Photo 7.33 The foam is cut by an outside contractor.

Photo 7.34 The foam is rough-cut by hand.

Photo 7.35 The foam is not cut to shape, just pierced by the tool.

3. Commas and Dots. The yellow angles in Photo 7.36 are called "commas," sometimes used for smaller workplace things, instead of continuous borders. But I am not a big fan. Though commas seem to enclose the real estate, I find they are poor substitutes for continuous borders. First, a comma does not provide enough visible information to create a pattern. Second, commas provide no place for the addresses so vital to reducing motion and building a workplace that speaks. My advice is to use commas sparingly—if at all.

Photo 7.36

Inset 7.3. You & Your Company's Technical Staff

Operator/Tech partnership.

You will almost certainly need and want support from your company's technical staff as you implement inventive visual solutions, including innovative borders. Make sure to ask your trainer and/or supervisor to schedule time for tech staff to meet with you.

Technical staff want to build a relationship with you too. Make sure to tell them not just what you need and want—but also what you envision. They are there to help. Ask questions. Keep an open, experimental frame of mind. Many remarkable visual inventions have resulted from the rich, informed interaction between operators like you and technical staff. Develop this partnership.

Photo 7.37

The red dot of paint is border enough for the bucket in Photo 7.37. But a worry applies here as well. While there is room to apply an address, the item that resides on that dot will hide that address. There are ways around this, and I am sure you can figure it out. Here are two hints: Think about using nearby architecture and think about *air*.

Photo 7.38 (right) shows you an innovative use of dots. The red circle on the wall makes it easy for us to find the fire extinguisher with a minimum of motion. Because when we need an extinguisher, even the tiniest bit of motion (time) can be disastrous. "Look for the red dot!" That is the safety standard in this facility.

Photo 7.38

4. Person-Width Borders. Person-width borders are another innovative adaptation of borders, with many valuable applications. They are especially important in companies that are not yet lean—the ones with lots of WIP, especially in the warehouse. Here is a learning sequence that shows how person-width borders can help (Photos 7.39-7.41 and Photo Cluster 7.42-7.44).

Here is a far too typical loading dock (Photo 7.39). Miles of piles. Tons of motion. Zero visual information. Let's improve the area and our performance first by installing the visual where, beginning with borders.

Photo 7.39 Tons of stuff/tons of motion.

That's better! A loading dock with three designated lanes—the exact volume needed to fill up an 18-wheel truck (Photo 7.40). That is a start. But, though improved, these borders need to get smarter. Can you see why?

Photo 7.40 The basics of visual order.

Yes, when stacked, there is no easy way to access the pallets if, for example, we need to verify that we packed the J-190s (Photo 7.41). We ask Joe, the move man. He moves it all out. We find the J-190s. Joe moves it all back again. We need a better way.

Photo 7.41 But more is needed.

What can we do instead? We can install person-width borders, as shown in Photo 7.42. Person-width borders provide two functions: boundary and access. That means: They allow me, you, or Joe to find out if the J-190s are on the dock and ready to be loaded, without moving a single pallet.

Photo 7.42 A better way.   **Photo 7.44** See it?

Photo 7.43 Look closely here for a clue.

There is more to discover. Study the floor itself. The close-up in Photo 7.43 gives a good view. Notice anything? See the scraps of yellow in between the borders (red arrow)? What are they? Think. (*Hint:* Notice the yellow paint scraps at a right angle to the wide yellow borders.)

That's right! They are leftovers from a previous set of person-width borders that were laid at right angles to where they are now. Because the old borders were not removed completely, they left us a kind of archeological record of the previous location logic.

And what was that previous logic? What were they like before and why? The answer is in front of your eyes, at the tip of your nose. Look. Sharpen your visual thinking. (*Hint:* Look at the red arrow at the far end of Photo 7.44—at the far end of the existing personal-width aisle. What is that at the far end?)

"Oh my gosh," you say, "That's the dock door!"

That's right! The previous person-width layout ran counter to the dock doors. It blocked them. That meant each pallet had to be handled twice: once when it was delivered to the dock area and again to move it around to face the loading doors. The new layout is smarter. It lines up with the dock doors precisely, allowing pallets to flow directly onto trucks.

> *Note:* The previous person-width borders had been laid out so forklifts could easily deposit pallets directly from the main warehouse floor, a straight shot that seemed easier at the time. That logic was eventually set aside for the new one—pallets ready for loading from the get-go.

The company got smarter so its borders got smarter, too.

Here is another *Before-and-After* example that shows you how practical person-width borders are for any area.

> ***Before:*** Pallets of WIP (Work-In-Process) were constantly delivered to this spot because it was vacant and therefore looked available. The pallets always blocked one of the entrances to the cell directly behind the WIP (Photo 7.45).

> ***After:*** So the operator worked with Maintenance to install: 1) a person-width border, allowing her easy entry and exit; and 2) an official bordered location for WIP pallets (red arrow) since that spot was going to get used anyway (Photo 7.46).

In Photo Series 7.47 you see a selection of person-width borders at Denison Hydraulics (Ohio) before the company went lean. Remarkably consistent applications throughout this WIP-loaded facility.

5. Dashed Borders. Dashed borders allow us to designate locations that are only sometimes used. Photo 7.48 shows a corner of the production floor that is in use—only sometimes. But because it houses an im-

Photo 7.48 A temporary location, vitally needed from time to time.

portant function when it is used (customized materials for only certain orders), we provide a designated, bordered location. (Royal Nooteboom Trailers/Holland)

6. Photo-Copied Borders. Benchtop borders can be as innovative as those on the floor. Bob Comeau, resident visual genius at United Electric Controls (UE), had worked there for 20 years when he started looking for a shortcut to laying down borders. That is when he invented photo-copied borders (Photo 7.49).

Photo 7.49 Photo-copied borders.

Bob simply carried his hand tools over to the photo copier, laid them on the glass (very gently), and pressed the button—instant borders! Next he cut them out, put them precisely in place, and glued them onto heavy paper. Then he covered them with Plexiglas. Bob's innovation spread like wildfire through UE—and across the world.

Can you tell which tools are missing? Yes: the scissors, a level block, and two spring screwdrivers (lower right). But it is a bit tricky to tell, creating another form of motion, unintentional though it was.

That small dilemma was addressed when Grace in the shipping department of Alpha Industries (Massachusetts) adapted Bob's photo-copy invention for her calculator and tape measure, two items she used a

Photo 7.50 There or not there?

lot. Great idea—except the likeness was too exact. As a result, from time to time, she'd get mixed up, thinking one of the items was in place when it was only its photo (Photo 7.50).

What to do? She added a telling detail: a red mark on the face of the two real items so she could tell the difference between there and not there—at-a-glance (Photo 7.51).

Photo 7.51 Now I can tell.

7. Slanted Borders. We introduced slanted or angled borders in Chapter 6 when we discussed the smart placement principle: *Use the natural flow line.* Remember we said: "Very little in life outside of work happens at right angles—so why should life at work be different?"

Borders that are set at a slight angle allow forklift drivers easy put-and-pick when moving material. The photo Series on the next page (7.52) provides more examples. As you examine these, remember that these splendid borders are the result of smart placement thinking. As always, the thinking came first.

Photo Series 7.52 Slanted Borders at Denison Hydraulics (Ohio).

Bill Podolski, day-shift move man triggered the invention of slanted borders with the famous words: "Gee, those right-angled borders make it awfully hard for me to maneuver my forklift.... Would you mind if I cut the corner?"

This slanted border in Jimmy's area is on the main aisle, letting material handlers pickup and deliver with ease. Notice how he used borders to squeeze every inch from his cell real estate.

LEFT: Slanted borders for material pick/put on the main aisle.
MIDDLE: A long, broad yellow person-width border allows easy access.
RIGHT: A grid of squares for pallets in long term storage.

8. Double Borders. Remember this double-the-function example (Photo 7.53) from Chapter 6? Gary in the FB-27 Cell invented it so that he could tell, merely by looking, which model was next. This is a highly innovative and economical use of floor real estate. Called "double borders" in the visual where, they helped Gary be ready for his next changeover. Now discover your own applications for double borders in your area.

Here is another double border story. Photo 7.54 shows you a desk piled so high with debris, the value field looks like it has moved to the

chair. You and I know that as soon as the chair fills up, the value field will shift again—this time to the floor. Whose desk is this anyway? We want to know!

Photo 7.55 shows a better way to handle a desktop. This is the desk of Francis Davies, visual workplace coordinator for GM Plant #19 (Indiana). See how Francis identified her value-field with a simple black border. This was her way of reminding herself to keep that area free of clutter—because that is where her actual work happened (her primary value field).

This example makes some people worry that their boss will ask them to implement, as a standard, the same bordered layout on their desks. This would be the boss's mistake. First, it would be a weak use of the power of standardization (see *Leadership Task 8* in Chapter 3). Second, desk layout is a fairly personal segment of the operational real estate. Cookie-cutter imitations are rarely effective.

Here is a better desk standard: Set up a single drawer in every desk (say, the upper left) with a basic set of supplies (pen, paper, etc.) and allow anyone away from their own desk to pick up an incoming call there and access those supplies. United Electric Controls implemented this as a standard in Purchasing and improved their customer responsiveness and saved a ton of motion.

Photo 7.55 Francis's desk at a level of visual order that she found useful and pleasing.

For right now: Watch the phone. Francis put a border around it (Photo 7.56). Then she added a second border (Photo 7.57). Question: Why? Why did she add that second border? Look. Think. Consider.

Photo 7.56 Close up of phone.

Photo 7.57 Francis added a second border, but why?

Photo 7.58 A courteous visual solution. Thanks!

Did she make a location for her pencil? Perhaps. That would be clever; but that is not why she did it. Think some more. Here is a hint: I discovered that second border—and its purpose—when I sat in the side chair at Francis's desk and asked to use her phone (her office, deep inside the plant, was a dead zone for cell phones).

Get it? Yes! She gave the phone a second border so if someone in the side chair (me!) asked to use her phone—kaboom—she turned it to face that person (Photo 7.58). As a result, the phone was never out of visual order. The visual where is embedded.

· Again, just because Francis decided to go this far does not mean you must. She put a double border down because it made sense to her. She did not share her desk with anyone so she implemented as she saw fit.

Next question: Where did Francis get her idea? Yes, Gary's double border function in the FB-27 cell at Fleet, the one we just discussed.

Does it surprise you that someone in an office should learn from the shop floor? In fact, it happens all the time—and vice-versa as well. We also see manufacturing employees learning from hospitals—and vice versa.

Contrary to popular belief, seeing examples from other industries can actually help us better understand the principles of visuality than if we restrict ourselves to same-industry solutions. Bear this in mind when you start thinking about expanding your visual conversion. It is the principles that teach—and they are found in all great examples.

See Photo Series 7.59 as a reminder of the many double-border applications shared earlier in this book, plus a few new ones. All but the airport solution were inspired by Gary's invention.

Photo Series 7.59 Double Borders.

Color-Coded Borders

We color-code borders in order to strengthen or reinforce the address element of the visual where (Photo 7.60). Color-coded borders, however, cannot—and should not—substitute for crisp, clear addresses.

When a company adopts this mistake as "standard," color-coded borders not only trigger mix-ups (motion), they also fail to contribute their full potential to operational excellence. Because color-coding is associated with addresses, we will discuss it further in Chapter 8.

Meanwhile, understand the following when color-coding borders.

High-contrast, double-colored borders

When you place two high-contrast colors side-by-side, the colors vibrate. Each color competes for the eye's full attention: white-black, yellow-black, red-black, magenta-black, and so on. ANSI and OSHA, federal agencies for workplace health and safety, have standards (requirements) governing the use of such color combinations for borders in high-risk situations. They also publish guidelines for their use elsewhere. But note: This second set are guidelines, not requirements. Don't confuse guidelines with rules.

Photo 7.60 Visuality lets us ell the difference merely by looking. This border system identifies international packages, sub-divided by country address, enhanced by color coding. The colors let us see from a distance that there is difference. But color coding is shorthand. It requires addresses to share the telling detail. (Seton Name Plate/Connecticut)

The point is: Don't use high-contrast borders for everything. Here's why. Look at the hand truck in Photo 7.61. It is in perfect visual order with a border that surrounds it, an address that names it, and an ID label on the thing itself. But the use of high-contrast yellow-black tape for its border creates risk. OSHA federal register regulation 1910.144 requires yellow-black for hazardous areas because that color pairing is specifically engineered to put us on the alert. But what is the danger here? Will that hand truck jump up and throttle us if we walk too close to it? I doubt it.

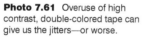

Photo 7.61 Overuse of high contrast, double-colored tape can give us the jitters—or worse.

Photo 7.62 Aaaah, that's better. We no longer harbor the suspicion that this hand truck might ambush us. Nice hand truck.

"Well, it is just overuse," you may say. "What's the harm?" The harm is this: When the eye lands on high-contrast colors, the eye is not able to rest. When the eye cannot rest, the brain cannot rest. That is why a high-contrast color mix is used in situations of risk: to disturb the eye in order to disturb the mind and get our attention. We pay attention.

But when these combinations are overused in a factory (as in aisle after aisle of yellow-black or white-black borders), our eye and therefore our mind are continually disturbed. As a result, we enter into a state of hyper-vigilance and alarm, a condition that our bodies register as stress. Use solid colors instead (Photo 7.62) and reserve high-contrast mixes for situations of actual risk.

Again: OSHA and ANSI issue rules (obey them) and guidelines (consider them). Know the difference. See Photo Series 7.63 for more.

Photo Series 7.63 More Correct and Incorrect Use of High-Contrast Borders

Right Use These white-red borders alert us to an emergency exit.

Over Use Why use black-white tape when this solid wood work bench and supplies pose no danger?

Right Use A plain yellow border serves this location and its contents very well.

Leadership Task 13: Developing a Companywide Color-Code Border System*

Long before the first border is laid down, management needs to define and finalize a companywide color-code system for borders. The following eight-step procedure works well for a group of 5-7 knowledgeable individuals (doing the below sub-exercises in small teams of 2-3). I recommend you undertake this process. If you already have a color-code system for borders, use this sequence to vet it.

1. Each small team lists all items that have a floor print or wall print.
2. Each small team clusters those items into like categories.
3. The whole group gathers to compare notes and create a combined cluster of categories.
4. Each small team then separately attempts to whittle down that combined cluster to no fewer than five and no more than seven.
5. Each small team presents its cluster to the whole group and discusses its thinking.
6. Separated into small teams again, each team assigns a color to each category in the cluster.
7. Gathering together, the teams share and compare colors, and then develop an agreed upon set.
8. The group posts this for feedback (from associates too), waiting *a few weeks before finalizing*.

See the next page for an example of a color-code border system template (Figure 7.6).

* See our step-by-step *training video by the same name (www.visualworkplace.com)*.

Applying Borders: Follow a Step-by-Step Process

Borders are the indispensable first element for implementing the visual where. Now you know in detail why that is so and how borders anchor the operational functions in your area and make them knowable to everyone—at-a-glance. You also know that borders will make your area look terrific—operationally and cosmetically beautiful.

It is now time to walk through the steps of putting borders physically in place. I call it: "Laying down the lines. Laying down the law."

NOTE: So much of what you/your company need to know about laying down borders depends on the specific area and floor type already in place—epoxy, concrete, stone, wood. Select your border material based on those—paint (oil or latex), paint plus sealant, striping paint, vinyl tape, electrostatic tape, speciality brands, and so on. Many choices/many decisions. Before you decide, contact a reputable supplier, seek guidance, and get educated. (See *Leadership Task 14* for more, page 146.)

Floor Border Color Code System: Examples*

We suggest a color-code system with between five and seven colors.

Color	Part Number for Tape***	Part Number for Paint***
1. YELLOW: For transportation and forklift lanes; for walkways for people walking between departments; for parking places.	2R276	
2. GREEN: For outgoing material or finished goods; could also be for WIP location when ready to move internally from one area/operation to another).	2R266	
3. ORANGE: For incoming material, supplies, consumables, parts.	2R677	
4. BLUE:*** Around machines (all sections); for machine-associated carts & racks, such as change over carts; for dies and tooling racks and cabinets.	2R731	
5. WHITE:*** For racks/return racks and pallets; for desks, filing cabinets, and other workplace furniture; for lockers and break areas; for trash cans.	2R332	
6. RED: For inspection, rework, scrap, defects, on-hold items, and red-tag area/pallet locations.	5E312	
7. YELLOW/BLACK (or red/black): For hazardous areas or items; for indicating that caution is required when entering or working in a given zone; for chemicals and chemical zone, Fire Zone, fire extinguishers and fire equipment, used rag cans. (Use high-contrast borders appropriately. They are designed to create optical stress as a means of catching our attention; overuse can be tiring.)	5G688	

* There will always be a close corollary between colors for floor borders and those for work surfaces (such as work benches).

** As a rule, borders around and outside the department are 4 inches wide; borders within departments are 2-3 inches wide. (The numbers you see here are examples of part numbers in one particular company.) Also, if you end with paint, begin with tape. If you end with tape, don't forget to wax.

*** You may find the distinctions between blue items and white items too refined for your environment. In that case, they can be collapsed into a single border color: either white or blue)

Other Border Considerations

Purple is a useful next color. Light gray works on some surfaces. Dark gray is better for others.

Brown is hard to see on dark floors. For long-lasting easy on/easy off floor borders, check out Floor-Mark and DuraStripe.

Here are two ways you can use two colors on borders to make more differentiation. Think about it.

At this company, this stripe approach identifies structure, pipes, air lines, electrical lines that cross overhead an aisle way, walkway, etc. Used as a *heads up* for personnel transporting items that a structure is overhead. 4" black and 4" white alternating stripes.

Figure 7.6 One company's color-code system for borders (LM-Aero).

Guidelines and Tips

Laying down borders is important work. Prepare for it.

1. This chapter introduces you to ten border types (person-width, slanted, dashed, etc.). Decide which border type best serves the item it will enclose and that item's function.

2. Keep your supervisor and Maintenance staff in the loop. You cannot move forward without their involvement, agreement, and direct help. If yours is a union company, learn about and abide by the same requirements and procedures as you would in any improvement initiative. Talk with your supervisor to see if certain requirements can be relaxed for the WTMS roll out.

3. Many areas begin by testing out their border placement in plain masking tape (or chalk); then they move to more permanent materials.

4. Some areas decide to use a striping machine to lay down borders because it is so quick and easy to apply. Just fill the machine with paint and walk, pushing it ahead (Photo 7.64). Because the paint must be thin enough to flow through the machine, it takes less time to apply and dries faster than paint applied by roller. But those borders rarely last a month and need to be refreshed often. Some people see this as an advantage since they might get smarter in the meantime and will not have to remove the old borders in order to apply new ones. Wait a few weeks, the thinking goes, and the existing layout will fade, ready for the next level of smart placement.

Photo 7.64 The striping machine for borders.

5. If you decide to use paint, consult with Maintenance and/or Facilities for tips and expert advice. Your supervisor will either gather the knowledge for you or hook you with the right people. Again, make sure to talk to reputable suppliers.

6. If your company has a color-code system for borders, find out about it. There may be parts of the existing system that need to change, including the colors themselves. In most companies, this will be beyond your reach. Check with your supervisor or trainer. (See *Leadership Task 14* on page 144 for more.)

Nine Tips for Effective Bordering (Photo Series 7.65)

Tip 1. Get Clean: Before you lay down your borders, make sure the floor is squeaky clean, dry, and dust free. Thoroughly remove any old tape. If yours is a stone floor, you may have to grind off the old borders or mask them with paint matching the current color of your floor.

Tip 2. Be Precise: Whether paint or tape, take the time needed to be precise. Precision is key to outstanding results. Use a tape measure, straight edge, or chalk line to make your borders straight and true, especially if a border is free-standing (not close to a structural edge like a wall or machine).

Tip 3. Right Size: Leave a margin between the item and its border—breathing room. That is, do not lay a border flush against the item itself. If you do, you and other will spend far too much time getting the item situated within that tight border. Instead—and as a general rule—leave 2.0-3.0 inches between the floor item and its border and 0.5-1.0 for work surface items.

Tip 4. Masking Tape First: If you decide to use paint, map out the width and length of your borders in masking tape first. Here you see Tommy making his way around a machining center, measuring out the tape width and length. Maintenance follows with the paint.

Tip 5. Round Shapes: Circular borders (for example for bins/floor fans) can be tricky. Try using a trash bin lid to get a nice round shape. Then work your way around with small strips of masking tape. The circular shapes in the photo were filled with paint—a big dot instead of just a bordered edge.

Tip 6. Mark the Color: Mark the color for each border on cardboard or, as applies, on the masking tape itself so that painters (usually Maintenance on an off-shift or over the weekend) will know at-a-glance what the selected color is. Do this even if you are doing your own painting so you don't forget.

Tip 7. Double Seal: Extend the life of your newly-painted borders with a double coat of sealant, especially in heavy forklift traffic. When you seal, use a roller wide enough to get 1-2 inches of overlap on both sides. Check with your paint supplier first!

Tip 8. Don't Stretch Plastic: If you are using plastic tape, remember not to stretch the tape as you lay it. If you do, it will curl and never adhere properly. Instead, lay it gently off the roll. This is *always* a two-person job. Warning: Regular waxing is essential to keep tape edges sealed. Once dust gets under an edge, the tape will quickly start to loosen.

Tip 9. Think Smart: Remember, borders are meant to change as the flow of work changes. Set aside thoughts of laying down borders once and only once. Borders are dynamic—as dynamic as your own improvement thinking. The same goes for waiting to get the flow *just right* before borders get implemented. Do not wait. Borders are far too important to delay. Instead, learn how to lay them down smoothly and remove them quickly.

Next Steps

You just learned a lot about borders. Now bring your visual workplace hit list up to speed on your new thinking (Figure 7.7).

Working alone or with a buddy, study your Could-Be Map and identify

border opportunities. Make a list of them by name. Think through the ones you want to tackle and post then on the hit list—even if you do not plan to tackle them yourself. Remember: Just because you thought of an application does not mean you have to do it. And just because no one else seems interested in it does not mean it should not get done. Post them all. Your trainer, coach, or supervisor will help keep tasks moving forward.

Figure 7.7 A hit list keeps track.

Good for Laughs
Associates at Denison Hydraulics were big fans of borders. Highly inventive and thorough, they also had a lot of fun. Because this is a union plant, Maintenance lays down the paint, based on the notes that associates leave for the night shift. Junior was the person—and he had a sense of humor.

Look at Photo 7.66 for an example of a border that made me laugh right out loud. What happened? Bill

Jones left a note for Maintenance to paint the border you see in the photo yellow—but he neglected to move his coat tree out of the way. Maintenance, always ready for a laugh, decided to take Bill's request literally and painted everything along the way. Everybody enjoyed the joke (Photo 7.67).

Photo 7.67 Bill's neighbors laughed too.

Here is another great joke at the expense of the border requirement "for everything that casts a shadow."

Photo 7.66 *Everything* in the line of fire got a yellow border.

One day, the guys from Assembly Test came running over to get me. Lloyd, they said, had finally gotten on board with borders. They went on to state that he had decided to begin by putting a border around his red tool box. "At last!," I thought. As I arrived in Lloyd's area, a crowd had gathered. Then Lloyd showed me his rolling red tool box and crisp yellow border. I was delighted. And, with the words "My tool box is never without a border," he pushed the tool box—and the border went with it! We fell over laughing (Photos 7.68 and 7.69).

Photos 7.68 and 7.69 This red tool-box is never without its border—and that was the point of Lloyd's joke.

Leadership Task 14: Maintenance Gets on Board

The role of Maintenance is crucial to the success of your WTMS conversion. Early in the planning stages, you as a leader need to meet with your Maintenance Department for at least four reasons.

1. To learn about the company's color-code system for borders, if there is one. If there is not, make sure Maintenance participates in creating one (*Leadership Task 13*). Maintenance will prefer to keep to a few colors to keep supplies to a minimum—and you will need to convince them to support five to seven.

2. To gain Maintenance's involvement in developing (or validating) a standard procedure for laying down borders efficiently—and for removing them fast. This will go a long way towards easing people's worries about changing the layout.

3. To work out with Maintenance how much time (or percentage of time) it can provide the WTMS conversion effort on a weekly or monthly basis. The goal is 5% minimum. But 10% would accelerate the improvement process handsomely. This is the time that Maintenance assigns, for example, to help on smart placement tasks, building fixtures, laying down borders, and so on. Improvement activity is usually slow for the first month or two of a conversion; then it steadily builds. Prepare for this now.

4. To work with Maintenance to develop a special work order form just for the areas targeted for WTMS training and, therefore, the visual conversion. Make the form a different color, preferably bright. Work out a simple system for submitting and tracking orders. And get all this done before you launch. Then pilot the new system and work out the bugs.

Discipline is remembering
what you love.

Albert Einstein

Chapter | Eight

Visual Where:
Addresses and ID Labels

Address Basics

We now move to the second element of the visual where: addresses. In this chapter, you will learn about the waste—motion—that gets triggered when addresses are inaccurate, unreadable, incomplete, weak, or simply absent from the workplace.

In far too many companies, addresses are overlooked or merely given lip service. It is not enough, for example, to throw some parts on a shelf, hang a sign that says "parts storage," and leave the rest for other people to figure out. This non-approach is not just inadequate. It is a sure prescription for accidents, mix-ups, defects, long downtime, long lead time, unhappy employees, unhappy customers, and plummeting profit margins. Like a road map without names on it, shelves, racks, benches, cabinets, drawers, walls, and floors may hold items we vitally need—but without excellent addresses we have no clear way of finding them.

You are about to see dozens of addresses that work—and work well. Many are highly specific; others are generic. That makes no difference because as soon as an address triggers even the smallest question (even the tiniest bit of motion), we know the address needs an upgrade.

As we walk through this chapter, make a point to expand your understanding of what makes addresses effective and how you can make them even more so. What is that I hear? "I already know everything there is to know about addresses. I mean how much can there be anyway? It's just a label with a name on it!"

Photo 8.1 The three elements of the visual where: border + address + ID label.

If that is you speaking, then hear this: You are wrong. Despite over thirty-five years (as of this writing) of researching and implementing visuality all over the world, I learn more about addresses all the time.

There are more than seventy addresses in this chapter, and they merely scratch the surface of what is possible. I include them in order to ignite your thinking and trigger your inventiveness so you can create addresses that go even further and serve you precisely and completely. In fact, there are many types of addresses I do not discuss here—either because of space constraints or because premier examples have not yet been created. This is especially true for offices and hospitals where deep visuality is yet to be developed.

Pattern Recognition

The need for addresses goes beyond our need to know where things are in a fixed and reliable way—that is to say, visually. In a larger way, addresses support our earlier discussion about the mind as a pattern-seeking mechanism. Addresses help us find and recognize the full pattern of work. As a result, they help us feel a new level of psychological and physical safety. Without addresses, the pattern is incomplete. To underscore the mind's remarkable ability to find and recognize patterns, study Figure 8.1.

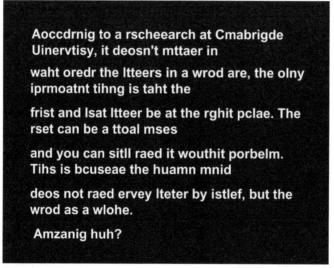

Aoccdrnig to a rscheearch at Cmabrigde Uinervtisy, it deosn't mttaer in

waht oredr the ltteers in a wrod are, the olny iprmoatnt tihng is taht the

frist and lsat ltteer be at the rghit pclae. The rset can be a ttoal mses

and you can sitll raed it wouthit porbelm. Tihs is bcuseae the huamn mnid

deos not raed ervey lteter by istlef, but the wrod as a wlohe.

Amzanig huh?

Figure 8.1 The mind will always seek a pattern.

At first, the above letters look garbled. Then we find that we can read them. Even though every word longer than three letters is spelled incorrectly, we still recognize each of them and understand each sentence. We could even read the text aloud despite its many typos. Pettry amzanig huh?

How is that possible? It is possible because your mind—which is fully linked with your eyes—does not read letters. It recognizes pattern. It recognizes the profile. In this case, it recognizes the profile or shape of each word as defined by its first and last letter.

In a similar way, this powerful ability of our mind allows us to know the time on an analog clock (Figure 8.2) nanoseconds faster than on a digital readout (Figure 8.3). That is because an analog clock allows us to recognize the whole and its meaning in order to tell the time—instead of sub-vocalizing each number, as we must on a

Figure 8.2 Analog Clock.

Figure 8.3 Digital Clock.

digital clock. Both types of clocks (analog and digital) are installed in the high-risk environment of a fighter jet's cockpit for the sake of redundancy. But it is analog instrumentation that allows for decisive responses that are nanoseconds faster in that high-risk location.

We harness that same power of the mind for the benefit of our company when we lay down borders and then apply their operational partner: addresses. So let's begin to create work that makes (more) sense by understanding and applying addresses—for everything that casts a shadow.

Border + Address

The premise behind an address in the workplace is the same as an address on your home. In one case, "you" are the resident. In the other, the work item or material is. But at work we can go one step further in making this link crystal clear: an item's address tells us what belongs in the "real estate" you claim through borders.

Photo 8.2 shows the home for *Completed Parts*—and you know it because of the address. Without the address, you would have to guess or try to remember or ask someone—all forms of motion. A border without an address works only when the item is in that location. Only then can we know what "lives" there for sure.

Photo 8.2 A good address means you don't have to ask.

Photo 8.3 Occupant unknown.

In the case of Photo 8.3, it is anybody's guess what "lives" in the yellow bordered area. Only habit (called *tribal knowledge*) can help you. But it cannot help newcomers or visitors. The purpose of borders is to put separate, physical boundaries around material, tools, machines, furniture—and anything else that occupies real estate in your area—whether on a floor, wall, bench, or shelf. The purpose of addresses is to name those occupants.

Addresses can be fixed to an array of locations: 1) embedded in the border itself, 2) fixed on a surface that is above or near the item, 3) posted on a standing sign, 4) posted behind the border, 5) posted over the border (airborne), and so on. See Photo Series 8.4. The one place an address cannot be is "nowhere."

Photo Series 8.4
An array of address applications.

In my many years of hands-on implementation and coaching, I have found only two situations where an address for a border location are not required: traffic lanes and pedestrian aisles (Photo 8.5). Because the aisle and traffic functions are continuous and cut across the entire production site, they do not require addresses. Still many companies handle this acceptable gap by embossing on icons of forklifts and pedestrians (Photo 8.6). But mostly, these lanes simply snake their way through the facility, without an identifying address of any kind.

Photo 8.5 Traffic lanes and aisles.

Photo 8.6 Pedestrian walkway.

For Everything That Casts a Shadow. With those two exceptions, the visual where requires a border plus address for everything that casts a shadow (more about ID labels later). That is the hard-and-fast requirement that serves your business purposes exceptionally well—not just at the outset as order begins to emerge visually, but also later when the focus shifts to sustaining and extending visual functionality. When you adopt the everything-that-casts-a-shadow rule, you are using that rule both as a tool and as a standard for self-examination, self-audit, and continuous improvement.

This is the *go-to-yellow* level on the laminated map (Chapter 3). A *yellow dot* means the visual where is entirely in place in that area. In many companies, that also means the area reached a 15% to 30% increase in productivity, as I noted at the start of this book. See Photo Series 8.7 for three more examples.

Photo Series 8.7

Without an address on the bright yellow border of this blue paperwork desk, we would not know its specific purpose: *Hold and Ship.*

Without the "Change Over Cart" address on the border, we cannot know what belongs in this spot when the cart is in use, where to return the cart—or if the wrong cart (an intruder) is in this location.

Eight air hoses "live" on this wall. Make it more exact. Number each circle and add a matching ID label on each hose. Then you know the number of hoses, without counting + which, if any, is missing.

On All Surfaces. As with borders, begin to apply addresses on the floor and work your way up—to the walls, work surfaces, and then on to short shelves and tall ones, and into cabinets and drawers.

Six Rules for Addresses

When you apply addresses, follow the next six rules. Make your addresses workhorses of performance.

Rule 1: Large Enough. Make each address large enough to easily read—and easily grasp—at a distance. The basic rule is: An address must be perfectly readable at two feet when on foot and perfectly readable at four feet when on a cart or forklift. That means your addresses must be "right-sized" from the start. You can rarely make an address that is too big. But folks often make addresses far too small. When an address is small, we work too hard to see it. The address (which is supposed to be a motion-buster) becomes a motion-producer.

Rule 2: Upper and Lower Case. Whenever possible, use upper case and lower case letters in your addresses. Avoid the popular but troublesome ALL UPPER CASE (ALL CAPS) address. Using all caps prevents the mind from identifying the pattern. Why? Because all caps flattens the profile of the letters and turns them into block. As a result, the pattern of the word disappears and we are forced to read, rather than recognize, the words. (See Figure 8.4 and Photo 8.8.)

Figure 8.4 Upper/lower case rules.

A word in all CAPS—as in this very sentence—stands out when (and only when) the words on either side of it are not in all caps. Why? Because the upper/lower case words that surround it create a profile that makes the caps stand out. BUT WHEN WE CAPITALIZE ALL THE LETTERS OF ALL THE WORDS IN A SENTENCE, THE PROFILE IS LOST—and our quick understanding with it.

Photo 8.8 Easy to read address.

When given a choice, use upper and lower case letters. You may be challenged to find this in stencils. The last time I checked, most came in all caps only. Label-making machines, however, now offer a choice of upper/lower and all caps. Nearly all such machines come with a computer interface, making effective addresses easy and affordable (Photo 8.9). For more, check with your local supplier. If they don't carry upper/lower case machines, ask them. They will.

Rule 3: High-Contrast. Another common address error is the lack of color. Just because black appears to be the opposite of white does not make *black and white* the best color combination for addresses. In fact, black letters (and numbers) tend to fuse on a white background into a nearly unreadable grayness. Black-on-white is the least easily seen as an address and yet the most commonly used.

Photo 8.9 A popular label maker for making upper/lower case and ALL CAPS addresses. Also in the preferred black-on-yellow color combination. (See **your local supplier**.)

What does work? Uncle Sam has already done the research for us: bold black letters (or numbers) on a dense crayon-yellow background. In a field of colors, the human eye sees yellow first. When given a choice, create high-contrast, easy-to-read addresses in a yellow-black or black-yellow color combination. (See again, Photo 8.9.)

Look around the community and notice black-on-yellow combinations are everywhere (see Photo Series 8.10 on next page): a) crime scene tape, b) crayon-yellow school buses (a color reserved in 1939 for school buses by U.S. Federal Law), c) customer/gate signage at many airport terminals, and d) license plates of many states in the U.S.A. (also in England). Take a lesson from all of these applications: Use high-contrast yellow/black and black/yellow color combinations to make your addresses highly readable.

Rule 4: Color-Coding. You may think that color coding is a border function. It is not. Technically speaking, color coding is a form of address (that is sometimes embedded in borders). Color-coding lets us quickly sort (at-a-glance)—but addresses provide the telling detail.

The look-alike fixtures on the lower cabinet shelf in Photo 8.11 are each clearly addressed. Color coding makes it even easier to select the correct one. After all, we are human and lead busy, often compressed lives, especially nowadays. And we forget. And then we forget that we forgot. That's when we can get into big trouble.

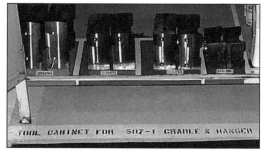

Photo 8.11 Color-coded fixture cabinet with patch borders + perfect addresses.

Look at the handsome color-coded drawer in Photo 8.12. Attractive though it is, can you see what is wrong? Yes, there are no addresses for the two collar gauges. The purpose of color coding is to enhance an address, not replace it. Do not make the mistake I see in many companies new to visuality: they use color-coding instead of addresses—as a substitute. Though that seems to be a time saver, this "short cut" easily turns into a long cut, leading to mix-ups, accidents, defects, long lead times, and unhappy customers.

Photo 8.12 These collar gauges need more.

There is another reason we combine color-coding with words (or numbers): Some of us are color blind. Studies show that 8%-12% of all men (and 1% of women) are some degree of color blind, usually in the green and red range. So words and numbers come first—then add color-coding.

Rule 5: Surround Addresses. It is always better to put an address on all sides of a floor item—rather than on just one side—especially if the item is large. In Photo 8.13, three of the four sides of border that surround that tool dolly are plainly addressed. This becomes critical for items with a large floor footprint such as monument machines (Photo 8.14). In that case, locate the machine address on all sides (whether airborne, border-embedded, or both) so vital address details can be seen and known, whatever the angle of approach.

Photo 8.13 Surround address for a fixture for fixtures.

Photo 8.14 Surround address on a machining center.

Rule 6: Standardize Names (Nomenclature). You and your colleagues have to agree on a common set of names for the items in your work area. Take a pause before creating addresses so everyone can settle on a single name. For example, you may refer to a certain machine in your area as the "JTM-1." But other people refer to it as the "2-Axis CNC." Still others call it "Big Blue." Get together and decide on a single name and use it. Supervisors and staff also weigh in on this for positive cross-departmental impact.

In visuality, we refer to this as *determine a standard nomenclature*—a find a common name for things. This is an important activity not just for things within your department but for items, materials, machines, and processes that are shared across departments. Your supervisor can, will, and must help. As visuality spreads, the added support of the Visual-Macro Team (Chapter 3) can help further.

> ## Leadership Task 15: Naming by Consensus
>
> Supervisors & Managers: Finding common names for the things within your area is an opportunity for you to help associates reach a balance between I-driven and group preferences—and so it is an opportunity to create *true consensus*.
>
> Do not be tempted to use your position as "boss" to shortcut the process, save time, and get your favorite names adopted. Instead of gaining time, the I-driven process will grind to a halt. People who report to you will simply let you have your way—and you will have short-circuited the spirited associate engagement you have worked so long and sincerely to cultivate through WTMS. I guarantee it. "Naming" is a team sport.

Make Your Addresses More Effective: Five Tips

Many companies casually undertake the mighty opportunity that well-developed addresses offer. This is usually because they have not yet realized how powerfully addresses can contribute to the bottom line. In many such facilities, white addresses (with black letters or numbers) are plastered on everything, cookie-cutter fashion—usually under a 5S umbrella—in the mistaken belief that this fulfils the requirement.

It does not. Small wonder that the very people who are asked to put such dull addresses in place lose the will to maintain them and the heart to look for ways to make them more effective. The standard has already been set; it was called "good enough," a sworn enemy of excellence.

Let's do something other than that. Let's begin with the premise that: 1) addresses are indispensable to operational excellence, and 2) addresses should improve, just as borders do—because as we get smarter, our addresses should get smarter.

Here are five tips to keep in mind as you seek to make your addresses as effective as possible. By "effective" I mean: easy-to-see, easy-to-read, accurate, complete, and related to the task-at-hand.

Tip 1: Use Arrows

When you start to apply addresses to racks and shelves, do not subtract from your efforts by failing to make it clear which address applies to what shelf.

The positive impact of the bold yellow-and-black shelf addresses in Photo 8.15 is reduced as we hesitate and wonder if CD30C applies to material above it—or below it. Add arrows and the question is never asked. Any hint of that form of micro-motion evaporates.

Arrows + Barcoding. Product barcoding is an operational necessity for asset tracking, inventory control, unique identification, and automatic data collection. It is also vital for RFID (Radio Frequency Identification Data)—a technology developed in World War II as an IFF (Identify Friend or Foe) tool for aircraft. Tall warehouse shelving is a key application opportunity (Photo 8.16).

Photo 8.15 Better, but ....

For the purposes of workplace visuality, however, barcode addresses weaken visual viability because the tag is white, inches small, and filled with equally

Photo 8.16 Tall shelves.

small black letters, numbers, and bars unknowable without a reader. Plus, many companies apply the barcode strip directly onto the shelving units. If the shelves are beige (Photo 8.17), the barcode tag is even harder to locate, whether from far away or close up.

But barcodes are so widely used, we had better not ignore the problem or complain about it too long. Instead, we apply visual principles to make barcodes more user friendly. Here are two ways:

1. Add a contrasting background. Add a backing to barcode tags through paint, colored cardboard, or a color magnetic strip. See the dark green cardboard backing, behind the black-and-white barcode tag? Readable at last! (Photo 8.18)

2. Add arrows. As mentioned earlier, a hidden motion (hidden question) in many shelf addresses is this: To which shelf does that address apply—the shelf above the address or the shelf below the address? Add arrows and clear up the mystery (Photo 8.19).

Photo 8.17 White gets lost on beige.

Photo 8.18 A dark backing helps.

Photo 8.19 Arrows clear up the mystery.

Gwenie's Rant on Arrows. In my view, arrows on all shelving should be mandatory (made a standard)—not just in the warehouse but everywhere. "Why?" says the newcomer to visuality. "After all, the time lost in figuring out which shelf the address applies to can be measured in nanoseconds. The motion is tiny." But the visual thinker knows better. The visual thinker knows to add up the nanoseconds of motion triggered by a single vague address—in this case, one without arrows—over the course of a single day, then a week, and then a month. That is when the cost of the absence of arrows becomes screamingly apparent. Go a level higher and multiply those now-thousands of nanoseconds per month by the number of individuals who go to that same shelf, day after day, month after month, year after year, and the screams grow louder.

I don't believe anyone has ever had the internal fortitude to go to the next level—multiplying all that by the number of products on that shelving unit and then the number of shelving units in the department, company, and corporation. Why torment yourself? Better to just get arrows going and watch them spread as the intelligent, forward-thinking people who work with you get the message—as inevitably as the sunrise.

Tip 2: Use Driver-License Level Addresses

Unless you make the decision to use a purely generic address (Photo 8.20; discussed in detail in a mo-

ment), your aim is to add telling detail to each address, making them ever more specific. In that way, you and others will have sufficient information to act immediately, independently, and correctly, without questions or hesitation—that is, with minimal motion. Said another way: The address must anticipate people's need-to-know. When an address does that, I call it a *driver-license level address.* It is packed with relevant detail.

Your driver's license shares your name, photo, home address, birth date, height, vehicle restrictions, driving restrictions, the license number—and what you want us to do with your vital organs should you get into a fatal accident. In short, it contains the information needed for us to make positive identification, make correct and timely value-add decisions, and take effective, timely action.

Photo 8.20 Generic addresses.

In the same way, a good workplace address shares many levels of information about its residents. The more complicated or look-alike an item, the more you need to include specifics in the address in order for us to put/pick that item quickly, without the slightest hesitation or any possibility of mix-up.

Examine the four-address system in Photo 8.21 that John Pacheco developed (United Electric Controls/ Massachusetts). It was the first address of its kind I had ever seen. I named it a *driver-license level address.* John's addresses made us see the difference between the four sets of look-alike rods to which they applied. The rods were identical in length but not in material. They had identical ODs (outer diameter) but different IDs (inner diameter).

John wanted an address approach that minimized mix-ups across these look-alike rods. Here is how he did it:

1. John alternated the location of rods by material: stainless steel/copper/stainless steel/copper.

2. He placed the ID specification of each rod type at the top of the address to make it easy for us to spot the telling attribute.

3. John paired similarities: *ID .015* together and *ID .021* together.

4. He colored the copper addresses yellow to break the apparent symmetry a bit further.

Photo 8.21 John Pacheco's first driver-license level address.

This exceptional address type perfectly demonstrates the principle of *how to tell the difference merely by looking*, a principle of all workplace visuality. Providing driver-license level information is as useful as it is satisfying. Effectively implemented, this elegant address approach has the capacity—in the manufacturing—to reduce picking errors, speed up material handling, and prevent stock-outs. In hospital and medical settings, the benefits are even more pronounced. Look for ways to adapt and apply this principle to all situations that need crystal clear, detailed addresses. What situation doesn't!

Tip 3: Use Generic Addresses

With addresses, begin with the intention of creating the most accurate, precise, and complete address possible (driver-license level). But also be prepared to change your mind when the polar opposite is required. That polar opposite is called *a generic address*. Generic (or general) addresses have many applications. Typically, they are used when co-located items are so different that they cannot be defined by a single address.

Here is a story of a generic address (Photo 8.22), triggered by an uncommon form of motion: searching for a lost pizza. The night shift at Greene Rubber (Massachusetts) phoned in for a pizza. Expecting delivery within 30 minutes, people continued working and were surprised an hour later when the pizza still had not shown up. They called to inquire. "But we delivered it 40 minutes ago," was the response. "No, you didn't!" "Yes, we did." "No! You didn't!" "YES! WE DID!!"

Photo 8.22 Now we can find that pizza!

A team member went to the night delivery desk and asked. The reply was: "Sure it came. I took it back to your department ages ago." "Well, where did you put it?" "In your department!" was the response.

The pizza was eventually found, needless to say, cold and hard. That was when the night shift decided that this would never happen again. They designated a location they simply called "Drop Zone." Everything and anything delivered to the department was put there—parts, cardboard, tools, and piping hot pizza. This is a very good example of a generic address.

Tip 4: Avoid Meaningless Addresses

Look at the addresses in Photo 8.23 (plus Detail). They are: 12089499, 12065401, etc.—part numbers of the components you see here in bins in an automotive assembly area. Lots of numbers but no meaning.

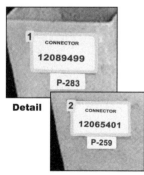
Detail

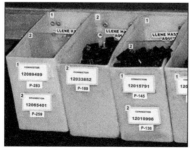
Photo 8.23 Lots of numbers but no meaning.

We do not doubt that these number addresses were developed with care and a desire to be of help. It *is* of help and certainly far better than nothing. It is something. It is a beginning.

But if we sit and observe the micro-activity triggered by such addresses, we see a lot of earnest, hard-working employees engaged in a lot of micro-motion. First, we see operators bent over, straining to see the numbers. If we keep watching, we observe the strain that this almost-good-enough approach causes material handlers, re-stock people and/or water spiders—every person responsible for keeping the bins filled. Lean in a bit closer and you might hear them muttering: "Hmmm, does this box of parts match the bin number? Well, almost, I think .... Gosh, maybe not. Wait a minute let me double check. Darn, where are my glasses?" We would see a ton of motion.

What is the remedy? No, not a better pair of glasses. The remedy is to think visually—first by recognizing that folks are struggling, not working. Then start improving these addresses, with the active involvement of the people who have to use it.

The first thing we do is *not* to remove those long part numbers (because someone needs them). The first thing we do is to add a thing I call *handles*.

Tip 5: Add Address Handles

Adding handles to an address strengthens it and makes it crystal clear. Handles are like additions or repeats. They make an address sharper by adding an echo or a second way to convey that address but in a different manner. The fancy term for this is "deliberate redundancy." Here are some handles we can add to long part number addresses in Photo 8.23 that will do the trick:

- Trade name
- Photograph
- Drawing
- Whom to call when the part is low or out
- That phone number

Look at the blue parts holder in Photo 8.24. Each blue pocket holds the specific part whose number is indicated directly above it. Pocket 3 holds part number 12064171. Directly above that is a drawing (a handle) of that part to make the match (see Detail).

Then, in case we forget exactly how to assemble that part, the number of the standard operating procedure is included in the address as well: SOP 19 (another handle). Fully and visually informed, we move forward with confidence and leave work satisfied that we contributed to our company and earned our keep.

This is a blistering great address! Visible, accurate, correct, specific, precise, complete, and very effective.

Detail.

Photo 8.24 So many visual devices to help assemble correctly.

With that, we conclude the five tips for developing highly-effective addresses in your area so you can create brilliant addresses in your work area. Next we look at innovations that are bound to make your addresses even more powerful—and, we bet in some cases, make your socks roll up and down.

Make Your Addresses More Powerful: Eight Innovations

Addresses are a major element in the operational language you embed into the workplace through WTMS. Sometimes it seems that there are nearly as many ways to apply effective addresses as there are words to put on them. Here are eight examples of address innovation.

a. Stacked Address. What happens when you combine a floor border with stacked bins? You get stacked addresses (Photo 8.25). Two stacked bins are home to three part numbers. (Notice that the bottom bin has two sections.) Each bin has its own address (two addresses on the bottom). Plus these three addresses are also on the floor border. (Fleet Engineers/Michigan)

Detail.

Photo 8.25 Stacked Addresses.

b. Photo-Copied Address. Do you remember Bob Comeau's invention of photo-copied borders discussed in the last chapter? Never to be outdone (even by himself), Bob proceeded to develop another layer of innovation on his innovation. You see it in Photo 8.26: a photo of the tools needed to changeover the Nichifu machine (to the left). That tool photo acts as an address—not a border—because it tells us what tools are in the blue bin above it, a type of Bill of Tools. (United Electric Controls/Massachusetts)

Photo 8.26 Photo-copied address for changeover tools.

c. 3D-Tab Address. A powerful yet largely under-used address option is three-dimensional (3D) tabs—addresses that stick out into space so that you do not need to stand in front of the address to see it. One of the most useful applications of 3D tabs is in rows of racks. The challenge with rows, especially if there are a lot of them, is that you rarely discover if what you need is in a row until you walk down it—and discover that it is not. With 3D tabs (Photos 8.27 and 8.28), you can tell at a distance, from either end of the row.

Smart retail stores use 3D tabs to improve the customer experience while keeping floor staff to a minimum. Empowered consumers, we can be self-regulating because the retail environment is self-explaining, as shown in the splendid end-caps in Photo 8.29.

Photo 8.27 This series of 3D tabs tell us from-a-distance that what we are looking for is—or is not—down this row.

Photo 8.28 The closer we get, the more value-add information we get.

Photo 8.29 Blue end-caps are very large 3D tabs. Notice: 1) generic addresses combined with words, 2) the use of yellow, and 3) major and minor sorts in the airborne addresses.

d. 3D-Tab Addresses Linked to Borders. Melody Sparrow's bench was located near five rows of hard-to-find diodes, resistors, and transistors. Although those rows were not her area, nearly everyone who went to them assumed, since she was close by, that she knew where things were. They were wrong. But that did not stop them from repeatedly asking for her help to find what they needed.

By default, their information deficits rapidly became hers—and that translated into the endless motion of interruptions and searching. Melody took the situation in hand and created the array system of 3D-tab addresses you see in Photos 8.30 and 8.31. She further improved that visual solution by adding a second color to the already color-coded borders that framed the tall racks (Photo 8.32). In that photo, you see the yellow for resistors running the length of that resistor inventory. Brilliant visual thinking. (Harris Corp./Illinois)

Photo 8.30 3D tabs along the row.

Photo 8.31 Yellow 3D tab for resistors.

Photo 8.32 Yellow border defines the resistor inventory.

e. Generic 3D Tabs. While Melody's addresses needed to be very specific, a set of tall shelves in a different company (Photo 8.33) needs to accommodate a constant flow of ever-changing parts. This time

the 3D-tab addresses are generic. This lets the same spaces be used and re-used for an ever-changing product mix, with the same visual logic. The tabs remain unchanged: B1, B2, B3, B4, and so on. (Delphi/Mexico)

How many places can you find in your own area where 3D-tab addresses can help reduce motion?

Photo 8.33 Generic 3D tabs.

f. Number Address. We human beings are complicated. So is our behavior. We are also error-prone. That is one of the main reasons why visuality is so important. That is also why there are so many excellent visual solutions in community places: so many people—so many opportunities for mistakes.

(Study Photo 8.34 for the principles it holds, noting that this approach was replaced by the smart phone.) Similar to the above Delphi 3D-tab solution, numbers can help us deal with too many differences.

Because there were too many phone numbers in a seven-county area to fit in a single book, an agency developed a set of seven phone books that were organized by numbers (one through seven) instead of by county name. The match between book and county is made without titles, thanks to the color-coded map on the backboard. Can you see the next step in making this solution even smarter? Yes, color-match the numbers on each book to the map.

Photo 8.34 Number addresses match the phone books to the county map.

Photo 8.35 Numbered pipes, a tiny detail that results in big savings.

Another example of using numbers as addresses is the pipe application in Photo 8.35. When you see a company that bothers to address pipes in a facility, you are among advanced visual thinkers—those who look ahead into the repair and maintenance function and take steps, in advance, to reduce the potential downtime. "Picking up the money lying on the floor" is another way to say this.

g. Metric vs. Standard. Numbers are often able to make addresses more specific than words can, as in the case of the two types of rod stock shown in Photos 8.36 to 8.38.

The rods are identical materials—but one set is cut in metric units (for European customers) while the other is cut in standard units (for US clients). Bill Jones made sure each address captured that key difference by using numbers, not words. He spelled out the distinction further through color-coding (yellow for metric/red for standard). As we saw earlier in John Pacheco's driver-license level address, by alternating the color, Bill minimized mix-ups. (Denison Hydraulics/Ohio)

Our final number-as-address solution belongs to the world of cams—tools used for machining complicated parts such as screw threading.

Photo 8.36 Metric rod stock in yellow.

Photo 8.37 Standard rod stock in red.

Photo 8.38 Rack from a distance.

h. Cam Storage. The shocking *Before* in Photo 8.39 shows how cams used to be stored. The equally remarkable *After* (Photo 8.40) gives you a sense of the hundreds of cams this company utilized across more than 30 screw-making machines—and why creating visually-coherent storage for them was an operational requirement.

Photo 8.39 Cam storage, *Before.*

Notice how the operators who created this visual solution situated the cams on a backboard, using cam size as the address (Photo 8.41). Though they did not realize it at the time, when these operators painted the board with broad white and blue bands, they automatically made finding specific cams—as well as returning them—faster, more accurate, and easier. Why? Because of the now-familiar principle of harnessing the mind's power to recognize and make meaning of patterns. The blue and white bands created enough of a pattern for it to register (Curtis Screw/New York). CNC machining has since replaced cams with a new technology. But the visual principles reflected in this address solution are well worth your study and consideration.

Photo 8.40 Bands of color make it easier for our brain to recollect the right location.

Photo 8.41 The address is the cam size.

Addresses By Function

Visuality is a form of operational language. Addresses can do more than simply tell us where things are and where they go. Used inventively, they can support day-to-day operations specifically and admirably well. Now we study four address categories, for a total of eleven different types of address solutions:

- Tool Checkout
- Process Sequencing
- Departmental Addresses
- Material Handling

1. Tool Checkout-A: Magnetic Address. New magnetic materials bring useful options to the address function. The department in this example (Photo 8.42) has manual processes, requiring small but highly-specialized tools and fixtures. These tools are too costly for each associate to have an individual set. Instead of chasing down tools all the time, associates invented a simple checkout approach to maximize tool sharing and traceability. Here is how it works.

- Tools and fixtures are placed on a low metal rack in visual order. (This is an electrostatic area and the only available bordering tape was red.)

- The name of each associate is marked on a magnetic tag. The tags are lined up on the rack front. A sixth tag is marked *Repair* for tools that leave the area for that reason.

- When an associate needs a tool or fixture, he/she takes it from the rack and leaves, in its place, her name magnet. If the tool needs repair or calibration, she turns it in and leaves that magnet in its place.

Photo 8.42 Magnetic address approach for specialized tools.

- In this way, if others need that tool, they know where it is and either wait—or find the current user and ask for it next. Minimum wondering. Minimum wandering. Minimum motion. (Alpha Industries/Massachusetts)

2. Tool Checkout-B: The Chit Address. A chit is a note or voucher and, as such, is linked to something of value. In the following example that valuable thing is tools.

The approach in Photos 8.43 and 8.44 uses chits for tool checkout and traceability in the Warranty Department at Volgren, a bus manufacturer in Australia.

Notice that this system tackles two separate outcomes: 1) checking out a tool so the person who takes it can be held accountable for returning it, and 2) providing a colleague that needs an unavailable tool a way to find the current user and schedule a turn.

Before this chit system, repair operators spent a great deal of time chasing down highly-prized tools—or were

Photo 8.44 Special tool corner. See yellow circle for the chit/tool checkout board.

Photo 8.43 Close-up/tool checkout board.

forced to wait for people to return from lunch/rest room/meeting/etc. in the hope that they knew a tool's whereabouts. The layers upon layers of motion triggered by the lack of a systematic visual approach defies quantification. Here is detail on how the chit checkout works:

1. Specialized tools are co-located on a stand on the production floor.
2. Each operator is provided with six chits in a given color with their respective name on them.
3. When the operator takes a tool, he leaves the chit in place.

The aerospace industry makes good use of the chit checkout approach. Typically, each operator carries individualized chits on a large key ring, with a personal photo and barcode that is scanned when a tool is taken.

3. Process Sequencing Address. I never fully realized how much an innovative address can silently, reliably, and precisely reveal process sequence until I saw the following series at Curtis Screw (New York).

Notice that all four of the addresses in Photo 8.45 have the same top-level information: M8219. But they are not repeat addresses. The information below the M8219 address maps out the process sequence—four operational stages. This is the part that is brilliant. Look.

Photo 8.45 Four addresses that only seem identical.

Photo 8.46 Stage 1 address.

In Photo 8.46, the Stage 1 detail reads: "AFTER WASH/COUNT/WAITING FOR TUMBLE."

In Photo 8.47, Stage 2 is: "AFTER TUMBLE/WAITING FOR HEAT TREAT."

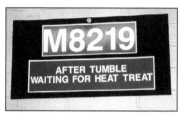

Photo 8.47 Stage 2 address.

This makes so much sense. It is often difficult or even impossible—by sight alone—to see the difference between parts at various stages. For Curtis operators, that was exactly the point. They were not able to reliably tell the difference merely by looking at M8219 parts as those parts went through a four-stage process. For example, parts after heat treat looked almost identical to those that had not.

Lots of mix-ups resulted, followed by lots of scrap. The solution was to created a series of addresses that stated those differences as part of each address. Bins of parts got placed under the address that named their current operational stage. This address sequence is a remarkably simple and effective visual solution that brilliantly combines smart placement principles with highly functional addresses.

4. Departmental Addresses. We already discussed that addresses are not only about retrieval. They can have other important purposes—the IN-and-OUT function and departmental addresses, for example.

a. IN-and-OUT Address (when not to standardize). Many people rightly link standardization with the journey to excellence. But far too many think this means making everything the same, uniform, and identical. Here, they are mistaken. Take addresses, for example. People who say they want everything the "same/uniform/identical" almost always want addresses to be like that: the same size, shape, and color. That is not a move towards standardization. That is cutting cookies (Photo 8.48).

As far as visuality and addresses are concerned, cookie-cutter standardization is no standardization at all. Instead, it is death by sameness. This robs the enterprise of high-performance excellence and its employees of the satisfaction that comes from genuine inventive engagement—aka, thinking—and the robust, creative solutions that derive from that. For me, one of the hallmarks of a spirited and engaged workforce and a genuinely effective visual conversion is what I call the "weird" factor—or, in polite company, the "local" factor.

Photo 8.48 Cookies anyone?

If a company's array of visual devices looks suspiciously similar and appears to occur on the same level of mind or imagination, something is not right with the rollout. Usually that means two things. First, the "good enough" bar is set too low. As a result, the company standardizes on visual improvements too soon and too quickly. Second, no time or not enough time is set aside for improvement activity. As a result, people simply do not have the time or quiet to think and invent—to test their own ideas and experiment. In either case, the visual improvement process is short-circuited.

Instead of standardizing on a specific outcome (for example, requiring a specific type of address), companies are better served by requiring that a specific functionality be put into place—not requiring a specific form in which to do that. For instance, companies will rightly require that each area have IN-and-OUT addresses—but not necessarily mandate that they look alike, cookie-cutter fashion, from the outset.

There are dozens of ways to create such a set of addresses. Let the experimentation begin! Managers, don't seek to control that. Seek to make sure each department has: 1) a highly-visual location for newly delivered goods and materials, and 2) a separate, highly-visual location for goods and materials that are ready for removal or pick up.

Now that is a smart standard. What those addresses look like is not the point. What is the point is that each department has a pair.

You may have seen better in your lifetime—or imagined better in your mind—but for me the IN-and-OUT locations shown in Photos 8.49 and 8.50 are simply delightful—though I would love to see a border define the limits of OUT. Why not widen the scope: Apply the same IN-and-OUT requirement to workbenches too. That could go a long way toward ending senseless mix-ups from picking up material that is not yet ready.

Photo 8.49 Address for incoming.

Photo 8.50 Address for outgoing.

The department next door may go about this another way. And the department next to that yet another. Let each area go through a period of trial and error as it discovers what works for it. At some point, your company will want to adopt a more or less uniform format for the IN-and-OUT function—a so-to-speak "standardized practice."

But that comes later, after people who use those locations many times a day have a chance to explore the possibilities and experiment with, for example, location, look, and feel (form, fit, and function). That is how inventive visual solutions can transform into true *Visual Best Practices*—a term that values uniformity while leaving plenty of room for upgrades.

b. Addressing the "Entrance." In much the same way, your company can (I think *should*) require each department to visually indicate/show its name. When you name your work area, name its entrance—name the "top" of the stream.

Many departments have no actual doors, no designated threshold. As a result, it is not easy to tell where the area actually begins. If you not know that, how can you know the flow-in and flow-out points—the flow of materials/WIP? Begin that process. First, select the main entrance of your department. Then give it a name—an address.

Most departments at Trailmobile/Canada had no walls. The site manager made naming the entrance to every area a requirement. Many unspoken questions were immediately answered, as you see in Photo 8.51: Rear Headers Department.

Photo 8.51 The Rear Headers team built their departmental address into the floor at the "top" of their area (red arrow) (Trailmobile/Canada).

Big Challenge. Another big challenge in locating the so-called "entrance" is that many departments cover a vast amount of floor space (Photo 8.52). With that much undifferentiated square footage, it is a challenge to find the perimeter (the outside edge), let alone the top of the stream (the entrance). The department in Photo 8.53 attempted to solve this by plastering signage high in the heavens of this very large space. Despite their best intentions, they merely substituted one confusing universe with another.

Photo 8.52
Nothing.

Photo 8.53
Not much more.

To tell you the truth, in 35 years in the field, I have never seen this handled in a way that makes sense. As a result, I have no benchmark. But I do suspect why: Area addresses tend to possess the same cookie-cutter look and the same cookie-cutter failure because the "signage" task is typically given to busy engineers or an equally busy Facilities department—usually triggered by a visit from corporate. "Get some signs up quick!" cries the CEO, "Corporate will be here in three weeks!" A list of departments is compiled, sent to an outside contractor, and two weeks later three dozen look-alike signs are hung.

While usually well-made ("to last the ages"), such signs rarely offer a way for us to see—to discern—the differences between departments. The signs themselves do not help. They do not show a difference in shape or color or information. Only the departmental name is different. As a result, we remain uninformed despite the sizable investment in professional signage. Many of us might prefer the previous absence of an approach because at least we had a reason to ask questions—instead of wandering around with our heads bent upward, looking for answers or clues amidst the new population of vinyl.

A week later, the corporate team arrives, sees the mob of airborne signage, and declares the "darn signs" a best practice because they are identical in look and feel to the signage the corporate team saw in the showcase/best practice plant they toured last month— another example of mis-placed standardization.

So much more is possible.

A Bribe. At the moment I have nothing to contribute to this sorry situation except my complaint—and a bribe. Will you help find a better way—a way for departmental addresses to make a genuine visual contribution to the operational excellence of the company?

If you develop one—a practical and functional visual approach to departmental addresses in large spaces, send it to me with an explanation. If I agree that it works and moves the thinking along, I will present my one-day visual workplace/visual thinking seminar at your company for expenses only, as my schedule permits. I won't restrict this to one satisfactory approach—or the first one. Send them all.

I am happy to recognize multiple approaches from different companies. This is untested ground. I will keep this offer open in this second edition of this book, in the hope of an array of splendid approaches so we will have reason enough for a third edition. (Send to: contact@visualworkplace.com. Thanks!)

c. *Homemade Address vs. Commercial Address.* While I realize departmental addresses for large companies are usually made by an outside contractor, I favor homemade addresses, as you might guess. Photo Series 8.54 provides an assortment.

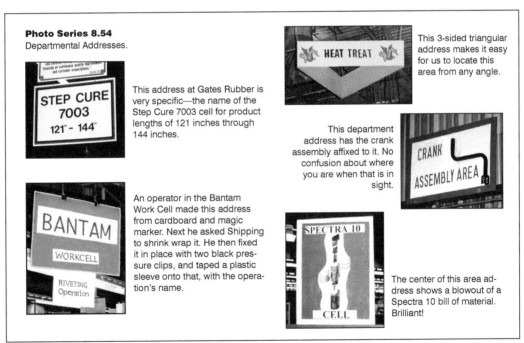

Photo Series 8.54
Departmental Addresses.

This address at Gates Rubber is very specific—the name of the Step Cure 7003 cell for product lengths of 121 inches through 144 inches.

This 3-sided triangular address makes it easy for us to locate this area from any angle.

This department address has the crank assembly affixed to it. No confusion about where you are when that is in sight.

An operator in the Bantam Work Cell made this address from cardboard and magic marker. Next he asked Shipping to shrink wrap it. He then fixed it in place with two black pressure clips, and taped a plastic sleeve onto that, with the operation's name.

The center of this area address shows a blowout of a Spectra 10 bill of material. Brilliant!

Museum Quality Addresses at Fleet. Fleet Engineers (Michigan) had two goals in mind when it decided to go visual: 1) reduce the mountains of waste that were choking the company at that time, and 2) awaken the workforce to a greater sense of ownership and accountability. The surprise came by just how much and how quickly both goals were met.

Business-wise, for example, materials handling was reduced by 70% within the first year, quality improved by over 50%, and overall manufacturing lead time shrank by a third (and the facility was still four years away from implementing lean). Employee-wise, operators did not just take ownership, they got ignited, even about something as ordinary as meeting the new requirement that each department prominently display its address. Photo Series 8.55 shows you two superb contributions. Who knew such talent existed?

Photo Series 8.55 Museum quality area addresses.

Jeff Hamm and Gary White wanted the departmental address they created for the FB-27 Cell to communicate the team's commitment to quality and productivity.

The FB-27 address hung high over the welding booth for everyone to see and admire (red arrow).

The area address for Fleet's Cut-Off Department featured a green cutting machine and a superhero competing for supremacy. Robert Oldaker (inset), the artist, titled his work, *Man against Machine*.

5. Material Handling Addresses. Wikipedia defines material handling as:

The movement, storage, control, and protection of materials, goods, and products throughout the process of manufacturing, distribution, consumption and disposal. The focus is on the methods, mechanical equipment, systems and related controls used to achieve these functions.

Let's see how visuality makes a powerful contribution through addresses for this core function in (Photo Series 8.56) below.

a. Variable (Temporary) Addresses. A temporary address is home to items that can change often in type and/or quantity; they are variable. Because of this, the address mechanism has to be flexible but also timely, accurate, complete, precise, and readable. Here are five good examples.

Temporary Address Solution 1. The excellent example on the left (Photo 1) is a standing sign for components in short-term storage. As soon as the pallet is moved, the standing sign is removed—unless or until a pallet of the exact same part number occupies that floor space again.

Notice the three handles that amplify the address: 1) exact part number, 2) common name, and 3) a photo of the part itself. The potential motion of mix-ups is minimized.

Temporary Address Solution 2. In Photo 2, you see a different type of temporary standing sign. This one provides the temperature and duration for a batch of units already in the oven for an epoxy cure cycle. This address, strictly speaking, represents a temporary location for that material. We have only one place to look for accurate timely information: this standing sign near Oven 2.

The information on the white sheet of paper changes from shift to shift. Why not laminate it, then wipe it clean for new use? Notice the mix of bold/non-bold letters and upper/lower case. In this case, the mix forces us to read each word to get the meaning—a smart idea in this case.

Temporary Address Solution 3. Here's another address challenge, solved with a temporary address. Freudenberg-NOK manufactures a wide range of elastomeric seals and custom-molded products, with over 30 sites worldwide. That translates into a large variety of dies (tooling) at each site. The Georgia facility in the U.S.A. tackled the challenge of dies complexity by developing a flexible storage system, built on two key visual principles: temporary address and point-of-use.

The aim was to make sure that only dies for a given week of work were brought to the production floor. The solution hinged on two factors.

First, the dies rack had to be large enough to hold a week's worth of dies—but small enough to prevent unneeded dies from accumulating. Once the right-sized rack was chosen (Photo 3a), it was moved close to the production floor (point-of-use) and to the machines it served. (The dies not in weekly use were stored nearby but out of the main value field.)

Second, the approach needed to be flexible yet accurate and complete. Magnetic addresses were the solution. A magnetic tag was made for each die in the inventory and stored at the end of the dies rack in a type of physical table of contents (Photo 3b is a great example of *use the existing architecture.)*

Yes, like you, I would love to see these black-on-white addresses upgraded to black-on-yellow. Still, this is an excellent example of the permanent power of temporary addresses!

Temporary Address Solution 4. Innovation—the use of our imagination in the workplace—is often our only chance at developing a solution to unusual operational challenges, at Fleet Engineers for example.

We already know the Fleet team is a wildly creative group. Here's what they did when faced with sheets of steel with specs so similar, they were nearly impossible to tell apart without special instruments and a lot of time. As a result, material handlers would "eyeball" the sheets, make a best guess—and often be wrong. What to do?

Only a highly-specific address for each steel type would work. But where to post it? People experimented and finally hit upon using the hollow supports in the rack structure itself (Photo 4). They made blocks of wood to fit the slots (see red arrow), marked part numbers on them, and inserted and removed them as needed. Challenge met!

Temporary Address Solution 5. Our final example of a temporary address solution is one of the most innovative, brought to us by those brilliant operators at Denison Hydraulics (Ohio). As you will see, their visual answer reflects many address principles discussed in this section and previously.

The challenge is familiar: a high variety of parts (this time on pallets) that move in and out of the same physical area—in this case, the Test Cell—all needing to be found quickly, accurately, and easily. Each pallet (Photo 8.57) holds an array of part numbers, with new pallets replacing the previous as testing is completed. The upshot: There was no way to post specific addresses on those beautiful yellow borders.

Photo 8.57 Test Pallet: *Before.*

Photo 8.58 Yellow Temporary Addresses: *After.*

Knowing this, the Denison Test team created a set of yellow laminated cards with all current part numbers on them and stored them in a nearby bin. When a pallet is delivered, the material handler matches the part numbers on the move order to the correct yellow card and places that card on the part (Photo 8.58). Presto-change-o! Highly accurate *temporary* addresses and exceptional material handling.

Please note that, because these cards are lightweight and not anchored down, drafts could scatter them (Detail). How would you deal with this issue?

Detail Close-up: *After.*

Warehouse Addresses

Despite our best efforts, forty years after JIT/Lean arrived in the West, most companies still have not achieved one-piece flow or its material corollary, zero inventories (not more than three hours of WIP). On the contrary, many companies are still packed to the rafters with stock. The following address solutions can help, whether you are a manufacturer, or a distribution center like the ones in the examples below and responsible for processing large quantities of just about everything.

Such centers have acquired a sophisticated understanding of the challenges associated with large inventories and have solved them in ways that I hope you find instructive for your own purposes. We begin with a widely-seen address application: the airborne address.

Airborne Address: Basic. An airborne address is simply one that hangs from the ceiling—those yellow and black placards above the rows in Photo 8.59 (see red arrow). Here again we have generic number addresses (9, 10, 11) that support the continuous loading of the stock in temporary residence between each person-width border. These airborne addresses are easy for forklift drivers to see at a distance.

> *Question.* What is the readability problem with these airborne addresses as you see it here?
>
> *Answer.* Blocked by mounds of inventory, we cannot see the airborne addresses when we are close without craning or stepping away from the rows.
>
> *Solution.* Add floor addresses at both ends of each row (Photo 8.60; see red arrow).

Photo 8.59 Airborne address on loading dock.

Photo 8.60 Redundant floor addresses.

Airborne Addresses: Advanced. Make no mistake, warehouses and distribution centers have special needs—vast expanses of concrete, stories of racks, and a roof that is far, far away. And beneath it, motion potential that ranges from suffering to near insanity. For most companies, the silver bullet is not SAP, TecSys, or any other asset management software system—though a nifty RFID mechanism could lend a welcome, powerful assist in the pick-and-put process (if you can afford it). But if you cannot, why not decipher the operational logic of your warehouse approach and embed that logic, visually?

We travel to one of the world's great automotive suppliers, Delphi (now "Aptiv"), for a set of first-rate visual applications. I have been to dozens of Delphi plants, some when the corporation was still Packard Electric. All the sites were visual show stoppers, having been schooled by Sumitomo Electric in the 1980s. The group continues to grow in its use of visuality. Let's take a closer look.

First, in the photo sequence that begins with Photo 8.61, we see large (visible at 30 yards) airborne addresses: 01 and 02, the first of many rows. Each blank space below these two numbers holds a plastic pocket for more details. This is visible in Photo 8.62: Double Row 03.

Look at that hanging placard address. See how the same product shares two rows of finished goods. Look more closely and you will see the double arrows, under "03." Each of them points to a separate column. The sheet below the "03" is a list of the 12 plants on the delivery route, the telling detail that will help us do a better job (see Detail).

Photo 8.61 Lane addresses visible at 30 feet.

Photo 8.62 The list of plants on the delivery route is inserted in the plastic pocket of the placard for the two rows of "03."

PLANT 61 - ZACATECAS	PLANT 86 - LINARES
PLANT 62 - FRESNILLO I	PLANT 87 - ANAHUAC
PLANT 63 - FRESNILLO II	PLT 91/92 - VICTORIA I/II
PLANT 81 - N LAREDO I	PLANT 96 - GUADALUPE
PLANT 82 - N LAREDO I	PLANT 97 - CENTEC II
PLANT 84 - GUADALUPE	PLANT 98 - CENTEC I

Detail.

Let's go to the tall shelves and locate the home for the 5700s (Photo 8.63). Photo 8.64 shows the "5900 Mochis" in a low-cost flexible format—paper in a plastic sleeve. The row address (Photo 8.65) is an ever-splendid 3D tab. But look how it is constructed—not of costly metal, fabricated by an outside supplier but folded, laminated paper, printed by you. Low cost, hands-on, flexible, and highly readable.

Photo 8.64 Simple plastic sleeve plus tape.

Photo 8.63 Two rows of part number 5700.

Photo 8.65 3D tabs you can make yourself.

Take a look at Photo Series 8.66. It shows how you can go to Rack Row 60 and find a handy *Table of Barcode Contents*. Travel further and see more detail—a vivid demonstration of driver-license address— the closer you get, the more information you get.

The point in showing this RFID barcode rack system is not to persuade you to buy one. If your company has the money and time to convert to RFID, it probably has already done so—or is in the process. The point in sharing this is so you can study the components of this sophisticated address system. Study the ideas and the elements; then select which will help make your current approach more visual and therefore more useful.

Look again at Photo Series 8.66. Notice the low-cost way in which the 3D tabs are created: just folded paper, laminated to give the material enough heft to make it into a 3D tab; then mounted on a strut. You may not be able to purchase the kit for this—but you sure can afford the idea. Put your home-made version in place with masking or duct tape. This becomes your pilot—your beginning. All beginnings are important. That is the nature of starting anything. Beginnings are also powerful because they represent the new. They are the horizon and you must seek it.

Photo Series 8.66 RFID Elements. (How many can you adapt for your warehouse?)

ID Labels

Now the final element of the visual where: ID labels (red circle, Photo 8.67). Once a location is claimed by a border and address, put an ID label on the item that lives there. Make the match: Border + Address + ID Label.

ID labels are how items find their way back home if they wander off, go for a "walk," or just get lost. The location information you build in by the visual where is functioning. But the lack of an ID label on any tool could mean that tool may "belong" to someone else by the morning. Similar to a soldier's dog tag, an ID label moves with the item—because it is on it! Look at the three examples in Photo Series 8.68. The first is an example of what not to do!

Photo 8.67 The final element of the visual where: ID label.

Photo Series 8.68 ID Label Opportunities.

This design-to-task system does such a great job controlling tool placement that we may not notice that it lacks the ID label level—probably because the boxes are made by a vendor. Add ID labels and complete the visual where.

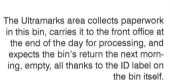

The Ultramarks area collects paperwork in this bin, carries it to the front office at the end of the day for processing, and expects the bin's return the next morning, empty, all thanks to the ID label on the bin itself.

This hand truck reflects the simple formula for the visual where: border, address, and ID label on the thing itself.

Time to clear up one small point: My "hard-and-fast rule" about the visual where for everything that casts a shadow loosens a bit related to ID labels. Why? Because you cannot put ID labels on consumables—the stacks of packing cardboard, those brackets, this bubble wrap, those commodity parts.

While you should (and will) put an ID label on the red bin that holds your wood screws, you will not—and cannot—apply ID labels to each of those screws. In much the same way, I can ID label my coffee cup ("Gwenie's Cup") but not the coffee that is in it. But you already know that.

Addresses and ID Labels: Next Steps. Review what you just learned about addresses and ID labels and how your thinking has grown in how you can make your area safe and more operationally effective. Then, working alone or with a buddy, make a list of opportunities for them and update your visual workplace hit list (Figure 8.4). Post *all* your improvement ideas, even if you do not plan to tackle them yourself.

Figure 8.4

The Visual Where: A Personal Testimony

We have completed our journey through the basics of the visual where—two chapters and over 150 examples in action. You have probably already begun to apply this powerful visual combination to your own work area and seen struggle/motion decrease and work begin to make much more sense.

In Chapter 11, you learn about visual mini systems and ways to drill these basic principles deeper into the information deficits of day-to-day work. Then in Chapter 12 (*Four Power Levels*), you learn how to make your visual solutions more and more powerful. This is when visuality becomes more of a language than an application—and you become masterful at *letting the workplace speak*.

Photo 8.69 Joyce Clark, ace visual thinker.

Before we do that, let me introduce you to Joyce Clark, a member of the Shipping Team at Seton Name Plate in Branford, Connecticut (Photo 8.69). Joyce took to visuality like a duck to water. For her, the visual workplace—beginning with the visual where—was the long-hoped for answer to the everyday struggles that she and her spirited co-workers found discouraging. She, like many of you, came to work to make a contribution. Like you, she wanted her day to make more sense. Here are some of her words:

"I worked out back at Seton Name Plate, in the stacks, picking products that needed to be shipped. Those stacks used to feel like a gigantic maze. And I used to feel like the mouse traveling through it. I could never get to what I was looking for. It aggravated me. I felt like I was wasting my time.

Now that I put the visual where in place, I go to where I need to go, get my product, and come right back. That's the first thing that's great about visuality—I'm saving my time.

Everything is in its place. Everything is sorted. That's my smart placement. I cleared wasted space in my area that I use now to get my packages shipped. And because it is so organized and neat, my returns dropped from over ten a week to nearly zero!

My mistakes are down drastically. My returns—whether a mis-pick or wrong quantity or the order got the wrong label—are totally almost non-existent now. I got an award for it too. I had eight weeks straight without a return. No one has touched my record yet. I say it is because of the visual workplace. Because prior to that, I had a lot of mistakes!"

Thank you, Joyce, for your visual leadership and your inspiration. Truth be told, Joyce's colleagues sometimes enjoyed teasing her about her enthusiasm for WTMS and workplace visuality. When they gave her the title of *Queen of Visual Order*, Joyce responded—visually, of course.

You can see her reply in Photo 8.70. I called it *ID Label Mania*. She called it *Joyce's Revenge*.

Photo 8.70 ID Label Mania: Joyce's Revenge.

> People don't come to Toyota to work.
> They come to think.
>
> Taiichi Ohno

People and Results

Congratulations, you have come a long way since we started. You've attacked many forms of motion in your work area through smart placement and the visual where—and so made many of your day-to-day struggles disappear. Motion is on the run! You've learned a lot and will soon learn how to drill deeper into information deficits and invent even more powerful visual solutions.

But right now, here in Section 4, let's take a pause and consider other parts of your journey to date.

For example, have you noticed that some of your colleagues are really excited about WTMS and want to forge ahead? You are probably one of them. Others seem to hold back. Still others don't seem to like WTMS at all. In Chapter 9, the first of the two chapters in this section , I share ways for you to think about these different responses—and ways to understand and handle them.

Chapter 10 is all about results—results that value-add associates like you and companies like yours have achieved by using WTMS in the ways you are learning about in this book. These results are remarkable for their financial impact (the bottom line) and their equally positive impact on the work culture (people). They are also what is supposed to happen when operator-led visuality is effectively implemented.

Chapter | Nine

Ourselves and Others

For some people, the Work That Makes Sense method makes "a lot of sense." Who wouldn't want to make an intelligent visual partner out of the things in the work area? Who wouldn't benefit from a workplace that speaks? Yes, for some people (perhaps including you), operator-led visuality is not only a "no brainer," it is also a fascinating process and fun, too.

But other people act like they couldn't care less. They are indifferent. Still others loudly complain and object to change, any change, including WTMS—but they often don't tell us why.

WTMS principles and practices cannot take root in your company, let alone create a workplace that speaks if not enough people are on board and participating. For that to happen, some of us may need to engage in activities and behaviors that are a bit different from the usual. We may need to learn new habits—new habits of doing and thinking, and new habits of mind and heart.

Adopting new habits is not always easy—because learning them often means unlearning old ones. You know what I know. Old habits can hold on tightly, especially when tied to values and beliefs about how we see ourselves and how we see others. Still, from time to time we may discover that some of our values and beliefs need a slight revision because we realize they are no longer entirely true.

Revising values and beliefs and taking on new ones can either be exciting or uncomfortable. It depends on how you look at the situation.

In this chapter, I share some of the values and beliefs at the heart of WTMS, along with some terms and definitions. You will also read a story, called The Parable of the Rowers. It shows those values and beliefs through the actions of people very much like you. Like you, they recognized that things had to improve in their work areas and that operator-led visuality could help, a lot. It's just that not everybody agreed with them.

Terms and Definitions

When we believe strongly in something and see it as the answer that we (or our company or the world) has been waiting for, our eyesight can get a little muddled.

Our tendency is to put a "resistance" label on everything and everybody that do not agree with us. We tend to see their lack of support as opposition or a lack of cooperation.

Without a doubt, some people will actively resist your ideas, however terrific you may think those ideas are. But there is another section of people—usually a larger section—who are either too busy to support your idea or just not interested in doing so. That's the section that is experiencing some manner of *inertia*—a response that is very different from *resistance*.

We better be precise about these types of responses. Let's start with a definition of inertia.

Inertia: The Two Stages

The dictionary defines *inertia* as: "the tendency of a body that is at rest to remain at rest—or that is moving to remain moving—unless acted upon by an outside force." Yes, inertia has two parts or stages: non-moving inertia and moving inertia.

Non-Moving Inertia/Stage 1: Imagine a roll of masking tape that sits on a table. It is not moving; it simply sits. The tape is in the stage called "non-moving inertia." The tape will remain that way until and unless it is acted upon by something outside of it (an outside force). For example, you may flick the roll of tape with your finger, and it starts to roll.

Moving Inertia/Stage 2: When the tape starts to roll, it moves into the second stage of inertia: "moving inertia." The tape will continue moving until and unless something outside of it stops it from moving. It hits a book that is lying on the table and comes to a standstill. It has once again entered a state of non-moving inertia. See Photo Series 9.1.

Stage 1/Non-Moving Inertia: The tape sits still on the table top.

Stage 2/Moving Inertia: Push the tape with your finger and it moves.

Stage 1/Non-Moving Inertia: The tape hits books and stops again.

In people terms, moving inertia occurs when people are already involved in an activity (whether an improvement effort or getting production out); and they simply keep on in that direction. They keep doing the thing they are currently doing until and unless something comes along that causes them to stop—or to move in a new direction. They are not resisting. They are simply continuing.

You'll know a person is in a state of moving inertia if he/she says something like this to you when you ask that person to get on board with WTMS:

> "I'm too busy right now."

> "It's not important to me."

> "Please don't bother me. I'm already doing all I can."

Non-moving inertia sounds more like: "Sorry, I don't want to be bothered," "I'm not interested," or "I really don't care." You may not like those responses but do not make the mistake of thinking that they are lazy or being difficult. Take them at their word: They don't want to be bothered. Not right now, anyway. They are busy maintaining their current state of non-movement. You may not like their choice —but they are not resisting you.

Resistance is very different.

Resistance: Positive and Negative

The dictionary definition of *resistance* is: "Any force that tends to oppose or retard." As with inertia, resistance has several meanings, only this time they divide neatly into positive resistance and negative resistance.

Positive Resistance. Here are four forms of positive resistance. These are not only *not* harmful but natural and beneficial. (You may know of others.)

> *Positive Resistance 1: Electricity.* In the science of electricity, resistance is the property that causes heat to be generated when an electric current passes through a channel.

> *Positive Resistance 2: Flight.* In the science of flight, resistance is the upward pushing force against the surface of a bird's (or plane's) wings that keeps it airborne.

The positive resistance found in electricity.

The positive resistance found in flight.

The positive resistance found in sports training.

The positive resistance found in medicine.

Positive Resistance 3: Sports. In sports, resistance in training makes your muscles work against a weight or force and therefore helps to build greater muscle strength and endurance (as in free weights, resistance bands, and weight machines).

Positive Resistance 4: Medicine. In medicine, resistance refers to the body's ability to ward off disease, as a part of a healthy immune system.

Who would complain about any of those? Not I! See Photo Series 9.2.

Negative Resistance. Negative resistance is the second main category and very different from the positive type. Here is a dictionary definition of negative resistance: "The refusal to accept or comply with something; the attempt to prevent or oppose something by action or argument."

When negative resistance opens its mouth, you are looking "No!" right in the throat. There are countless ways to say it. But it is still "No!" This is the decision to push back. See Photos 9.3 and 9.4.

What to do. When you want to see operator-led visuality take root in your company and the forces of resistance and inertia are afoot, it is fair to ask, "What can we reasonably expect from other people? If some people don't care or resist, is there a way to get them on board? How should I (or could I) respond?

- When people are enthusiastic?
- When people who don't care—or are too busy?
- People oppose and resist?

My response is in the form of a story I call *The Parable of the Rowers.* As you will see, *you* play a major role in this story.

Photo 9.3 Negative resistance is the decision to push back.

Photo 9.4 The NO of negative resistance.

The Parable of the Rowers

So there you are, listening to the top executive in your company talk to everyone about the need for change. With the company facing increases in costs, lead times, and sub-par quality—along with unhappy customers and even more unhappy employees, the top boss announces her decision to transform the enterprise. She shares her vision. "We need to reach a new land—a new operational level so customers are delighted, quality is excellent, profit margins are growing, and YOU are spirited and engaged.

"To get there," she continues, "we must leave the Dreadful Land of Waste and cross a great ocean, the Ocean of Continuous Improvement. We will need a sturdy methodology to get us there—a worthy boat to carry us. Our boat is called the *SS Visual Workplace*" (Figures 9.1 and 9.2).

Figure 9.1 The Ocean of Continuous Improvement.

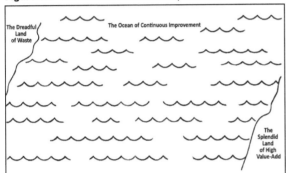

Figure 9.2 Our sturdy vessel, the *SS Visual Workplace*.

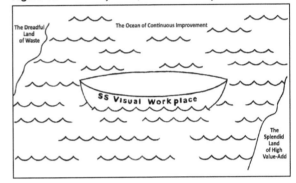

You are on that boat, joined by others like yourself, each with a set of oars in hand. Together you are rowing towards the new land. Your cheeks are flushed, your eyes are steady. You breathe deeply and often. You see the vision burning brightly and are full of ideas and hope. You are the Rowers (Figure 9.3).

Rowers are not alone on the board. Others are with you—a larger group. And they are watching. They are watching you row. They are the Watchers (Figure 9.4).

Figure 9.3 The Rowers.

Figure 9.4 The Watchers.

For the purposes of this story, the four Rowers you see make up 25 percent of the workforce. That means that eight Watchers make up 50 percent. Between the Rowers and the Watchers, 75 percent of the workforce is on the boat. But 25 percent and 50 percent do not equal 100 percent (Figure 9.5).

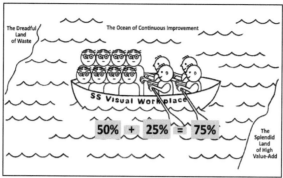

Figure 9.5 50% plus 25% do not add up to 100%.

Where is the other 25 percent of the workforce? Where are the remaining employees?

You look around. You see some people off in the distance on the beach, sitting in the sun in the Dreadful Land of Waste, complaining about the new changes. Others are in the water, paddling about, grumbling. They are the Grumblers.

Wherever they are, whatever they are doing, two things are certain. The Grumblers are not happy and not on the boat. Yes, 25 percent of the workforce is not happy about the changes. See Figure 9.6.

Figure 9.6 The other 25% are the Grumblers and not on the boat.

Wait a minute! One of the Grumblers is swimming toward the boat, with something on her mind. Better do something quick, Rowers! But what?

But what? A good question—and an important one—because what you, the Rowers, do next may well make the difference between getting to your destination or getting stuck in the glooms where the wreckage of countless other improvement efforts can be found.

For example, you and your co-Rowers may decide that you need to find out what is making the Grumblers so darned grumpy. So each Rower invites a Grumbler for a chat in order to find out what the problem is so maybe the Grumbler will have a change of heart.

Afterwards, you Rowers meet and discuss what happened. You may all still be in the dark. Maybe some Grumblers said things that also made you feel uneasy. Worried, you Rowers become even more determined to find a way to get the Grumblers on board.

What Not to Do

The above is not only exactly what not to do, it is a big mistake. Here's why.

One of the main things to understand about Grumblers is this: They grumble. And, for whatever reason, many Grumblers enjoy grumbling. Others may indeed have a genuine complaint. But either way, you as a Rower are not in a position to address their complaints. Management is—and in most companies, management will, carefully and respectfully.

When you run up against Grumblers on your journey, as you surely will, your next move is not to try to get them on board. Your next move is to continue doing what you are doing: rowing. Attempting to get the Grumblers to change their minds and get on board almost never works. The Watchers could have told you. They know from years of watching.

Watchers watch. That is what they do at the start of anything new. They watch the Rowers row. They watch the Grumblers grumble. They also watch to see what the Rowers decide to do about the grumbling. They watch what the Rowers choose to pay attention to.

Watchers know about attention. They know attention is energy. That is one of the reasons they do so much watching. They are waiting until they can be sure that the investment of their own energy investment will pay off. Watchers also know that many Grumblers are capable of eating up just about all the energy that comes their way—usually in the form of rowers trying to persuade them to get on board.

The more the Rowers try, the more tired they get—and disheartened. When their well-intended efforts do not pay off, Rowers can begin to doubt themselves and question their own vision.

When the Watchers see this, they see the implementation going down the tubes (as they have often seen before). They then do the only thing that makes sense to them. They jump ship. They join the Grumblers. One, two—then eight (Figure 9.7). Then Rowers take the dive (Figure 9.8). The Grumblers won.

Figure 9.7 Watchers jump overboard.

Figure 9.8 Rowers take the dive.

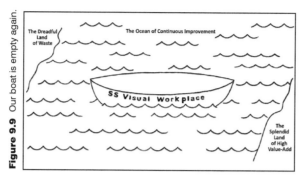

Figure 9.9 Our boat is empty again.

What We Pay Attention to Grows. In the 1930s, a scientist named Elton Mayo studied the effects of light (as in light bulbs or illumination) on the productivity of operators who worked near Chicago in a factory with very low lighting called the Hawthorne Works. Mr. Mayo assumed that people would be more productive if they had more light to work by. He was amazed, however, to discover that people became more productive whether they were provided more light or less light. It did not matter. The level of illumination was not a factor in productivity.

Puzzled, he repeated the experiment many times. He always got the same results. Mayo finally concluded that the productivity gains were due to the interest being shown in the operators as subjects of the study—the amount of attention they were paid—whether the lights went up or down. This is called the *Hawthorne Effect*, an outcome that demonstrated the power of attention.

Later, Werner Heisenberg, another scientist, discovered the same thing in his research on atoms. He discovered that atoms changed their activity whenever Heisenberg simply watched them under a microscope. He confirmed the power of attention.

Attention is energy. What it rests upon grows. It is a powerful force. The Rowers in our parable ended up paying more attention to the grumbling than to their own rowing. When they did this, the tide began to turn against the WTMS outcome they wanted.

The Power of Choice. One of the main points in the parable is your own right to choose—the right of every individual to choose.

At the outset, the Rowers in our parable made a choice. They decided to put their shoulders to the oar and row. We respect that. Watchers chose to wait. We respect that. And some people chose to grumble. We must respect that too. Even though we do not agree with their choices, we must respect people's right to choose.

Grumblers chose not to participate. They may never change their minds. Perhaps they have their reasons. Some Grumblers can get noisy about this. Some may even try to be disruptive. Sooner or later, your company will decide if it wants the extra baggage that Grumblers carry. And Grumblers will decide if they are willing to meet the company partway. Most Grumblers do.

Perhaps the most surprising switch is when a Grumbler on Tuesday decides that she wants to start rowing on Thursday. She will not explain herself. If you ask her what happened, she is likely to say, "I changed my mind" and walk away.

I guarantee you that she is telling the truth. All you have to do to see more of this is to do your part: Keep rowing.

A Different Ending

Here is another way this parable can end.

Even though the Rowers see Grumblers doing nothing to help the effort, even though they see Grumblers coming toward them with trouble on their minds, Rowers fix their eyes on their goal and keep rowing. Their oar strokes are strong and steady. The boat pulls away. They keep rowing. As they do, the Watchers notice the calm intent of the Rowers, who stay firm and true even as sweat pours down their brows.

A Watcher shifts around a bit and puts on a crooked smile. A few moments later, she picks up a set of oars and starts to row, clumsily at first, and then more smoothly. A watching neighbor follows suit. Then another joins in, and another, and another.

Soon, the boat slips into a tailwind, and the crew raises a mast and sail. The sail puffs and fills. The Grumblers are barely visible now. A dinghy hitched up to the boat is sent back to pick up anyone who wants to get on board. It comes back full.

The lesson now is an obvious one. What you give your attention to grows. It is a universal law, and it can work for or against your goals. You decide. So be careful what you pay attention to—and keep rowing.

Leadership Task 16: Your Own Rower Leadership

As a company manager/supervisor and Rower yourself, you know your visible commitment to excellence matters. Fretting over indifference and resistance will not win over associates. What will win them over is seeing your steadfast dedication to continuous improvement through visuality.

Here are four things that can help. One: Recognize and appreciate all visual devices (big and tiny) created by operators. Thank individuals publicly and privately. Two: Leave people who are not yet Rowers alone—but you already knew that. Three: Model the behavior you want. Find ways to make your own work visual. Watchers and Grumblers are more likely to get on board when they see you, as a company leader, reducing the motion in your own work by converting information deficits into visual solutions. Four: Once visuality catches on, invite outsiders in for tours. The glow of their recognition will be cause for everyone to celebrate, even the grumps (if any are left).

You'd be amazed how these four actions dissolves inertia and resistance and turn your most unresponsive Watcher and loudest Grumbler into enthusiastic Rowers. When that happens, quietly welcome them into the ranks. Why not also ask them to help educate others. Success breeds success. It happens all the time.

I don't mind if you change things.
Just don't try to change me.
Author: Nearly Everyone

Chapter | Ten

Results: People and the Bottom Line

Creating a workplace that speaks through operator-led visuality does not just produce transformed operations with a vastly improved bottom line. It also results in a transformed workforce: value-add associates who recognize and understand the enemy—information deficits—and know how to track down that enemy's footprint—motion—so they can eliminate both through solutions that are visual. They have become visual thinkers. This is the path you follow as well.

In this chapter, you consider a set of bottom line and cultural results from six of the many companies that have successfully implemented Work That Make Sense. These same companies often learned and applied other power visual methods for other organizational functions—visual displays for supervisors; visual leadership for executives; visual machine® for machinists and maintenance; visual guarantees/poka yoke for the quality function; visual problem-solving for all levels; and so on and so forth.

Still, for our purposes, I share only those cultural and financial results tied directly to WTMS/operator-led visuality. The six companies are: Lockheed Martin, USA; Skyworks Solutions, Boston; Motorola, Texas; Trailmobile, Toronto; Bio-Medical, New Mexico; and Brandt Engineering Products, Canada.

Results-1: Lockheed-Martin Aerospace

Lockheed-Martin Aerospace (LM-Aero) is a legendary competitor in jet fighter aviation, building and sustaining such premier systems as the F-35, F-22, F-16, and C-130, with seven main sites in the USA, a vast world-wide supply chain, and over 30,000 employees.

Photo 10.1 LM-Aero, Fort Worth.

LM-Aero, headquartered in Fort Worth, Texas (Photo 10.1), was already on its journey to operational excellence when Mark Swisher, head of 6S/Visual, asked us to train operators in visuality. The company was facing its arch-rival, Boeing, for the Joint Strike Fighter contract, valued at $200 billion in future revenue. In time, LM-Aero won the contract. Visuality helped.

Photo 10.2 LM-Aero production floor.

At the time of the JSF challenge, lean concepts and tools were already in place on Fort Worth's mile-long production line, mostly learned and applied by LM-Aero engineers (Photo 10.2). When we began to train operator-led visuality, frontline associates had been given the green to learn and apply. The process flourished. Operators became visual thinkers and invented hundreds of remarkable visual solutions to problems (motion) that engineers didn't even know—and couldn't have known—existed.

When you get to Chapter 11, for example, you'll study the splendid contributions of Margie Herrera, LM-Aero visual superstar. Right now explore the stunning "Red Apron" visual mini-system invented by John, one of Margie's colleagues (Photo Series 10.5 on right). Make sure to read the telling detail.

The Red Apron array became one of the many Visual Best Practices that operators created that accelerated lead time—and with it, quality. These two outcomes factored mightily into the JSF win. Effectively implemented, operator-led visuality in many companies consistently generates a spirited and engaged workforce and a minimum 15% increase in productivity, exactly because it was operator-led. That is also what happened at LM-Aero.

Photo 10.3 LM-Aero skunkworks.

But some LM-Aero lean leaders and lean coaches wondered if visuality wasn't just a different name for lean. "Was the remarkable success of operator-led visuality just lean in disguise?" they sincerely asked.

Senior managers decided to put the question to the test. They assigned a team of visual thinkers to apply 1,000 hours of visual improvement—*only*—to a Jet Fighter Modification Station in the company's skunkworks (high-security R&D facility) located in Palmdale, California (Photos 10.3 and 10.4). No lean tools or techniques would be used in this test—only operator-led visual methods.

> Note: A *modification* or *mod* station is workspace or area where jet fighters are refurbished and upgraded.)

Photo 10.4 Long view: Jet Fighter Mod Station at the Palmdale site.

The application of those 1,000 visual improvement hours took place over a period of seven calendar months. Because Palmdale was and remains top-secret, I am not able to share the actual visual solutions that were invented there. But I can share the results that LM-Aero shared with me to share with you. (Note: "one unit" means "one jet fighter.")

Photo Series 10.5 Operator-invented *Red-Apron Visual Best Practice* system at LM-Aero's Fort Worth, Texas site.

1. This blue platform is work space for building the yellow intake valve on the outside and inside. See brown lift (double red arrows). Before working on the inside of the valve, the assembler grabs tools and parts, gets on the brown lift (red arrow), and presses the lift button. Like a tiny elevator, the lift carries the operator up, inside the valve.

2. But there was a hidden problem. Assemblers took the lift into the valve, only to realize they forgot something. So they'd have to down again, get what they forgot, and go up again. Only to realize they forgot something else. So they'd go down again. And go on and on.

3. Nobody gave this a second thought until they began the WTMS training and learned about motion and info deficits.

Red arrow points to an intake valve on this jet fighter.

4. Margie's friend, John, had worked in the intake valve areas for decades. He was an expert. When he got trained in WTMS, he understood what he had to do to eliminate the motion of going up/down over and over again. He needed to visually build-in the answer to the question: Do I have everything I need to go up that lift and do the task?.

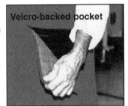

Velcro-backed pocket

5. The center of John's visual solution is the red apron on the right. That black rectangle is Velcro. On the left are sets of pocket, backed in Velcro and secured to a Velcro panel that attaches to the blue platform with Velcro ties. The tools below are too heavy for Velcro so John hangs them on yellow metal hooks.

6. Notice: The pockets are color-coded to task—yellow, orange, blue, green. John's visual invention became a Visual Best Practice and spread across all seven LM-Aero sites in the USA.

7. But as John and his colleagues learned when mix-ups began to occur: One in 12 men is some degree of color blind. So John added the addresses you see below. No more mistakes.

8. Later John added pockets and holders on the opposite side of the blue platform.

9. John's Red-Apron visual mini-system used so many smart placement principles:
   #1: Locate function at/near the point-of-use
   #10: Co-locate different functions (Design-to-Task)
   #11: Use the existing architecture
   #12: Store things not air
   #13: Double the Function

- Productivity Increase: 15 percent

- Permanent reduction of 700 hours of labor content per unit (per jet fighter)

- Complete payback on the 1,000-hour investment after 7 units (after 7 jet fighters)

Those who questioned the purpose and power of operator-led visuality now had their evidence, the actual results of the above experiment. The numbers met or exceeded, in the eyes of many, the impact of the company's lean improvements to that point and made a place for associate-driven visuality as a separate and formidable improvement strategy at LM-Aero.

Like the two wings of a bird, visual and lean belong together, working side-by-side on every company's journey to excellence (Photo 10.6).

Photo 10.6 Visual and lean, like two wings of a bird.

Results-2: Skyworks Solutions

Skyworks Solutions (Skyworks) manufactures analog semiconductors, with one of its main factories in the Boston area. Previously the site was home to Alpha Industries, with 200 value-add associates in its multi-lingual workforce. That company had asked me to run a pilot on operator-led visuality a few years before Skyworks acquired it. The process met with a great success (see my book, *Visual Workplace, Visual Thinking*). Later Annie Yu, a licensed visual instructor of exceptional skill, became manager of training at the new Skyworks plant and continued the implementation across 30+ work cells.

Here are the results in just one of those cells, after four months—with the *before* given as a point of comparison.

Before
- Ran out of chemicals on average of 1-3 times each shift
- 42 hours per week of downtime

After
- Eliminated all stock outs
- Zero hours per week downtime
- Increased production by 25%

Annualized Results Across the Cell
- Reduced walking by 54%
- Eliminated all (100%) rework in plating process
- Eliminated 7,132 hours of downtime and operator cycle time per year
- Reduced scrap by $2,555,000 per year

Annie Yu and Skyworks operators continued to multiply those monetary outcomes, cell by cell. With each, associate self-leadership and self-accountability grew, along with the spirit of their engagement.

Results-3: Motorola

The Motorola facility in Sequin, Texas manufactured smart phones 24/7, with a workforce of 1,600 value-add associates across three shifts (Photo 10.7). Sequin was a very busy plant. As with many high-volume, multi-shift sites, management searched for a way to strengthen the work culture in order to improve safety, quality, and on-time delivery.

After researching effective approaches, they decided on operator-led visuality, at the time called *Visual Workplace/Visual Order*. As is also the case now, the package was available as an off-the-shelf training system—10 DVD videos and a Resource Folio that was full of other instructional materials. Motorola in Sequin proceeded.

I never set foot in the Sequin factory nor did any VTI trainer or affiliate. It was only when the Sequin training director called a year after the launch that we learned of their great success. That is to say, the visual conversion of this massive site was achieved solely by Sequin employees using the DVD system—and their good hearts and minds, the other true engines of operator-led visuality.

Photo 10.7 Operators at their benches at Motorola in Sequin, Texas.

Here are some of the other details she shared with us. She and her staff of four trainers trained all supervisors across all shifts. Then the supervisors trained all operators in the steps, values, principles, and practices of visuality—the building blocks, smart placement methods, the visual where, and so on.

After only 12 months, she reported, the site's inventory had been reduced by over $15 million, and the work culture was entirely and positively transformed. Everyone was, to use her words, "blown away by the power of the visual workplace and the level of engagement." So were we, just hearing about it!

Implementing operator-led visuality with 1,600 operators is a challenge the methodology is designed to meet. Doing that in a period of 12 months is a rare accomplishment. Kudos to Motorola in Sequin.

Results-4: Trailmobile

In October of 1999, Trailmobile headquarters in Chicago completed its purchase of a privately-owned and run trailer factory in Toronto. Who at the moment could have imagined that three years later that Toronto site would have become Trailmobile's largest plant—and, not long after that, its *only* factory in the United States and Canada? (See a Trailmobile trailer in Photo 10.8.)

Photo 10.8 Trailmobile trailer.

The story had a tough start. Trailmobile inherited monthly measures (key performance indicator/KPIs) from the former owner, that were shockingly negative: accident frequency was at 46 percent, operational efficiency was at 86 percent, and pre-delivery warranty costs (work that had to get done on each trailer *after* the client bought it but before it was delivered) stood at a whopping $40,000/each trailer. When employees showed up for their first day of work for their new Trailmobile bosses, they were already discouraged and disheartened.

When Tom Wiseman, the new plant manager, took over in November, he knew he needed two things fast—dramatically improved operations and a revitalized workforce. He asked me to launch operator-led visuality as the crucial first step on the site's journey to excellence. I arrived in a blizzard. It was January in Canada. We dug in. The training began, following the same learn-and-do process set forth in this book.

Six months later, the accident frequency rate stood at 11 percent (an 80 percent drop but, of course, still not acceptable); operational efficiency had soared to 117 percent (36 percent increase); and pre-delivery warranty costs were at $3,000, a 92.5 percent plunge. The bottom-line turnaround had begun.

The news got even better. Employee absenteeism had dropped to 10 percent, down from 80 percent (meaning 8 out of 10 employees had not come to work at least once a month. Fifty percent of the production floor square footage had been liberated and re-deployed. Plus, instead of supervisors constantly walking out the door, supervisor retention was up 25 percent. What's more, when gas prices rose and the trailer market dried up, Tom Wiseman had to cut back to one shift (50 percent fewer employees). But you know what? Operational efficiency didn't just remain at 117 percent. It increased by 7 percent. This was a whopping great turnaround.

Operator-led visuality didn't just improve the bottom line. The culture was entirely transformed. See Photo Series 10.8 for a taste. When asked to describe the impact of visuality on Trailmobile associates, April Love (her real name)—who in January began as visual workplace coordinator and was promoted to continuous improvement director in August—said this:

> *Operator-led visuality has un-locked the potential of our employees. The potential was always there. We just couldn't see it. Now associates are the driving force behind not just change but our journey to excellence. And new employees can light a candle from an existing flame where before there was nothing.*

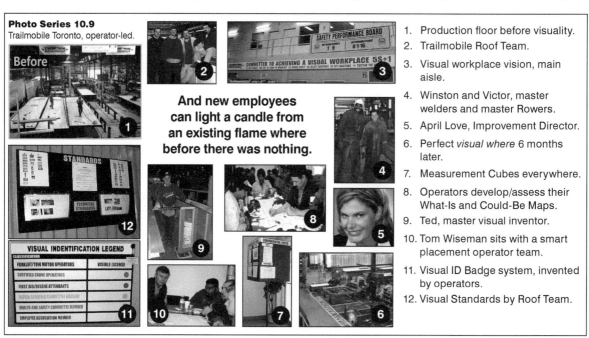

Photo Series 10.9
Trailmobile Toronto, operator-led.

1. Production floor before visuality.
2. Trailmobile Roof Team.
3. Visual workplace vision, main aisle.
4. Winston and Victor, master welders and master Rowers.
5. April Love, Improvement Director.
6. Perfect *visual where* 6 months later.
7. Measurement Cubes everywhere.
8. Operators develop/assess their What-Is and Could-Be Maps.
9. Ted, master visual inventor.
10. Tom Wiseman sits with a smart placement operator team.
11. Visual ID Badge system, invented by operators.
12. Visual Standards by Roof Team.

Results-5: Bio-Medical Facility

One of the most amazing set of results I've ever encountered happened at a non-union, bilingual (English-Spanish) facility in Albuquerque, New Mexico, one of the many factories in a giant bio-medical conglomerate. As part of a corporate initiative, I had trained that site's strategic improvement director in an array of my visual methods—along with directors from several other facilities. One of those methods was WTMS, which was available off-the-shelf, as a stand-alone system so companies could become self-sufficient but did not have to master the training content since they could teach through online modules.

When the director returned to her plant, she enlisted the help of her in-house training staff to launch WTMS in Albuquerque.

> • I'll call the site's director *Elizabeth* (not her real name) because the contract terms my company signed prohibit sharing the company's name, people's names, or photographs of them or any site.

Operator training began, following the same WTMS methodology described in this book (corporate called it the *Visual Factory*). Associates learned about I-driven and the other building blocks of visual thinking; they learned about smart placement. Because the WTMS modules have a complete Spanish version, people learned in their native language. Another big plus. Value-add associates were excited, engaged, and inventive. In Elizabeth's words, "The whole thing took off like a rocket."

Elizabeth later told me about what happened next, something that had never happened before anywhere in the world. Just as operators were about to learn and apply the visual where, they asked to train themselves! They made an appointment with Elizabeth, went to her office and said: "Since WTMS is I-driven, and since the instructions are on video, we don't see why we can't just train ourselves."

As Elizabeth later told me, she was speechless. At first, she didn't know what to say. Then she realized there was no reason to say *no*. In fact, it made sense to her too. "Let's give it a try," she replied.

And they did. Value-add associates began to train themselves in April. Many met for "Lunch-and-Learn" sessions. They had a lot to share and talk about. By May, operators had implemented 82 new visual solutions. In June, they added 101 new devices—and 122 more in July. By November, the cumulative count was 1,031 visual devices. See Figure 10.1.

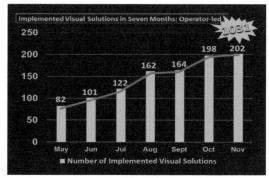

Figure 10.1 The total number of implemented visual solutions in the first seven months of operators training themselves: 1031.

Keeping track of so many new visual solutions became a challenge all by itself. So operators decided to make that visual as well. Not only did a star get posted on or near each new device, but each area maintained a map that showed the location of each star.

Though contract terms keep me from sharing photos of those stars and those area maps, I hope you will get a sense of this from Photo Series 10.9.

Photo Series 10.10 Star Maps showing 50 visual devices across three production lines (16 + 24 + 20 stars).

Stars were everywhere. It's one thing to imagine fifty visual devices (stars) at a site. Can we really wrap our minds around what 1031 individual visual devices look like in a company—and for a company? Figure Series 10.2 may help. And operators at this Albuquerque site were just starting to roll.

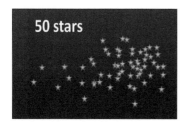 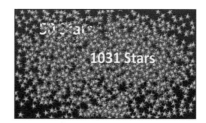

Figure Series 10.2 Comparison of 50 stars versus 1031 stars—the number of implemented visual solutions in the first seven months when operators began to train themselves.

And there's more. Associates decided to set up a three-step visual hit list process. In step 1, operators named area-specific problems they encountered tied to information deficits. Step 2 happened when "someone" invented a visual device that solved that specific problem. Step 3 was spreading that solutions to all others areas that had the same the of problem. This became the engine for triggering the exploding number of devices in this facility and keeping building blocks we discussed in Chapter 2 front and center in everyone's thinking. Operators became scientists of motion, which is one of the main WTMS outcomes. They came to work to think, create, and contribute—seamlessly linked to their daily work.

The tool at the heart of this 3-step process is a 15-column grid, one column for each of the 15 cells or work areas at that site (Photo 10.11). Each visual solution is listed on the left (some 90 are listed in the image). Traffic-light status is shown under each of the 15 columns, telling us the stage of implementation in that area for each device: red for not started or stuck, yellow for mid-way complete, and green for done/fully in lace. Blue means the device is not related tot he needs of that department, and—here's the really clever part—everyone knows it.

Every part of this operator-led process delights me, especially the remarkable new practices local operators created to help them invent, spread, and track their solutions and make them sustainable. There is a great deal of discussion about the importance of respect for every individual in today's workplace. A big portion of that happens when management—a source of great authority and ability—turns the principle of respect into policy and required behaviors and procedures.

We certainly see that in Elizabeth's ground-breaking decision to affirm and support the desire of site operators to train themselves and hold themselves accountable for outcomes that were previously her job.

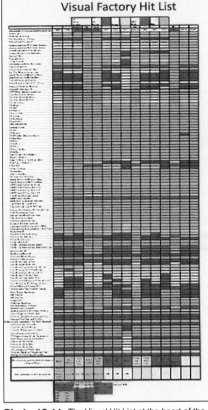

Photo 10.11 The Visual Hit List at the heart of the 3-Step Process.

As significant, this bio-medical mini-case study also demonstrates the inspiring level of respect that operators had for themselves—and for their colleagues, no matter the department. I encourage you to consider both sources of respect as you move forward in this book and learn more about visuality and the contribution of operators just like you.

Results-6: Brandt Engineering Products

Brandt Engineering Products (BEP), based in Regina, Canada, designs and manufactures heavy-duty, customized equipment systems for the construction industry, one of the five companies in The Brandt Group. Some 200 frontline employees work on the high-mix/low-volume production floor in BEP's main facility of 100,000 square feet. As BEP discovered when it began its improvement journey, that type of operations requires a combination of lean and visual strategies to meet its challenges.

Photo 10.12 Stewart Bellamy, ace visual thinker, inspired leader, and gifted trainer and coach.

Stewart Bellamy, BEP Improvement Manager, headed the visual transformation, with a passionate understanding that, in his words, "work and improvement are the same thing" (Photo 10.12). BEP began in the late 1990s with 5S. For the first few years traditional 5S audits were used as the main driver. As is often the case with audits, frontline operators showed little interest. Without their buy-in, the process stalled. No one yet knew how to go beyond 5S as a clean up tool, including Stewart. Ownership and responsibility grew somewhat when the focus changed to random audits, conducted by operators.

Then Stewart and trainer/coach team learned about visuality, first through my early book, *Visual Systems*, then by attending several of my introductory visual workplace seminars. That led them to expand BEP's 5S approach to go beyond neat and clean, and labels and lines. They targeted a "workplace that speaks." Operator buy-in improved, hovering around 20 to 25 percent. But individuals had not yet been asked to focus on their own value field; everything was done through agreement—consensus thinking.

Another five years passed. There were now four or five pockets of excellence across BEP's very large production floor. Nothing, however, grew of its own momentum. The process was not sustainable. Frontline operators still had a narrow understanding of visuality—that it was device-based. They had not yet learned about information deficits, motion, value field, or I-driven change. Visuality was not yet about a process of thinking, visual thinking.

The company was growing by leaps and bounds. In a 15-year period sales had increased by 800 percent, and the plant itself had expanded four times. Stewart knew a more structured, systematic approach to visuality was needed. He and his colleagues began to teach Work That Makes Sense, through this book and through the online modules. Associates attended classroom training sessions every two to three weeks. Hands-on application happened between sessions when associates visually improved their own value fields, operator-led.

The impact was immediate and clear (Photo Series 10.13). BEP realized, in Stewart's words, that "lean is not always the method of choice in our high-mix/low-volume production. Visuality got the job done. The visual solutions our operators create are not just highly inventive, they connect up work areas and build our work culture. We are getting what is really unusual in a low-volume/high-mix shop: an accelerated flow of work."

Here is how a BEP hourly employee put it:

"I used to spend at least 5 minutes an hour looking for...something—a tool or parts or information; or waiting for them. Or just wandering around. I added that up. Five minutes a day times seven daily work hours times 244 workdays a year means that I lose at least 19.6 days every year. And there are 200 of me on the floor! That's 31,360 lost hours every year."

BEP operators were becoming experts of their own work—scientists of motion. See Figure 10.3.

5 minutes/hour x 7 hours x 244 workdays x 200 operators

= 31,360 lost work hours/year

Figure 10.3 Operator equation demonstrating the true cost of motion and the information deficits that trigger it.

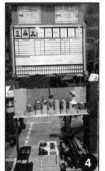

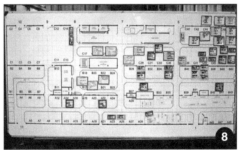

The more the process became visual, the more the production velocity increased.

Photo Series 10.13 WTMS in action on the BEP production floor.

1. The BEP production floor *before* visuality.

2. Array of Brandt products.

3., 9., 10, and 12. The visual where was implemented widely and systematically.

4., 5., 6., and 7. Operators developed design-to-task project boards on wheels, just the way they liked them. Water spiders keep them stocked, instead of operators having to wait in long lines at Stores, or hoarding materials just-in-case.

8. Low-volume/high-mix production requires information transparency. This project location board was a huge help.

11. Visuality and kanban revolutionized the PAINT booth. Operators invited suppliers to help them on the design.

More and more evidence began to pile up. When I asked Stewart for a good example of what operator-led visuality had done for the company's bottom line and its work culture, he sent Figure 10.4, saying that it was typical of results across BEP, adding with an energy and conviction that clearly came from his direct experience: "The more the process became visual, the more production velocity increased."

	BEFORE	AFTER
ASSEMBLY SPACE	more than 11,200 sq ft	less than 4,800 sq ft
THROUGHPUT	2 per week	8 per week
PRODUCTION TIME	250+ hours (average)	124 hours (average)
YARD STORAGE	>5,000 sq ft	Virtually eliminated
TEAM INVOLVEMENT	Good	Immeasurable

Figure 10.4 Results that show impact of operator-led visuality on BEP's work culture and bottom line.

Just the Beginning

The six WTMS mini-case studies in this chapter are just a sample,.We have dozens more with equally compelling people and bottom line results. Those who have been part of an effective WTMS implementation have come to expect these levels of results. Yes, the opportunity is there, and it is huge.

> And yes, we also have results from offices and healthcare settings. For example, a department of design engineers implemented visuality and increased their productivity by 34 percent, with the first big positive jump in four weeks. But those (and results like them) are for a different book.

As you also read in this chapter, there are many ways to personalize the process and make it colorful and exciting for your company and for your work area. But the fundamental method remains the same. First track down motion in all its many and irrational forms and find the information deficits that trigger them. Then eliminate both through solutions that are visual—the information deficits and instantly that motion. This is *visual thinking* and the I-driven process called Work That Makes Sense.

WTMS asks the question posed on the back cover of this book: "How much will value-add associates contribute—if you let them?" Now you know the answer: a heck of a lot. Let the workplace speak.

> ## You don't have to see the whole staircase.
> ## You just need to take the next step.
> ### Martin Luther King, Jr.

Drilling Deeper

Now that your area has a strong base of the visual where, many of the grosser forms of motion have begun to disappear and, with them, many of your day-to-day struggles. It is time for you to drill deeper into information deficits and invent visual devices that address them more completely.

Chapter 11 is the first of the three chapters in this section. In it, you learn to create *visual mini-systems* for carts, benches, shelves, corners, and other narrowly-focused areas in your department—and see examples of mini-systems inspired by master visual thinkers just like you. Then you travel deeper into motion and learn to eliminate unanswered (often *unasked*) questions for your customers by deploying your own need-to-share and turning answers into visual solutions. You learn about and apply *customer-driven visuality*.

In Chapter 12, you study how to build the effectiveness of your devices through the four power levels of visuality. From visual indicators to visual signals to visual controls, and culminating in *poka-yoke*/visual guarantees, these power categories can trigger round after round of new visual thinking. As a result, daily struggles dissolve and you master your work visually.

In Chapter 13, this book's final and very short chapter, we describe the basic human need for visuality both in the community and at work in order for our world to make sense.

Chapter | Eleven

Visual Mini-Systems and Customer-Driven Visuality

To this point, you have learned a great deal about implementing the visual where. Now it is time to drill deeper. You are about to learn about eliminating motion—and the information deficits that trigger that motion—by developing visual mini-systems and customer-driven visuality. We begin with visual mini-systems.

Visual Mini-Systems: Major Motion Busters

Visual mini-systems (mini-systems for short) are a major way to increase visual information sharing in your area. Here is the definition:

> *A visual mini-system is a cluster of visual devices that*
> *work together to promote a single performance outcome.*

Look again at some of the community and workplace solutions you already saw in this book (Photo Series 11.1, next page). They are *all* mini-systems—groups of visual devices that work together to make sure specific performance outcomes happen.

In the workplace, a mini-system can be as simple as a visually-defined tool cabinet—or a single shelf in it. It can be a drawer or the entire desk. It can be one side of the machine that you have visually organized around small tools, lubricants, and fixtures. Or you can make a visual system out of the entire machining center.

The point is, a mini-system has a tight focus. The visual devices in it share a purpose. They are located together and made visual for a reason: to create a specific outcome, to fulfill a fixed purpose.

Photo Series 11.1 Eight visual mini-systems, at work and in the community.

The paperwork gets done on time.

The plane can now load/unload quickly.

Gas for money, fast.

Consumables are handy.

I get to find the special tool that I need even if someone else has it.

Those parts and tools are for this assembly.

All my tools are at-a-glance; and I also know the ones that are missing.

Here is all I need to wire an 80-foot trailer chassis.

Consider the neighborhood school bus—packed with visual devices, all aimed at the single outcome of keeping our kids safe (Photo Series 11.2, next page).

When Visual Mini-Systems Begin

Start to apply mini-systems in your area after the visual where begins to take root. By then, you understand the basic visual vocabulary, know that details matter, and see the benefits of your own visual efforts beginning to grow—along with those of your colleagues.

This does not mean your area has completed its basic visual transformation. It means you and others continually apply core visual concepts—smart placement principles, slanted borders (for example), driver-license level addresses, color coding, and so on. You are learning to: a) operationalize your need-to-know (getting control of your corner of the world), and b) recognize your need-to-share (helping others). As a result, a growing number of visual devices populate your area; and they are I-driven. They come from your brains, hands, and vision—and those of other visual thinkers.

Motion is on the decline. Work (value-adding activity) is on the increase. Information deficits have begun to evaporate. You and your colleagues have firsthand experience in the early benefits of visual information sharing.

Plus, by the time visual mini-systems become the focus, your managers have set up many behind-the-scenes procedures that support your efforts. Improvement supply carts are regularly stocked, improvement time hours are made regularly available, maintenance has set up a special work order system for visual inventions, and visual blitzes have become a regular part of your area's improvement schedule. You can count on all of these. The visual conversion is gaining momentum (see *Leadership Task 18*).

But that does not mean you have to wait until things are perfect to launch mini-systems. In fact, mini-systems are so visually logical, I'll bet you have created several already. Now you are ready to implement mini-systems *by design*—and use them, intentionally, to drill deeper into motion and the hidden layers of information deficits in your work area.

The phrase that applies here is: *one-foot square/one-mile deep.* When you create mini-systems, you apply the elements of smart placement and the visual where in the greatest of detail. This takes a special effort. Now you have to develop the ability to: 1) See what is *not* there, 2) See the moment *before* the moment of motion, and 3) Detect *the habit of motion*—the habit of busy-ness versus work (adding value).

Take the story of John Pacheco (Photo 11.3, next page), visual workplace impresario and veteran machinist in the Model Shop at United Electric Controls (UE) (Massachusetts). We saw John's cut-saw bench in Chapter 3 and his pull-out paperwork shelf in Chapter 6. As you are about to read, John began his visual journey quite modestly—and grew from there. He generated dozens of visual mini-systems in the five years we worked together and many more since.

Photo Series 11.2 School bus visual mini-system, safety first.

Have you ever counted the visual devices on a school bus? (1) Bus lights are on all four sides that flash as the bus is stopping, plus the Stop Sign arm extends. (2) A cow-catcher swing arm in the front activates (see blue box) at unloading to make sure that kids walk into the driver's line of sight. (3) Cantilevered left and right mirrors on the bus hood are double insurance that small children will be seen if they walk in front of the bus. (4) An array of visual devices cover the back of the bus. (5) The shade of yellow used for school buses was reserved by US law in 1939, just for school vehicles. All this makes the bus's visual mini-system a visual maxi-system.

Leadership Task 18: Pay Attention to Beginnings

Pay close attention when you as a supervisor or manager go deeper into your own understanding of visuality—and when the visual thinkers who report to you begin to create visual solutions.

It is now that the conversion is in its most delicate state because even a single disparaging remark can undo the work of weeks or even months. Every contribution, however humble, has a huge value at this point. That value is said this way: *It is a beginning*. All beginnings are to be celebrated. They mark a break from the past and the promise of a tomorrow whose horizon is only partly understood.

Managers and supervisors, when you see that beginning—however small—make much of it. Give congratulations and take photos. Once ignited, people have such willingness to contribute. Though they may not yet have the skill to create a trackable bottom-line benefit, you still recognize their early efforts. You must project forward the tangible benefits that small early steps can produce as the momentum gathers. Pay attention. Notice the good and give praise. The success of your improvement initiative depends on that, as does the stability and improvement growth of the entire enterprise.

The Visual Inventiveness of John Pacheco

Like so many people, John was skeptical about visuality at first. He did not see how it would help him. Then he decided to give it a try and liked the result.

Photo 11.3 John Pacheco, ace visual thinker.

Part of John's early success was due to the wisdom of UE managers to recognize and appreciate his small efforts. For example, John's very first visual device was a border for his coffee cup. You can see it on the upper right of Photo 11.4 (yellow arrow). That photo also captures John's first mini-system—a visual home for stainless steel scrap and his water basket. If you look closely at that basket, you can see a series of six white ID labels that say "Water, Water, Water, Water, Water, Water." John was reaching. You could tell he wanted to do more.

Yes, John wanted to do more but ran out of ideas. So he asked his supervisor, Paul Plant, for suggestions (Photo 11.5). As the story goes, Paul mentioned the trouble the area had in getting visitors to wear safety glasses. Could John find a way to handle that?

You bet he could! The first thing John noticed was that the existing sign about safety glasses hung from the ceiling, 15 feet up (Photo 11.6). "Who looks up at the ceiling when they walk?" John observed.

John thought and thought. He also scanned ID product catalogues (like Seton Name Plate's). Bingo! John designed the fabulous safety glasses visual mini-system in Photos 11.7 and 11.8. This mini-system stopped you in your tracks and practically put the glasses on your nose! It provided safety glasses at the exact point-of-use. No searching. No excuses. No motion.

On your way out, the back of the STOP sign tells you what to do next: Return the glasses to the same box you took them from. John's system is self-explaining so we can be self-regulating. I make sure to stop at UE whenever I go to Boston to see the latest of John's remarkable and (so far) never-ending visual inventions. His *Stop: Safety Glasses* mini-system is always in place.

Photo 11.4 John's very first mini-system.

Photo 11.5 Paul Plant.

Photo 11.6 Why don't people remember to put on safety glasses?

Photo 11.7 Stop! Put safety glasses on right now.

Photo 11.8 Please return them as you leave.

Mini-Systems Opportunities

As you saw with John Pacheco, mini-systems have a narrow focus that often calls on you to drill deep. Because of this drilling action, you may need several hours over several days (or weeks) to complete one. This is part of the pleasure of creating a mini-system. You build the pieces gradually, gaining insight over time into what will make this system function better and better. As with all things discussed in this book, you are looking for a balance point between structure and creativity—between method and invention and even flights of fancy. That is the purpose of the WTMS methodology.

By *methodology*, I do not mean: Get *complicated*. No, I mean: Get *systematic*—do things step-by-step-by-step. When we create something systematically, the steps are in order because that order matters. Think of the steps in a cake recipe, an engine overhaul, or building a cabinet from scratch. In all these, the steps matter and so do their sequence. It is the same way when you build a visual mini-system.

Watch Your Steps

When you build a visual mini-system, follow the same visual conversion protocol (recipe) we have been using. The steps are identical. Only your focus has shifted—to that drawer, that shelf, that cart, or to some narrow purpose (such as: *Get people to wear safety glasses*). Here are the steps.

First do your prep:

> Tour your area and identify mini-system opportunities. Add these to your Visual Workplace Hit List. Pick the one you want to do first. Fill in your name (and a buddy's name, if you wish), along with your start and target dates. (Remember to divide complex mini-systems into smaller tasks that you post and track separately.) Gather your supplies.

Now follow these steps:

1. Clear out the clutter. Make the location clean and safe.
2. Think through and apply the principles of smart placement.
3. Implement the visual where for your mini-system. Be inventive.
4. Test out your mini-system through observation and use. Proof it.
5. Drill deeper: Identify the details and make them visual. (Look for hidden forms of motion and buried information deficits. Work through these as well.)

Follow this procedure, and you will create scorching good visual mini-systems.

Mini-systems are meant to be satisfying. So plan to build them gradually over time. That is the point. Creating a mini-system should not overwhelm you. Keep a tight focus and simply keep going until the system achieves a highly-detailed level of visual performance and it functions beautifully.

Finding Mini-System Opportunities

Let's go on the hunt for visual mini-system candidates. They are everywhere—in every cabinet, drawer, bench top and lower shelf, cart, tool box, and corner. The focus is tight and the need is evident. They are your *Befores*.

Mini-system opportunities are everywhere. Look at Photo Series 11.9 on the next page. (I put a red box around several—but not all—mini-system candidates.)

Photo Series 11.9 Visual mini-system opportunities are everywhere.

This maintenance department is full of small and large tools. It will take several visual mini-systems to pull these pieces together.

This is not just a mess. It hides a number of important functions that only a smart visual mini-system can reveal.

This HR office is a universe of mini-systems. Create them and you will achieve a well-functioning department.

Grab 15 minutes of improvement time on Monday and Wednesday, and some more on Friday and you will make tremendous progress.

Offices offer so many mini-system opportunities because of the many individual business functions. The red boxes indicate just some of them. Notice the bulletin board is included.

We will go to Fort Worth, Texas to see an example of a visual mini-system that drills deeper in the value field, one of the many invented by master visual thinker, Margie Herrera.

The Visual Inventiveness of Margie Herrera (I)

Margie Herrera is a long-time employee at Lockheed Martin Aerospace (LM-Aero) and a visual thinker of the first order (Photo 11.10). A material handler, Margie is in charge of stocking parts and materials for the Tube Shop (a tube fabrication and assembly area).

When LM-Aero started to roll out visuality in operations, Margie was among the first to create powerful mini-systems. Here is the first of the two visual mini-systems that Margie created that we discuss in this chapter.

Margie's Tube ID Tape Mini-System

Tube identification tape (tube ID tape) is used in aerospace fabrication to indicate characteristics of each type of tube on a jet fighter: part number, direction of flow, function (hydraulics, pneumatics, fuel, or air), etc. The color coding is also critical.

Photo 11.10 Margie Herrera, visual wizard.

For example, blue/yellow striped tape is used for hydraulics. This information is vital to the work of field personnel who are responsible for quick and precise repairs.

Tube ID tape has a shelf-life limit between 12 and 24 months. Towards the end of a tape's shelf life, its adhesive backing can lose surface stickiness, begin to ooze out the sides, and cause the entire roll to get glued shut. That is one reason tapes reaching their shelf limit need to be removed—another part of Margie's job.

Before: Margie had to police all the tape—boxes and boxes of them on seven tall blue racks. See those racks in Photo 11.11 on the left—stuffed with boxes of overstocked, out-of-date, or nearly empty tube ID tape. Despite Margie's determined efforts, an out-of-date roll of tape sometimes reached an assembler. Margie and her supervisor knew why. There were too many boxes of tape. Margie decided to tackle this problem. She began with the boxes.

Photo 11.11 Helen Cherry and far too many boxes in front of the tall blue racks.

With help from production control supervisor, Helen Cherry, and perishable materials engineer, Marty Harnish, Margie removed 130 boxes of tape (Photos 11.11 and 11.12). That's when Margie realized that she did not need all seven tall racks. She needed none of them. Instead, she set up a kanban pull mini-system that keeps her active inventory to a manageable minimum (two tapes per product code), ensures fresh tape, and makes certain no assembler ever runs out.

Photo 11.12 Marty Harnish with out-of-date tape.

Margie's new system was housed in a large blue tool cabinet, with partitioned drawers shallow enough to accommodate only two tape rolls per compartment, and enough drawers to store all her part numbers (Photo 11.13). With two rolls of tape per compartment, a second one is always ready for the next assembler if the first roll is in use or consumed.

Photo 11.13 Blue cabinet with "Need-to-Order" and "Already Ordered" cards.

Margie checks the cabinet daily. When she needs to order, she scans the barcode card she has placed in each compartment so she has exact information handy, at the point-of-use. Done!

Margie made the assemblers part of her mini-system as well. See the two plastic holders on the top of the blue cabinet (red box). The first contains a set of laminated cards that read "Need to Order." They are for assemblers, such as Dorita (Photo 11.14), to place in a compartment when they pull the first roll. This provides Margie with an easy, visual alert to replenish.

The second plastic holder contains "Already Ordered" cards. Margie, in her turn, exchanges that card for the Need-to-Order card she finds. As a result, assemblers know that Margie got the message. The communication loop is visually complete. Both customer (Dorita) and supplier (Margie) now know what each other knows. The partnership remains strong.

Photo 11.14 Margie's customer, Dorita, continues her work.

Margie's Tube ID Tape mini-system, brilliant in its visual detail, remained a LM-Aero Visual Best Practice until the industry developed print-on-demand technology that requires bare tape only, or tape that is pre-color-coded.

But for the purposes of this book, Margie has provided us with an excellent example of how to *make a system* out of the visual where—exactly what you and your colleagues are now focused on. Once you do, you move that much closer to exchanging red dots on your area's laminated map for yellow ones, indicating that the visual where is completely and thoroughly implemented in your area. Remember?

The Laminated Map: Tracking Your Progress

The laminated map is a tool you learned about in Chapter 3. It is used to track the progress of visual improvement in your area. A report card of sorts, this map is very valuable in driving WTMS—*systematically*—through your department. If you are already using it, please continue. If you have not yet adopted it, I urge you to set one up now. Here is a refresher on how.

You and your co-workers laminate a paper layout of your department. Then with ruler and removal marker, you divide it into its logical sub-area. Next you put a blue dot in each on those (blue means: *We are not going to improve this area yet.*). After you decide where to begin your visual improvement, you exchange red dots for blue dots. The red dot means: *Let's get started—we have a long way to go.*

Going-to-Yellow

That *red dot* is replaced by a *yellow dot* when you have installed the visual where thoroughly in a given sub-area. That means there is a border, an address, and (if possible) an ID label for everything that casts a shadow.

Your march to *yellow* gets even more focused when you undertake visual mini-systems. As discussed, mini-systems are about going deeper which is exactly what it takes for an area to *go-to-yellow*. You and your fellow associates keep replacing information deficits with visual devices.

Since the specific rules for yellow are built directly into this map, there is never any doubt when a sub-area gets

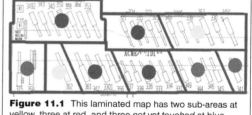

Figure 11.1 This laminated map has two sub-areas at yellow, three at red, and three *not yet touched* at blue.

to yellow. Set aside the audits, radar charts, and 5-point checklists. Your laminated map provides all that and more, with the added bonus that the standard—"for everything that casts a shadow"—is both I-driven and *not* subjective. This is how to use the laminated map on your way to yellow.

In a few pages, we'll talk about *going-to-green* and study a second mini-system by Margie Herrera. First, we need to deal with a familiar worry about mini-systems: How do we implement I-driven visual mini-systems in common areas where lots of people work but no one really "owns." There is no single "I."

Common Areas: The Pilot-Prototype Process

Here is what that worry can sound like: "*How do I visually improve this area when I share it with so many co-workers? How will I ever get them to agree? What do I do if they don't like my ideas?*"

First, the fact that you want to visually improve shared or common areas in your department is a big plus. It means you want to go further and realize other "I's" (your co-workers) may want to as well. It means you value creativity--yours and that of others. You know what people think and care about matters even though they may not agree with you. You want to move forward with visual improvement but not at the cost of good will. Be at ease. WTMS help is on the way.

The Pilot-Prototype Process: A Case Study

The WTMS method contains a proven process for testing different improvement ideas across shared functions and in common areas so everyone gets a fair chance to see how their own ideas work. It is called the *Pilot-Prototype Process* (the "2P Process" for short).

The purpose of the 2P Process is to give different people a systematic way to pilot or try out different visual improvement ideas (I-driven) for the same shared functions—common areas. Note the definitions of three key terms in the above sentence:

To Pilot: To test, try out, and explore an idea or design before it is accepted and used everywhere.
Protocol: A way, procedure, or practice that is well-defined and accepted as useful and relevant.
I-driven: To create a visual solution that satisfies one's own individual vision, first.

Background: Here is a mini-case study at Seton Name Plate on how the 2P Process works.

Seton's Shipping Department. Seton's Shipping Department was very large. Nearly everything in it was a shared resource or function for the 15 associates who worked there across three shifts: the nine packing stations, tons of packing material, dozens of order carts, five pallet jacks, and, of course, racks and racks of product inventory. The central task was: (1) Move through the tall shelves with a cart and a specific customer's order, (2) Pick and pull the items in that order, (3) Go to one of the nine packing stations and box up the order; and (4) send the shipment by conveyor to the loading dock.

WTMS Comes to Shipping. Shipping associates had to wait several months for their turn to get trained in WTMS. When it happened, they were all in.

Success: Smart Placement + Visual Where. They dug in, I-driven: cleared out the clutter/cleaned up the rest; and next studied smart placement principles/developed practical applications of the 14 principles. Then they implemented the visual where for floors and walls (Photo 11.15).

Photo 11.15 The visual where in Seton Shipping.

Stuck: Visual Mini-Systems. Everything flowed smoothly until it was time to turn the nine shipping stations into mini-systems. Nearly every associate had a ton of I-driven ideas and clamored to move ahead with them (and no one else's). And that was the problem. I-driven had become a barrier to moving forward. Everyone wanted their idea first! Emotions ran high. What to do?

Mistakes: Not Made. Richard Mini, Shipping supervisor, saw trouble brewing and knew four things: a) He wanted to keep the focus on visual improvement and moving forward, b) He did not want a battle for who got to go first, c) He wanted innovation—lots of different solutions, and d) He did not want to standardize too soon and homogenize people's ideas into plain vanilla. Rich wanted *Cherry Garcia* and *Coffee Heathbar Crunch*—I-driven visual inventiveness. He decided to implement the 2P Process.

1. At the monthly overlap meeting, Rick explained the 2P Process. He emphasized two main points. First, everyone will have plenty of chance to try out their own individual improvement ideas for turning a shipping station into a visual mini-system. Second, the benches did not need to look alike.

2. He asked the 15 associates to get into teams *by shift*, with two (but not more than three) people on each team. Or you could work solo.

3. Next, each team picked one of the nine Shipping Stations in the department as its pilot bench (benches were scattered around the area, with 6 to 8 feet on all sides). See Figure 11.2.

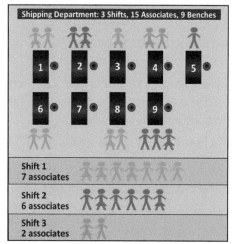

Figure 11.2 2P Process Packing Station Selection Map. This is a condensed floor plan of the nine packing stations (or benches) in the Shipping Department. In reality, these benches were scattered across a very large floor in locations convenient to associates. Here you see five teams of two people, two teams of one person, and one team of three people. On the chart, each shift is color coded so you can tell which shift "owns" which bench. Only Bench #7 has no owner. It remained a *before* until it was later upgraded d to the level of Visual Best Practice.

4. The selected bench remained that team's improvement focus for the next two months. Everyone else in the department used that bench, but only the "owner" team improved it. This applied to each team and its designated bench. (Only bench 7 was without an owner.)

5. For the next two months, each Shipping team applied the WTMS method step-by-step—detecting motion, uncovering information deficits, and inventing visual solutions that eliminated both. Then they implemented smart placement and the visual where on the bench-level, they way they saw fit (and tracked Improvement Time usage throughout). They tested ideas, changed their minds, innovated, iterated. Each team created their own version of a visual shipping station mini-system for that array of associated functions.

6. As part of the 2P Process, the teams also studied the other benches—5. You are urged to experiment, try out ideas, innovate, change your mind, and iterate. This part of the process would run two months. Check out the other benches. Compare, borrow, and build—and always say *thank you*. Some teams made good use of the Four People Process Tools, learned in Chapter 4: Brainstorm, Gatekeep, Talking Stick, and Consensus.

7. After about two months, Rich called the teams in for presentations, review, discussion, and appreciation. It was clear that a number of visual details migrated from bench to bench. As a result, benches were beginning to resemble each other. But everyone knew that standardization (a "single best bench") was not the goal. Let differences remain. The goal was to track down motion and convert missing information into high-performing visual solutions. Keep going. Better makes us best. A rich array of visual best practices began to emerge in Shipping. See Photo Series 11.16.

Widely Applicable. The 2P Process has proved very effective in the visual transformation of common areas and where there are many duplicated but shared operations, machines, and the like. NOTE: Unless you currently work in high-performance/self-directed teams, you will need to help of your supervisors and coaches in setting up and facilitating this process. Do it as a big team!

Photo Series 11.16 Shipping Station/before & after the 2P Process at Seton.

Shipping
Station

◀ Before

After ▶

The Visual Inventiveness of Margie Herrera (II)

Now let's look again at the visual wizardry of Margie Herrera and another mini-system she invented. Doing so will lead us to the second key principle of going deeper: customer-driven visuality.

Margie's PLS Mini-System

Margie created this next visual mini-system to solve a challenge her customers faced with commodity parts, called *Production Line Stock* (PLS) at LM-Aero. PLS covers a wide range of components that vary from shop to shop. PLS in one shop may mean fittings, caps, and covers. In another, it means nuts, bolts, screws, etc. Many such parts are look-alikes, differing only in minute attributes, for example, thread depth, spring-compression ratio, etc.

In the Tube Shop, PLS were available in small blue bins on double-sided, rolling carts that Margie kept stocked for several linked sub-areas.

When visuality came to LM-Aero, each area laid down a visual foundation of borders and addresses. Working from that base, Margie turned to visual mini-systems to drill into the details of her PLS approach.

First, she assigned an address to each side of the cart—the *Working Side* (Photo 11.17)—where assemblers (her customers) pull parts. The other was the *Stocking Side* (Photo 11.18), what Margie kept replenished.

Margie scanned the barcode address on each blue bin for ordering. When a bin ran out on the Working Side, the operator walked around to the Stocking Side and swapped the empty bin for a full one. This is classic 2-bin kanban.

Photo 11.17 PLS: the Working Side.

But, as Margie noticed, this didn't always happen smoothly. There were times when an operator found an empty bin on the Working Side and, when she went around to the Stocking Side to retrieve a full one, got stalled. Margie would see the operator reach for a bin and then just stand there. It didn't take long for Margie to realize that the person was trying to figure out which bin was the replacement. Was it the bin directly behind the one that was empty? Or, reading left to right, was it the bin on the opposite corner?

The bin's barcode held the answer, but it was far too small to read and compare—though Margie kept seeing people try. Eventually, they gave up and did nothing or looked for Margie so they could get an answer. In either case, they were doubtful, not confident—hesitant, not active. They were in motion.

Photo 11.18 PLS: the Stocking Side.

Margie's customers were in motion because of her—because of a missing answer (an information deficit) in her delivery system. Even though the PLS system she had developed to this point was far superior to the prior approach, it was clearly not yet complete. Margie knew she needed to share more information if she was to help her customers do a better job. But what information? And how? She was going to have to stretch her visual thinking.

Then in a flash, Margie understood the exact information deficit that had triggered that motion and what she would do to eliminate it, completely. She added a single, brilliant visual detail and the problem disappeared entirely.

Instead of making the bin address more specific or the information on the bar code larger, she simply added numbers—ordinal numbers: 1, 2, 3, 4, 5, and so on. In the visual language you learned in Chapter 7, Margie applied *generic addresses*.

Photo 11.19 The addition of a single brilliant detail.

She added a number to each bin (left to right) on the Working Side, starting with 1 (Photo 11.19 and Detail). Then she put a matching number on the related bin on the Stocking Side. Although the assemblers did not know the following (nor did they need to know it), in a 2-bin kanban system, the opposite side reads from right to left. As a result, when an operator finds an empty blue bin, she just goes to the Stocking Side and exchanges it for the fully-stocked bin with the same number. As with her tube ID tape mini-system discussed earlier, Margie included two sets of laminated cards—one to indicate the *Need-To-Order* and the other to indicate *Already-Ordered* (Photo 11.20).

Margie's PLS mini-system is a splendid example of customer-driven visuality—noticing your customer's motion and eliminating it through solutions that are visual. Photo 11.21 shows Margie with one of her happy assembler customers, Diana.

Splendid motion detective work. Splendid visual thinking. And splendid customer-driven visuality.

Photo 11.20 ALREADY ORDERED: Don't worry, replenishment is on its way.

Photo 11.21 Margie assisting her customer, Diana.

Customer-Driven Visuality

We know two things about Margie at the time of the above solutions. We know that she applied the need-to-know and the visual where vigorously to her own corner of the world and was well on her way to mastering it (she was nearly at yellow). We also know she had begun to apply the *need-to-share*, shifting her focus to the information she needed to share so that other people could do their own work with less struggle and in ways that were safer, smarter, and better. In the case of Margie's PLS system, those other people were her internal customers.

But they could just as well have been her internal suppliers—people inside LM-Aero who work upstream, downstream, and at stream from Margie. Add to these Margie's suppliers and customers, external to LM-Aero. All these groups were also her customers—customers of her information.

Margie had become active in her search to serve. She paid attention to the motion of her customers and suppliers. Sometimes, their motion would be in the form of questions they asked, or moments when they were stalled, felt confused, unsafe, or doubtful. Margie began to notice these things. She began to tackle them, one by one, by inventing visual devices and mini-systems that removed the information deficits that caused the motion in the first place. Driven by them, she was becoming a master visual thinker.

Photo 11.22 The yellow strip on this bin is a customer-driven device to help Margie better serve her customers.

Notice the small yellow strip at the bottom of the blue bin in Photo 11.22 (red box). Marge put it there for a customer-driven purpose. She color coded all PLS bins by department (yellow for Single Flare, green for Double Flare, etc.). She did not do this to "catch" an assembler "stealing" from another department. Her motivation was entirely different. She did it so that, if she found a bin with color code strip that did not match that area, she would know that area had run out of those PLS components. That's how she found more holes in her replenishment system and how she learned to better serve her customers.

This is the heart of the customer-driven process: To serve your customers (your internal and external customers and suppliers in that single term)—and to serve them better by visually sharing the information you know that they need to know.

Sharing with Your Customers

Think about your internal suppliers and customers. Who are they? What kind of information do they need to know from you? Do the same for your external suppliers and customers. Who are they? What kind of information do they need to know that you need to share? Are you currently sharing that? How? Could a visual device do it better?

Listen to their questions. Invite them into your area for a walkabout and ask them what information would help—even delight—them to be able to access at-a-glance. There will be a sizeable difference between what an internal customer (from, for example, a downstream process or planning) wants you to share—and an external customer, such as General Smith from the Department of Defense. Both have a need to know and will love it when, the next time they stop by, you have answered them visually.

In customer-driven visuality, your goal is to use visual devices and mini-systems to help your customers—all of them—feel safe, smart, and connected so they achieve greater success in their own day, in their own goals, and in their own work lives thanks to your visual contribution.

Going-to-Green

Green on the laminated map means you have drilled deeper into the information deficits in your area, so deeply that visuality is now sustainable. Part of that means implementing the customer-driven visuality you just read about. Another part is what you will read about in the next chapter: *The Four Power Levels of Visual Devices*. When your area *goes-to-green*, visual information sharing devices—and the visual thinking that produces them—have become a way of life there. Yours is a *Visual Best Practice* department. Your area has reached the *Showcase* level. It's a *Vision Place* within the company.

An area *goes-to-green* much the same way as it went to yellow—gradually, sub-area by sub-area (Figure 11.2). Unlike *going-to-yellow*, *green* has no specific defining criteria. Your area simply becomes visually powerful and complete when it moves to green. Using a word I coined in the 1980s, it becomes *visually transparent*. You can see into the operations of the department and retrieve…well, anything you want.

Like replacing a wall with a clear pane of glass, all is revealed. Nothing is hidden, secreted away or unavailable. When the area is green, the workplace speaks (Figures 11.3 and 11.4).

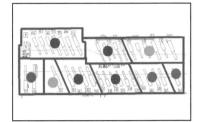

Figure 11.2 Gradually, sub-areas shift from yellow to green.

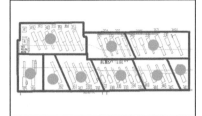

Figure 11.3 The entire area (department) has gone to full green.

Figure 11.4 When the area goes green, the dot on the company map goes green too.

You will know it—and you will like it. Besides the smooth flow of work and the absence of struggle, you will like the way it feels to work with others; they have become master visual thinkers as well. They know what you know and with you have designed and re-designed your work area. Your supervisor will also have a big smile on her face. Because you can get to your work, without struggle, she gets to hers. And by now she knows that her main job is not answering questions or chasing down materials.

She has become a leader of improvement—but that is a topic for another book.

Just one thing more (by now you know there is always "just one thing more" in this book). Don't assign green to your area too quickly. Don't assign it for effort—as in "they meant well and are trying so hard." Assign green because the results are evident. Make green worthy of the horizon you sought when you first got started on your visual journey. You were full of hope then—and belief and energy. And then you learned and applied a methodology, diligently over time. Not for a few days but over a number of months. You kept going. Make that pay off. Make sure your area is worthy of green. When a department goes green, it becomes a showcase—a vision place—for others.

They have been watching and will turn to your area to learn what a visual workplace is and how it functions long before they get started. Your company needs at least one visual showcase area (discussed in Chapter 3) to set the pace for others. When that happens, then instead of having to travel outside the company to see a vision place, people from other departments will simply walk across the floor to yours. Going to green is an achievement to celebrate.

The Visual Inventiveness of Rick Ell

Throughout this book you have seen many visual solutions invented by Rick Ell (Photo 11.23), precision machinist at Denison Hydraulics (now Parker Denison/Ohio).

Rick admits he was indifferent, even reluctant, when the *Work That Makes Sense* method was launched in his area. Later he decided to give WTMS a try. He liked the result and soon resolved to visually transform his entire area. You cannot see those results, unfortunately, because they disappeared virtually overnight when his cell was moved—before I had taken any photos.

Rick was assigned a new area and dug right in. The visual conversion of his first cell took nine months. Rick converted his second cell in less than three. It was the first thing on his agenda. Rick had already made a name for himself with his

Photo 11.23 Rick Ell, master visual thinker..

Photo Series 11.24 Denison's Visual Workplace Bulletin Board and Rick Ell's Dot Ceremony.

| With Steve Harvey holding the map, the author removes the yellow dot and hands it to Rick Ell. | A green dot is retrieved from the stash of dots and placed to show the new visual status of his department. | Congratulations to Rick Ell. Fellow Steering Team member, Deb Kelsey, joins in. |

first cell as a master visual thinker. In his second cell, he went beyond his own high standard. Machinists on the other two shifts competed to work there. They called it the *no-thinking cell*—because (as Rick explained) they didn't have to think when they were there; they just did the dance of work.

I was lucky enough to be on site the day that Rick's second cell went to green (Photo Series 11.24). Under the Denison Visual Workplace Bulletin Board which Steve Harvey (Denison's first-rate visual workplace coordinator) had created, Rick traded in his yellow dot for a green one, with champion Bill Cornell, Rick's supervisor, and Steering Team looking on. What a moment.

Take a tour of Rick's visual showcase in Photo Series 11.25. You saw many of these devices elsewhere in this book. Now they are grouped together to give you a greater sense of Rick's level of visual mastery.

Photo Series 11.25 The Visual Thinking Mastery of Rick Ell (*continues next page*).

The Pattern of Work

Smart Placement Principles Everywhere

The Machine That Speaks

The Visual Machine®

Rick's fan is never out of visual order.

Visuality Behind Closed Doors

Drilling Deep into the Value Field

Visual Mini-Systems and Customer-Driven Visuality: Next Steps

Figure 11.5 Keep track on your Hit List.

You have just learned about visual mini-systems and customer-driven visuality. Now it is time to look for opportunities to apply them.

Consider the mini-systems and customer-driven devices you just studied. Walk back through the pages of this chapter as you need to. How have they widened your thinking about ways that visuality can help you reduce motion, eliminate information deficits, and make your work area—and the work areas of your customers—safer and more operationally effective? Think about that now.

Then, working alone or with a buddy, make a list of visual improvement opportunities that occur to you. Add these to your visual workplace hit list (Figure 11.5), posting *all* your improvement ideas, even if you do not plan to tackle them yourself. Improvement is continuous so it all does not have to happen right away or happen through you alone.

You already know what happens after that: You keep going. You follow the methodology (the recipe). You keep thinking. And you keep using your hit list.

You also keep showing up for the visual blitzes scheduled in your area—and when I say show up, I mean all parts of you: hands, feet, brain, heart, vision, and sense of humor.

Converting to a fully-functioning visual workplace is about that—about engaging your hands, feet, brain, heart, vision, and sense of humor. It is about you and the people who work with you learning how to *function* on an entirely new level at work—a level that is captured visually and made tangible in the many devices you and they develop and embed into the living landscape of work.

Those who visit your work area see this tangible evidence as well. They see a remarkable level of operational excellence, made visual through those devices. They see work that makes sense.

> The future ain't what
> it used to be.
>
> Yogi Berra

Chapter | Twelve

The Four Power Levels of Visual Devices

Translating Information into Visual Devices

Let's go back to where we started. In Chapter 1, we said that visuality is about translating information into exact behavior through visual devices. That is because those devices share the needed information in a visual format—at-a-glance. Figure 12.1 puts tuns those words into an image. You have been learning about and applying that concept through this book.

Nearly every person who works begins the journey to workplace visuality in a value field that is starved for information. The *Before* photo you see Photo 12.1 is such a value field—a work bench with zero information sharing, flooded with missing answers (aka, information deficits) and their accomplice, motion.

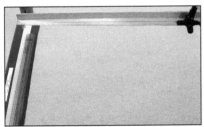

Photo 12. Before: Information-starved value field.

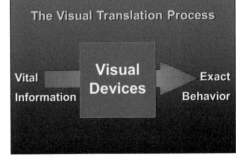

Figure 12.1 The translation of information into exact behavior—through visual devices.

But the situation does not have to stay that way. As we learn about visuality, we realize we can eliminate the info deficits—and the motion they trigger—through solutions that are visual. We become powerful visual thinkers, capable of creating increasingly powerful visual devices.

That is exactly what you see in Photo 12.2—the same work bench *after* visual thinking was applied—not once but repeatedly—until that value field functioned on a very high level. Here's how that happened.

Maryanne was one of the 23 Gold Cup assemblers in the WTMS training. The group had already learned and applied smart placement, the visual where, and visual mini-systems. They had become ace visual thinkers, always on the hunt for motion and its trigger, information deficits.

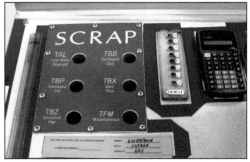

Photo 12.2 After: An information-rich value field.

One day, Maryanne noticed she spent the end of every shift first sorting the defects she found in the small parts she used in her work into six types. Then she counted each type. Then she used plugged those types and numbers into her Daily Defect Report. She noticed her motion and de-

Photo 12.3 Foam Cups.

cided to eliminate it visually. The final result is the red scrap separator plate you see in the upper left corner of Photo 12.2. It came after several iterations or cycles of thinking, allowing Maryanne to sort defects into one of the six types *as she finds them*. She drops the defect in the matching hole; it lands in a waiting cup. At the end of the day, she counts what is in each cup, gets a tally by defect type, and completes her report.

Maryanne's device did not eliminate defects. But it did simplify the task of tracking them. That, in turn, became an important step in streamlining her work. Nor did her invention begin as the snazzy red plate shown in the photo. It began as a set of six styrofoam cups (Photo 12.3), held together with masking tape, each cup marked with a different defect type. That was the first version of her solution. It saved so much time that other operators copied the idea for their own benches. Within months, Maryanne's solution was formalized into the powerful red scrap separator device in the photo and installed on every bench in the Gold Cup area. It had become a Visual Best Practice in her company.

Maryanne's solution includes many levels of visual functionality—not just the visual where. That is what makes it so effective and so powerful. And that is exactly what we are going to discuss and explain in this chapter: the power levels of visual devices.

Learning and Pacing Yourself

The purpose of this chapter is to show you many, many different visual devices. Some of these have already been discussed in this book. If you are familiar with my other visual workplace books, others could have been presented there. Why didn't I choose those other examples? The reason is simple: Certain devices are so outstanding they are classified in my mind as "teaching examples." They hold the principles of visuality so vividly and completely that they teach no matter the industry. That is why.

One more thing before we begin to study the four power levels of visual devices. Be aware that it may take longer than you think to absorb and apply what is shared in this chapter. My hope is that you do not rush through these pages, glancing at the photos, murmuring "uh huh, I get it," and moving on. Instead, I encourage you to spend time as you learn about each power category and consider how it can and does change human behavior. As part of this, think about ways to apply what you are learning in your own area in order to improve your own performance first—and then the performance of others.

If I were teaching you directly, we'd spend two to three weeks on each power level as you developed applications and track their impact. So don't rush through these pages. Build a better result. Ask your supervisor or trainer to walk through these pages with you—or organize a Book Study Group so you can study and apply the power levels with colleagues. They will be happy to help. This was the subject of *Leadership Task 11*, discussed in Chapter 5. Here is a recap, this time with you as the leader.

> This book, *Work That Makes Sense,* is an implementation manual. Put it to work for you and your colleagues by starting a Book Study Group. Your supervisor or trainer will help you set this up. Then meet regularly (weekly if you can) to discuss the ideas, concepts, principles, *and examples*—chapter by chapter. Meet in a quiet place for 30 minutes (management often provides an added 15 minutes). No interruptions please. Gatekeep for yourselves, use the Talking Stick as needed, rotate session leadership, keep focused, and set a reading schedule. Discuss what you have read. Listen, share insights, learn from each other. Identify possible applications. Get informed. Get inspired. Take the lead for steady visual improvements in your area.

The Four Power Levels

The purpose of this chapter is to show you that visual solutions exist on different levels of power—and to show you how to use those levels to give your own visual solutions more power. Power to do what? Power to get precise, predictable, and repeatable behavior. Power to make sure that what is supposed to happen, *does* happen.

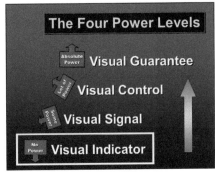

Figure 12.2 The Four Power Levels.

When you understand the four power levels, you begin to think beyond borders, addresses, and ID labels—because the visual where is only one category of visual function, and a very basic one at that. Other categories include visual standards, visual displays, visual metrics, visual problem solving, visual controls, visual pull systems, and visual guarantees. You are about to learn about most of these and how you can make your visual devices increasingly powerful through your own visual thinking.

Look at the four levels in Figure 12.2, starting from the bottom up: Visual Indicator, Visual Signal, Visual Control, and Visual Guarantee (poka-yoke). The red boxes describe and point to each level of power. Notice that the yellow arrow moves from less power to more. We begin with visual indicators.

Visual Indicators

Like all visual devices, a *visual indicator* delivers a message. The railroad crossing sign in Figure 12.3 shares information vital to drivers and pedestrians: "Be careful! Trains often pass here!" But indicators are placed at the bottom of the power progression because they have *no power* to make us slow down or stop. They simply announce the possibility of an oncoming train.

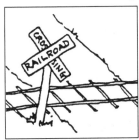

Figure 12.3 A visual indicator.

Because you and I are adults, we are likely to notice the indicator and, as a result, slow down. We understand the concept of consequences.

But teenagers? For far too many of them, the railroad crossing post looks like an open invitation to step on the gas—especially if a train is in sight—and try to outrun it and make it across the tracks without getting smashed. Immature? Childish? Dangerous? Yes, it is all those things. But no railroad sign can ever be powerful enough to change that. That is the point: Visual indicators have no power to make us do the right thing, even when it is in our best interests.

Look at Photo Series 12.4 for three more visual indicators found in the community.

Photo Series 12.4 Visual Indicators in the community.

"Stroller Parking" at Disney World. Nothing forces you to park there. No stroller police. It is up to you.

The most famous visual indicator of all. Its power lies in the possible consequences of ignoring it—an accident or a ticket. It has no power of its own.

We pay attention to street signs only when we need them. Otherwise, they are practically invisible. We breeze right by.

Visual indicators convey important, even vital, information, but they have no power to make us obey, comply, or adhere. They have no power to make us do the right thing.

This is not to say that visual indicators are not important. In fact, they are indispensable to our society and our work day. Imagine a world without street names, house addresses, stop signs, road signs, directions, maps, etc. Imagine your company without a name and an address on the front building, names on desks, departmental signs, names on each file drawer, signs that point us to the Mens Room vs. Ladies, and so on. Could you function without those? Probably—but why would you want to?

Photo 12.5 (plus Detail) shows you the glory of indicators: a great system of addresses at Seton Name Plate where thousands of catalogue orders are fulfilled weekly. Look at all the visual concepts captured here: big bold color-coded airborne and floor addresses and coded ID labels—plus *sort-the-universe, co-locate like functions,* and *put it on wheels.* The lowly visual indicator at its finest.

What self-respecting buyer could live without the two-sided, laminated, airborne driver-license address you see in Photo 12.6? Not Cindy Barter.

Photo 12.5 A mini-system of indicators.

Yes, visual indicators are valuable, but they are not powerful. Though we seem to automatically obey most indicators, in truth, anyone of us could decide—at any point—not to. Indicators leave us in charge of our own will. That is precisely why I once paid $54.25 for a cup of cappuccino—$4.25 for the coffee, the rest for the parking ticket—one day when

CINDY BARTER

BUYER #6   EXT. 207

RESPONSIBILITIES

SCREW MACHINE PARTS
SINTERED METAL
BAR STOCK
WIRE & CABLE
MOTORS
BELLOWS

ALTERNATE: JON BIRKETT

Photo 12.6

I chose to ignore a *No Parking* sign outside of a favorite cafe.

Ignoring indicators can trigger severe outcomes—or not. If someone, for example, does not see or follow the "Use First" indicator in Photo 12.7 (red arrow), the schedule may get thrown off—but no one dies. The reverse, however, is true for the STOP sign on the corner.

Visual indicators do not—by definition—*make us* do the right thing because they cannot. They have no power. We need devices with a higher level of power for that, the kind you learn about later in this chapter.

Visual Standards are Indicators. Managers love *Visual Standards*, such as the ones you see in the Photo Series 12.8. After all, their thinking goes, these visual messages make it perfectly clear what needs to be done, by when, and how—the technical and procedural details of adding value—so people are bound to use them. Yes? No.

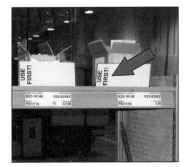

Photo 12.7 A visual indicator with an urgent request: "Use me first!"

Photo Series 12.8
Visual Standards from the shop floor.

While it is true that visual standards—indicators all—hold vital safety and quality answers, they have zero power to make us follow them. They depend entirely on our willingness to use them. If we accept that we need to know such detail and that the information is truthful and complete, we probably will decide in favor of reading them (step 1) and maybe even decide to follow them (step 2). In some organizations, those are two pretty big "ifs."

Here is the story that triggered a splendid visual standard, created by operators working in the blade grinding area at Hamilton Standard (Connecticut). When arguments between shifts began related to grinder cleanliness, it did not take long for people to recognize the complaints as a form of motion—bickering due to missing information. The missing information was what "clean enough" looked like. No standard had been set. Therefore cleanliness remained a subjective condition—an opinion. Needless to say, opinions differed.

But associates in this area were already visual thinkers. Their solution was brilliant: Photograph each grinder when it is "clean enough" and post that on each machine (Photo 12.9 and Detail). The quarreling stopped. This visual standard is an outstanding example of operator-led visual inventiveness.

By now, you have begun to understand that, though visual indicators can not force us to do anything, they can still influence practically everything. Take measures, for example.

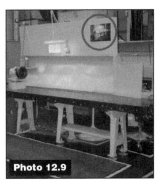

Photo 12.9

Detail

Visual Measures are Indicators. Nowadays, companies seem to watch, count, track, and measure practically everything. What supervisor does not hope that sharing such measures would automatically improve them? That rarely happens. Yet knowing the details of less-than-stellar results is important.

Look at the kiosk (or bird's nest) in Photo 12.10. This four-sided kiosk is built to show results across this area's key performance indicators (KPIs): safety, quality, delivery, and cost. Regular computer printouts get slipped into the plastic sleeves on each side (red box). The kiosk rotates. It is on wheels. You can take it to lunch if you want to. This is a very "talented" kiosk.

While this approach is a huge improvement over not collecting data at all, sharing results in this way is not, on its own, going to trigger improvement. Why? Because all this kiosk does is monitor and indicate.

All metrics (another word for measures) are indicators. They have no built-in power to make us improve or even care. But that does not mean they are not important. They are. The question is: Can they do more? The answer is yes, they can—and powerfully so, as long as: 1) they give you direct feedback on your own performance in as close to real time as possible; 2) they provide a point of comparison; 3) they help you discover cause; and 4) you use them.

Photo 12.10 Metrics on wheels.

Let's look at the first two requirements in more detail.

Feedback on Yourself and a Point of Comparison. First, separate the metrics that speak to your boss (usually because they speak to her boss)—and the metrics that speak to you.

The ones that speak to you will almost always give you feedback on your own behavior, your own performance. You will like that feedback the most when it is frequent, specific, and on demand—like the score at a ball game ... or the mirror in your bathroom. How interested are you in that feedback? The answer: very interested, never get tired of it, give me more.

Remember, the visual workplace is an I-driven methodology. You are at the center of it. That is not egotism; it is functionality. The self at the center not only directs your interest in performing well, it clamors for feedback on just how well. That is a main principle of I-driven measures. The motivation is on the inside—inside the measure and inside you.

Line operators at Alpha Industries (Massachusetts) were well on their visual journey when they decided to go after more feedback on their own performance, specifically related to on-time delivery. They constructed the airborne placard (visual indicator) in Photo 12.11 that announced their current on-time performance (93%) and boldly proclaimed what their own previous best had been—which in this case was even better: 100%. They held their own feet to the fire of continuous improvement and included a meaningful point of comparison to spur them on.

Photo 12.11 A visual metric provides a meaningful point of comparison.

There is much more to learn about visual metrics but this will get you started. Start experimenting with them. Put a metrics project on your hit list and explore. Your supervisor is sure to be interested in supporting your research, even delighted.

Visual Displays are Indicators. Similar to a visual metric, a visual display has no power to make us change, improve, or even pay attention. Its effectiveness comes from our interest in and need for the information that it contains. When we are motivated on the inside, we pay attention on the outside.

Photo 12.12 shows the maintenance display you saw in Chapter 1 when we discussed the ten doorways. Located on the main aisle of a 1500-person factory in Indiana, this board is divided into maintenance specialties across the top: electricians, millwrights, pipe fitters, and so on.

Its purpose is to share the truth about work orders, first so maintenance technicians know—then so everyone in the plant knows (this display was on a main aisle).

Look how honest it is. At the bottom of the display (in green), maintenance shows its completed tasks. In the middle (in yellow) are the new orders. At the top (in red) are the past due. Everyone can tell where most of the work is: past dues.

Visual displays are about telling the truth in real time, as the truth changes. You begin displays with the "I"—answering your need-to-know. Other people often need to know the same thing so it may look like you have built the board for others. But that is only a coincidence.

Photo 12.12 Maintenance shares order status visually.

Visual Display by Bill Antunes. More often than not, displays are developed by supervisors and managers. But there is nothing to prevent value-add associates—*you*—from inventing displays to support your own work and, nicely, that of your area. That is exactly what Bill Antunes did (Photo 12.13). You saw Bill's splendid work bench in Chapter 2. Bill began his display, triggered by *his* urgent need-to-know.

Photo 12.13 Bill Antunes, ace visual thinker.

Bill had worked in switch/control assembly at United Electric Controls (Massachusetts) for nearly 20 years before he learned about visuality. Before, his department was plagued by parts shortages *(stockouts)*. Management tried to remedy the problem many times but without success. The latest attempt was a three-sheet form you filled out when you saw a part running low. One sheet went to purchasing to alert the buyers. The second stayed with you as proof. Nobody knew what the third sheet was for—so it usually also got sent to the buyer as a reminder and double insurance. But that only confused the buyer since he already had one alert. So he set both forms aside to investigate "later." The part never got ordered.

As a visual thinker, Bill realized his area's approach to parts shortages was triggering a ton of motion—piling up information deficits (and part shortages) instead of reducing them. He decided to do something about it. He invented the visual display in Photo Series 12.14 (next page). Here's how it works.

1. The display is in two sections. The red column on the left is for part numbers that are out: *Hot Shortages*. The blue column on the right is for part numbers that will run out soon: *Low Stock*.

2. When an assembler notices a part is running low or an actual stockout, he or she marks the part number on the correct side of the display—and in the correct color (this is important to Bill).

3. The buyer (in this case, Lee Sacco) checks the display three times a day, noting any new items.

Photo Series 12.14
Stockouts Display of Bill Antunes.

Lee Sacco, the buyer, posts the promised delivery date.

Lee at his desk on the shopfloor.

4. Lee returns to his desk, calls the supplier, orders the parts, and secures a promised delivery date.

5. On his next trip to the board, he notes this information next to its part number—and, of course, looks for new items.

6. Bill (or whoever posted the shortage) then circles that delivery date to say "got it" and "thank you." The communication loop is complete.

This worked so well that within six months, Lee and the other buyers had moved their desks to the shopfloor. They knew they had to be where the action happened so they could better support operations.

See Photo 12.15 for an associate-led display in another company, this one related to production output. Work orders are marked on small magnets and re-arranged by operators themselves as the schedule is completed or revised. Other cells in the grid hold quality data, problems, and special needs or comments. As with all visual indicators, this display *tells only*—but it still makes a powerful daily contribution.

Visual Indicators: Next Steps. This concludes our discussion on visual indicators. Now it's time for you to consider them. How can the visual indicators you just studied expand your thinking about ways to make your area safer and operationally more effective?

Think about that now. Then, working alone or with a buddy, review the previous pages and

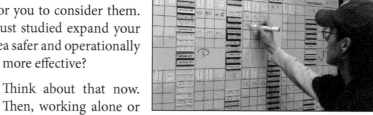

Photo 12.15 An associate tracks her daily production output, defects, and problems on a shared display.

list opportunities for visual indicators in your area, as you remind yourself of the many kinds of visual indicators that exist. Then add visual indicator projects to your visual workplace hit list (Figure 12.4). Remember to post *all* your improvement ideas, even if you do not plan to tackle them yourself. Improvement is continuous so it all does not have to happen right away or happen through you alone. *Thanks!*

Figure 12.4 Post and track your improvement ideas on your visual workplace hit list.

Visual Signals

We now move up the power ladder to *visual signals* and see how they strengthen adherence. Look at Figure 12.6. What changed? Yes, we added flashing lights to the railroad crossing indicator. Now when a train approaches, the lights start to flash and draw our attention to the fact that there is an oncoming train on the tracks we are approaching. We stop—the message was sent and received.

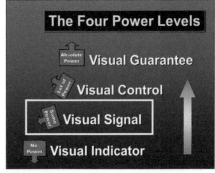

Figure 12.5 Power Level 2: Visual Signals.

That is, you and I stop. But our teenage friend might still gun the engine and make a run for it.

A visual signal has a bit more power than a visual indicator because it first grabs our attention—then delivers its message. But it is still up to us if we heed it. A visual signal is only slightly more effective than a visual indicator in making us do the right thing—and that means *hardly at all.*

Figure 12.6 A Visual Signal.

Examples of visual signals abound, from the stop light you see in Photo 12.16 to the beep-beep sound (annunciator signal) as the forklift backs up. Visual signals first get our attention—and then they deliver their message.

You can see this process in the simple rumble strip at the side of the road (Photo 12.17). You are driving home from turkey dinner at Grandma's house. The meal hits your nervous system, and you fall asleep at the wheel. The rumble strip springs into action the instant your tires touch it ... bounce, bounce, bounce! "Wake up wake up, you dunderhead!" it shouts. "You're heading for the ditch!"

What a perfect visual signal. The device simply lies there, mute but waiting, until the very instant you need it—when your wheels hit the strip on their way to the ditch. Instead of taking the dive, you swerve. Your behavior changes. You get back on a safe course, thanks to a few designed-in dents in the asphalt.

Photo 12.16
Traffic lights.

Photo 12.17
Rumble Strip.

What makes visual signals effective is the fact that they change. When a signal stops changing, we ignore it. Just like the stop light that gets stuck in the middle of the night in the middle of nowhere. Chances are high that we'll ignore it and speed on. It has lost the message it was designed to deliver. (Needless to say, I have never done that.)

Now let's look at some more examples.

Red Clothes Pin Visual Signal. Here is a story about a visual signal found in an unexpected place and in an unexpected form.

Camilla came in early every morning to prepare a report by 8:00 a.m. for Nate, the head engineer. Nate came in early every morning and hovered around Camilla's desk to make sure she got the report to him on time. Camilla put up with this for a while because, well, Nate was her boss. Then one morning she spoke up grumpily, in the language of visual thinking.

"Look Nate, I really respect you. But honestly you get me off to a bad start every morning because you hover around my desk, worrying about the report. Can't we do something about that?" Nate had also been trained in visuality. He knew grumpiness was often just another form of motion, caused by missing information, unanswered questions. He also recognized that in this case his unanswered question was his need to know exactly when his report was ready.

"Yes, Camilla," said Nate, "Let's solve this together." And they did—they figured out how to eliminate Nate's information deficit through visuality. Check Photos Series 12.18 to see how they did it.

Photo Series 12.18 A great visual signal solution.

Before. Is the report ready? Nate has to either go and look—or ask Camilla. He always asked Camilla.

After-1. When the report is ready, Camilla puts it in a blue bin and clips on the clothes pin—Nate's signal that the report is waiting.

After-2. When he picks it up, Nate removes the red clothes pin—his signal to Camilla: All is well with the world.

Machine Stacked Lights. The device in Photo 12.19 is a combination visual signal (the lights) and visual indicator (the words in Spanish that are fixed on the lights). Here is the translation:

Photo 12.19 The yellow light means planned downtime. No worries.

- Green-*Trabajand*: The machine is running. Everything is going smoothly.

- Yellow-*No Trabajand:* The machine in not running because of planned downtime.

- Red-*Ayuda Problema*: Oh no, we are having a problem. The machine is down, and we did not plan for that.

The purpose of this excellent visual signal + visual indicator application is to show the status of the process. In this case, the machine is down, but that is as planned (yellow).

***Andon*/Stacked Lights.** The technical name for these lights is *andon*—Japanese for "paper lantern." Andon is a system of stacked lights that share status information on core performance parameters: faults/stoppages, readiness, waiting state, help needed, and so on. But one of the challenges in using these systems is that the color order and number of lights are not the same from vendor to vendor.

Photo Series 12.20 An array of andons or stacked lights—but what do they mean?

An Andon Case in Point. The six sets of andons you see in Photo Series 12.20 were just some of dozens of stacked lights surrounding me at a mail processing center in Minneapolis. All were lit. But few had the same color sequence or number of lights. Plus, I had no idea what any of them meant, or if I was in mortal danger. When I asked, my escort replied, "Oh there's nothing to worry about. They're always on."

Instead of creating the sense of stability, control, and safety that visual devices are meant to provide, these stacked lights had the opposite impact. I was uneasy. When this happens, we either ignored the lights completely (because they are always on)—or feel a growing sense of danger for the same reason. Only a handful of people actually knew what they meant. This situation must be corrected. Here is how.

When you use lights to carry a message—whether a single light or a stack of them—add a name list or legend that translates each color into a precise meaning. The example in Photo 12.21 uses an adhesive label you fix directly onto the surface of the light. The other (Photo 12.22) uses cardboard and duct tape to post a two-sided legend. Stacked lights are an important way to share vital information, instantly, close at hand and at a distance. There must be no mystery about what that information is, what it means, or what to do in response. Do not let your andon lights cause the very motion they are supposed to reduce or even eliminate.

Photo 12.21 A stick-on label provides meaning.

Photo 12.22 Cardboard and tape is the answer here.

Visual Signals: Next Steps. This concludes our discussion on visual signals. Now it is time for you to think about and apply what you have just learned. How do the visual signals you just studied expand your thinking about ways to make your work area more visual, safer, and more operationally effective?

Think about that now as you review the examples in the preceding pages. Then, working alone or with a buddy, make a list of opportunities for visual signals in your area. Identify one or several that interest you the most. Then update your visual workplace hit list (Figure 12.7). Post *all* your improvement ideas, even if you do not plan to tackle them yourself.

Improvement is continuous so it all does not have to happen right away or happen through you alone.

Figure 12.7 Keep track on your hit list.

Visual Controls

A *visual control* is a mechanism that limits, restricts, and directs our behavior through structure—like the railroad crossing gate you see in Figure 12.9. Visual controls have a good deal of power. The gate now prevents vehicles from crossing the tracks when a train is coming. That physical barrier replaces the less effective railroad crossing sign (visual indicator), even with flashing lights (visual signal).

Figure 12.8 Level 3: Visual Controls.

Because visual controls are structural, they directly impact the power of the individual will—choice—except if a person is determined

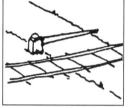

Figure 12.9 Visual Control.

to ignore them. Our teenage friend is still in jeopardy because his will is his main organizer. We can see him now, racing against the train, zigzagging through the very gates that are designed to protect him. Even if there were a cluster of *railroad cross buck signs* (their technical name), flashing lights, bells ringing, and a train in sight, that teenager might still make a run for it. Aaaaah youth!

For the rest of us, visual controls are powerful deterrents—or enablers, whichever side you look at. When we reach the control level, our behavior becomes less and less optional because the device itself structures (controls) our response. Here are examples.

The Power of Limits. To some, Photo 12.23 looks like a parking lot. They are wrong. It is instead a highly sophisticated visual control system. How do we know? Because 120 strangers will park 120 cars uniformly there. No injuries, dents, or even thinking twice from the very first moment they enter the property. How does that happen? It happens thanks to the position of the white borders (some called them "lines"), the length and angle of those borders, their number,

Photo 12.23 A powerful visual control system first—then a parking lot.

and the space between them. In short, it happens because of the power of limits: the strength of the pattern in the value field we call *a parking lot*. Adherence—control—is built into that landscape, visually. We seamlessly obey. That is the power of a visual control.

Photo 12.24 Snow erased the pattern.

You know you are in the presence of a powerful *visual control* system when the behavior evaporates if the control pattern is removed. In Photo 12.24 a heavy snow wiped out the control pattern—and with it adherence, compliance, and uniform behavior. In the absence of any control pattern, one wisely decides not to park there.

See the same effect in Photo 12.25 with the pallet jack parking: four bordered slots and four jacks—location and quantity in the same device. Add visual indicators (addresses and ID labels) for a complete visual solution (Photo 12.26).

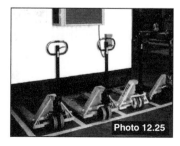

Photo 12.25

Photo 12.26

Borders as Structure. Are you wondering how 2-dimensional "lines" on a floor can have the power to control anything? After all, you may say, they are flat and have no tangible structure. The explanation lies in the discussion we already had about the power of pattern. Each of the floor (or ground) border examples shown above (including the parking lot) creates an enclosed space—a containment structure. Test this out by raising each of those "lines" up in your mind's eye. What do you get? Walls! It is those walls that we intuitively envision when we see or work in an area contained by borders. That is how "lines" can function as powerfully as structure. Consider this further as you study the three examples in Photo Series 12.27.

Barry Controls, a cellular manufacturer in Boston, favors broad bands of color as borders. These embed the pattern of work across the factory, creating a production environment that feels sane and stable. Question: Are these borders visual indicators or visual controls?

The green border for this rack has a gate—that front gap. The GM associates who created it push racks in and out through that gap as though it had walls on both sides—a measure of the power of pattern. What does this tell you about borders? Question: Are they indicators or controls?

Some see this work station and say, "Just a bunch of yellow lines." But you and I know it is the power of limits that regulates, even governs, this Scania takt-time driven assembly cell (Holland). This is the power of visual structure— the power of borders as visual controls. No question about it!

What do you think? If you are undecided, check it out further through your own visual applications and the behaviors that follow. Challenge your buddies in discussions about this. A clear and final answer, in this case, is not as important as exploring the question itself. You will all gain a much greater understanding of borders as controls through your lively exchanges and experiments. And that is answer enough. Now we will add to the mix.

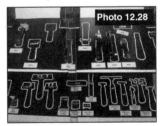

Raising Shadows/Making Walls. Photo 12.28 shows the visual application called *shadow boards* where a home for a tool is a bordered outline—the tool's shadow. Shadow boards keep tools in order, even though the shadow border is only a flat, 2-dimensional surface. They also tell you when a tool is elsewhere, *not at* home. But, visual thinker, why not go further?

Make the basic concept more powerful by raising up the shadow and making a wall—exactly what you see in Photo 12.29 (also shown in Chapter 7). Stiff blue foam is cut in the shape of tool profiles, providing a tight control function. A bright yellow background (in this case) allows us to spot at-a-glance when a tool is missing. The control element in this visual array—as with all visual control devices—is some manner of physical barrier, structured, or built into the device itself; in this case it is the foam.

While this particular set of tool boxes is made by an outside vendor, you can mimic the concept, using foam or even drawer liners from a hardware store (for more, revisit pages 105 and 133 in this book).

Changeover Tools/Visual Controls. Here is the same raising-walls action (Photo 12.30), applied to a machine changeover cart in the Tube Shop at Lockheed Martin Aerospace (Fort Worth, Texas). The thick foam on the top was carved to fit a needed set of hand tools and machine fixtures, making the tools not only handy and securely in place, but also automatically alerting us if something is missing.

Photo 12.30

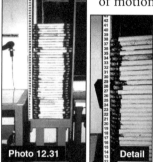

Photo 12.31   Detail

Counting as Control. The need to count is one of motion's most hidden forms. Jose and Roberto worked the day shift at Seton Name Plate, preparing anywhere from 48 to 52 silk screens for the night shift to process. They used to spend lots of time counting screens to make sure they had made enough. Already ace visual thinkers, they realized counting is motion—caused by the missing answer to the *how many* question. Photo 12.31 is their solution: a wooden box with numbers on the side and room for no more than 52 screens.

Visual Limits as Triggers/Min-Max Levels. In Photo 12.32, a dashed red visual control limit triggers safe human behavior by controlling the height for stacking bales of used cardboard on the loading dock at Seton Name Plate. Notice the good double use of existing architecture: the wall. Great visual thinking.

Besides the controlling aspect of the floor borders in Photo 12.33, the bright yellow "Re-Order Level" limit on each barrel (red arrow) is a visual control, triggering (or pulling) a human response when material level gets low. Add upper/lower limits (min/max levels) and you create more pull, which in turn embeds time into the process.

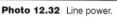

Detail

Photo 12.32   Line power.

Photo 12.33
Line power.

Photo 12.34 shows a storage spot for welding wire, used in the axle (aka, "bogie") assembly at the Trailmobile (Canada)—a simple visual where. Nothing more. Add a "limit" (see red arrow) to add an important dimension of meaning. You have defined what "enough" means—in this case 30 boxes of wire. In do-

Photo 12.34

ing this, you turn the visual where into *visual pull*. That so-called border represents a limit—and that limit triggers behavior. In exactly this way, human response is designed into the physical landscape of work.

A simple "limit" can help us—and everyone else—see when something is getting low: the *visual how many*. It becomes a min-max (minimum/maximum) device, a popular and useful visual control.

Photo 12.35

Min/max devices make it easy to tell at-a-glance when the item is in full supply or running out—whether raw material, parts, medicine, paper clips, or customers. Notice how the min-level of the visual controls described above triggers a pull from us (and/or material handlers) to replenish the supply. This is the link between visual controls and our next control application: *visual pull systems*.

Visual Pull Systems/Kanban. With visual pull systems, we reach the land of *kanban*—the imposition of limits *to control the pace of material consumption and replenishment.*

Photo 12.36 Visual pull.

There are many ways that visible pull can be installed. In Photo 12.36, the physical limits of the control border itself—four kanban squares—ensure that the nearby process never runs out of material. The squares convey the friendly message: *Don't worry; you won't run out—and you won't have to hoard stuff to keep on working.* There are four bins or squares of material (not three or two) because the site had only one forklift driver per shift. The drivers requested four squares so they could make their circuit without no chance of shutting down an area if they were running late (Packard Electric/Mississippi; then Delphi).

Actual cards were used to trigger pull in the inventive supply kanban system shown in Photo Series 12.37. "Kanban" means "laundry ticket" in Japanese.

Photo Series 12.37 Kanban replenishment system for welded parts.

With eight metalworking mills and over 800 employees manufacturing high-precision tubes and extruded shapes, Plymouth Tube Company started its excellence journey in 1999. It continues it to this day. In the West Monroe (Louisiana) facility, stock outages and parts hoarding were once a problem.

Then Robin Griggs, supplies purchaser, decided to solve the problem. She created the innovative kanban system shown here. If you think visual pull could help take some of the struggle out of work in your area, talk with your supervisor and/or purchasing.

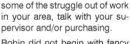

Robin did not begin with fancy laminated color cards. She did her thinking first; then she experimented with cardboard. Later she made things pretty.

1. Welding parts are stored in cubbies in this rack. Robin installed time card racks on the left and right (red arrows) because the parts bins were so small.

2. Each bin is marked with part numbers plus min/max replenishment levels.

3. Cards are numbered as well to correspond to each small bin and have clear instructions.

4. Each slot for a card is also numbered.

5. Parts running low? Turn the card upside down, put it back into the same slot. Robin will pick it up on her rounds.

Traffic Light Pull. Another popular visual pull method uses traffic-light color coding (red/yellow/green) to signal and control material delivery and pick up. This is an approach so simple, its effectiveness continues to surprise.

For a fine example, we go to the Delphi Rimir (Matamoras/Mexico; now part of Autoliv), air bag supplier to the auto industry, with value streams that include many cutting and sewing processes. In Photo 12.38, you see a roll of air bag material mounted on a cutting machine at the top of the stream (at the start of operations). The traffic light device is that painted placard on the side of the fabric roll, in plain sight of forklift drivers (red arrow). The drivers keep an eye on the color bands to make sure the fabric does not run out. If the fabric is within the green band, there is still plenty of time. If it drops to yellow, time to pay attention—a new roll will be needed soon. If it is down to the red, you are already too late.

Photo 12.38 Material Handlers pay attention.

An excellent system. Here's what else. This plant employed 1500 people at the time of these photos. This simple traffic-light pull system was the only material handling approach used throughout the facility. See Photo Series 12.39 for several more examples from this plant. Could such a system help your area?

Photo Series 12.39 Traffic light pull plant-wide: red-yellow-green visual control limits on every stack of material.

Animal Pull. Pull systems are so much a part of lean operations that we sometimes forget that these are also visual systems. Remembering this can help you improve an existing system. Here is a case in point.

The men and women on the machining floor at Freudenberg-NOK (Georgia) had devised a nifty pull system, using color-coded kanban cards to pull parts to specific machines. For example, match the "green" parts with the "green" machine (Photos 12.40 and 12.41).

This simple system should have worked well—but it did not. Costly mix-ups kept happening. Then, the site manager discovered that a number of male employees were some degree of color blind (the national average is one in twelve men). She was ready to shutdown the pull process. What to do?

Photos 12.40 & 12.41 A simple system that did not work.

The team met. "Gee, color coding is such a great concept. It would be a shame to close it down." They thought and talked and thought some more. Then they solved it. Here is how….

Eric, a night-shift machinist, mentioned that his toddler came to breakfast that morning wearing a shirt with a rabbit and an alligator on her pants. "So I told her—Tonya honey, you have to put a rabbit with a rabbit or an alligator with an alligator. The little animals have to match."

Photo 12.42

"That's it!," shouted the parents in the room. "Garanimals to make the match!" Garanimals is a kids clothing line of tops and pants with matching animals. The solution worked perfectly at NOK, making the kanban match with animal heads and bottoms, instead of color. Kanban at its most inventive! (Photos 12.42 and 12.43)

Photo 12.43

Visual Scheduling/Heijunka. Whether you work in a factory or hospital, the tool called *heijunka* can apply. "Heijunka" means "make flat and level" in Japanese. It is a system of logic for sequencing and smoothing out the flow of work. Kanban pull needs to be in place for heijunka to work, as does *standard work* (standard work is the pre-set flow of exact work content, based on the technical and procedural standards we discussed in Chapter 2.)

Heijunka is most effective when applied within a strong visual framework, especially when the base scheduling is computer-driven. With few exceptions, heijunka involves a physical box or structure that can segment work orders into actual physical slots. Photo Series 12.44 shows several of the many ways to do this. This need for physical structure is why heijunka is so rightly in the power category of visual controls.

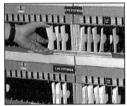

Photo Series 12.44 Visual scheduling/heijunka boxes.

Each card is an order, each slot, a time period (say 15 or 30 minutes). Cards are slotted in work sequence for the day.

Orders across the company are placed by days of the week in physical sequence.

The actual barcode labels are used as the work orders (the green card signifies a model change). The structure is a rack bought at K-Mart, turned upside down and secured on the workbench.

At Wiremold (Connecticut), heijunka has replaced paper scheduling completely. Each morning, hundreds of kanban cards are loaded into some 350 boxes—the site's production schedule for the day (Photo 12.45).

While both visual pull systems and heijunka require the heavy, active participation of engineers and planners, do not hesitate to envision them as possibilities for your work. Get inspired. Investigate them further. Ask questions. Experiment. Ask to run a pilot. See if your colleagues want to join in. Think *outside the box* as you consider ways to further visually embed the need to know and need to share in your work area. Become scientists of your work.

Photo 12.45

Figure 12.10

Visual Controls: Next Steps. As you just saw, visual controls have a wide array of applications. Consider these now, walking back through the pages as a review.

Then, working alone or with a buddy, list visual control opportunities in your area. Discuss them. Sketch them out in a notebook or on a flip chart. Present your thinking to others; and listen to theirs. When you are ready, post your ideas on your hit list, even if you do not plan or want to tackle them all yourself (Figure 12.10). Keep going. Keep learning. Keep improving.

Visual Guarantees

A *visual guarantee* is a mechanism that builds information so deeply into the process of work that it *becomes* the work. When that happens it also becomes impossible to do the wrong thing. Said another way: We can do the right thing *only*. A *poka-yoke*, fail-safe, or mistake proof device are three other names for this kind of visual solution.

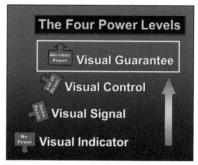

Figure 12.11 Level 4: Poka-yoke devices.

Figure 12.12 shows us what happened to the train and our teenager.

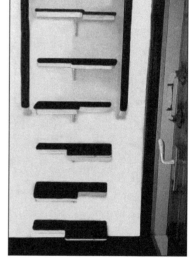

Re-routing the train to the bridge makes it impossible for them to collide. (This is a far more expensive option than usual when you move from visual control to visual guarantee.)

We go to the community for our first actual visual guarantee (Photo 12.46, provided by Annie Yu, WTMS Trainer, Boston). Study the photo and answer the following questions, based solely on what you see there. (To get you started, I will disclose that this device is located on ship.)

Question: What is the device? Answer: Some manner of ladder.

Question: How does the device work? What does it make sure you do?

Answer: You have to start climbing with your right foot. (You can try to start with your left foot. It's a free country. But you won't get far.)

*Question: What does the device (these stairs) make sure you do **not** do?*

Answer: The stairs make sure you do not skip a step. You cannot skip a step. Not even Julia Roberts—not even Michael Jordan—has the wing span to skip a step.

Good job! And those answers tell us that this device is a visual guarantee, requiring us to do the right thing while preventing us from doing the wrong thing. Visual guarantees or poka-yoke devices are the highest level of visual devices because behavior is so deeply embedded in it. Before we leave our ship, I have one more question: *Where did the idea for this visual guarantee come from? Why was it invented?*

Photo 12.46 What is the device? How does it work?

Here is a hint: Imagine yourself a sailor on a ship, sweetly asleep in your hammock, surrounded by 250 other sailors, likewise cozy in their "beds." Suddenly the alarm blasts: *Eurnh! Eurnh! Eurnh!* You leap up and, along with 250 others, make a mad rush for.... For what? Where are you? Where are they? Where are you rushing off to?

Yes! You are on a battleship in the middle of World War II, under attack. You and your buddies are rushing topside to the guns. Part of getting topside really fast is ensuring—*guaranteeing*—that the instant you put your foot on a ladder, you are already in exact unison with everyone else trying to go up that ladder. Right/left. Right/left. Right/left. Micro-seconds matter. *In visuality, the need leads.* This is a case in point.

The design of the stairs ensures you and your buddies will get topside, fast and safe. In visual guarantees, the attributes talk to each other. In this case, your foot communicates directly with each step. That is the point: *We humans are no longer part of the performance equation.* We simply do as the device dictates.

Photo 12.47 Dr. Shigeo Shingo, receiving an honorary doctorate from Utah State University in 1989, the inauguration of The Shingo Prize.

Dr. Shigeo Shingo. Dr. Shigeo Shingo nearly single-handedly brought visual guarantees to the world of work (Photo 12.47). He, along with Taiichi Ohno, was the co-architect of the Toyota Production System. Dr. Shingo called these amazing information-packed visual solutions: *poka-yoke* or "mistake-proof" devices. I call them visual guarantees to keep the message that they are part of the same continuum of visual logic that I call workplace visuality.

I had the honor of working with Dr. Shingo through the 1980s. Three years before he passed on, he asked me to use his book, *Zero Quality Control* (Productivity Press, 1986), as a base for creating a poka-yoke methodology for the West. As part of that, I developed a classification framework to help companies implement poka-yoke. Here is a part of that framework: the three types of poka-yoke devices. Like the power levels, we begin with the least powerful.

Type-3 Device: Detects the defect after the defect is made and contains it.

Type-2 Device: Detects the error causing the defect while that error is being made.

Type-1 Device: Eliminates the possibility of the error and therefore of the defect.

Type-3 Device: This visual guarantee from Chapter 2 is a Type-3 device because it captures a quality defect and prevents it from traveling downstream (Photo Series 12.48). Study it again, this time focusing on the power principles that make it work.

Photo Series 12.48 Type 3 Visual Guarantee: Detect the defect after it is made and contain it.

Problem: This hand holds a metal plunger, made by the machine at the back (red arrow). The outer diameter (OD) of some plungers are too large to slide inside the bushing. This hard-to-see defect is discovered in Final Test.

Challenge: Develop a way to ensure that no plunger with a defective OD travels downstream.
Solution: Embed the answer to the question "Is this OD good?" as deeply as possible into the process itself. Create a visual guarantee.

Visual Guarantee: First a plate is mounted on the blue bin, with a hole in the center the size of the bushing.

With the bushing mounted on the plate, the operator drops each plunger through, letting the bushing check the OD. If the plunger gets stuck, it is set aside. The attributes "talk" to each other.

Then think: *Could I create device like this to contain a defect in my area and prevent it from traveling downstream, only to fail in Final Test?* Look for an application. When you develop such containment devices, you are freed up to focus on solving the real problem—machines that often move out of calibration.

Sensors and limit switches, well-known poka-yoke devices, definitely help. If one were installed in the above machine, it would shut down that machine as soon as it moved out of calibration so it could not run even a single out-of-spec plunger OD. Look around. Sensors and limit switches are widely used in fast food restaurants, gas stations, airports—anywhere there is an untrained human/equipment interface. Misperforming machines simply shut down, often signalled by a sound or light annunciator (visual signal).

Type-2 Device: The second guarantee type detects errors as they are being made. At this level, we begin to hold ourselves directly accountable for product and process attributes—the execution of minute characteristics.

The example in Photo 12.49 shows us the 63 "pins" that need to be inserted into a subassembly. Instead of

Photo 12.49 Type 2 Guarantee: see your mistake as you're making it.

simply picking them out of a bin of hundreds, we count them out exactly in advance and position them on the board. In that way, we know at-a-glance if we have correctly completed the task—before we send it downstream.

Mounting a complete set of pins on the board makes it easy for the assembler to "see" that he needs to insert all of them. He will know, in real time, if he did not, without doubt or excuses. If he thinks he is done with the job and a clip is left on the board, he has made a mistake. And he will notice it in time to correct his error—instead of sending the unit downstream in the belief that it is complete and well made.

This is precisely why we say this level of guarantee allows us to notice when an error is being made as we are in the process of making it. As long as we stay alert and pay attention, a Type-2 poka-yoke is highly effective.

Type-1 Device. The final visual guarantee level is absolute. With a Type-1 device in place, whatever mistake you made in the past can no longer be made. Training is no longer a part of this success equation—nor binders, OJT, or your will. The device itself holds its own adherence. It is visually intelligent on that highest level.

A guarantee on this level cannot stop you from doing something *else* is wrong. But it can tightly control your behavior (or a machine's) towards a single attribute. For our example, we go to Finish Machining at the Rolls Royce plant in Oberursel, Germany. Gunther is an ace visual thinker and the machinist responsible for this final process—the high value-add segment of the value stream.

Photo 12.50. *Before:* An advanced level of the visual where is not powerful enough to keep Gunther from making mistakes.

He has taken pains to put all his yellow boxes of chucks and inserts in excellent visual order, even building a cubby unit to keep mix-ups to a minimum. Grab the wrong yellow box and you ruin the unit. Photo 12.50 shows his excellent green-cubby visual solution.

But Gunther soon found out the visual where could only reduce his mistakes. It was not powerful enough to eliminate them. He needed a surefire way to guarantee that his hand did not grab the wrong insert. So he made a model-specific masking template that: a) covered all wrong boxes, and b) allowed his hand to reach only the boxes right for what he was working on. This brilliant poka-yoke solution (Photo 12.51) shows a set of masking templates, color coded to product. Genius!

Photo 12.51 *After:* This masking template is product-specific, covering cubbies that hold the wrong yellow boxes so none can be wrongly taken. Gunther has access to the right ones only. Each of the other templates (blue, green, yellow) mask a different array of "wrong" cubbies.

Visual Guarantees: Next Steps

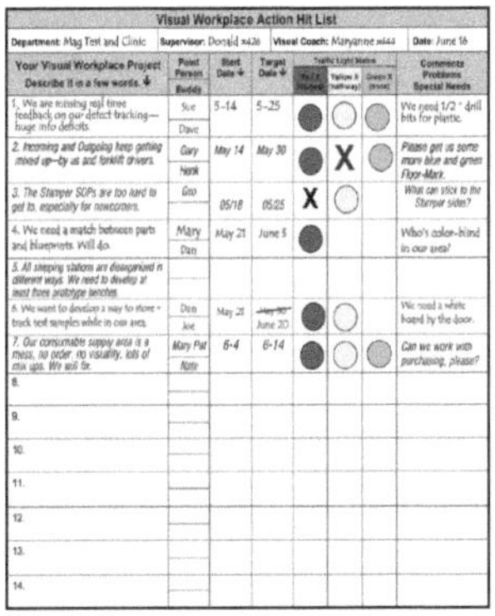

In this final section of the four power levels, I introduced the concept of visual guarantees/poka-yoke systems. There is so much more to learn about them—but not here, not today. Yet, I hope and believe you take the time to look for and find applications. Do that now. Working alone or with a buddy, make a list of guarantee opportunities in your area. Then post on your hit list, even if you do not plan or want to tackle them all yourself (Figure 12.13).

Learning to See

As mentioned, the purpose of this chapter is to show you many, many different kinds of visual devices, some repeats from this book's earlier chapters.

Figure 12.13 Track your improvement progress on your hit list.

These, along with many new visual solutions, are presented in a new way—from the vantage point of power. The four power levels of visual devices offer you a new way to explore workplace visuality and its ability to translate information into exact behavior. Remember the equation: "Translate vital information into exact behavior through visual devices (Figure 12.14), the foundation of visuality and your role as a visual thinker.

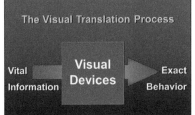

Because you have already learned so much about visuality, you are now able to see how visual devices convey vital information through any of our five senses. As with the teaching examples, every visual device has many layers or dimensions of meaning. Some of them are already captured in the devices we have studied. Others are waiting for you to discover and implement. But first you have to "see" the visual potential in the missing information that still surrounds you.

Figure 12.14 The foundation of all work.

I call this *inverted visual thinking* or *sight inversion*, and you must develop a skill at it and an appetite for it. It is one of the most rewarding and delicious aspects of thinking visually.

Because of that, expect to "see" visuality everywhere—even, as mentioned, when it is missing. Expect to go the mall and see cluster after cluster of visual devices influencing, even limiting your behavior. Expect to appreciate the thinking behind it. Expect to see this at the sport stadium, library, and hardware store. Expect to see it at your workplace and at the places where the world works. You'll see visual devices—or you will see the absence of them. You'll see the device that is not there—the device that has not yet been installed or maybe even invented—because you'll see the motion caused by its absence.

Visual thinker, apply the lessons of this book. Experiment with the possibilities. Visually answer your need to know until you are in control of your corner of the world through visuality. Then turn to others and recognize your need to share. Help other people gain control over their own work. When you do, the sense of safety, precision, alignment, and service becomes stronger in you and soon stronger in others.

> There is nothing so useless as doing efficiently
> that which should not be done at all.
> Peter Drucker

Chapter | Thirteen

We Are Visual Beings

We conclude this book appreciating visuality as a natural and inborn way of sharing vital information and connecting with others. When we recognize this as a birthright, our visual journey takes on new meaning. It becomes an opportunity to put us and our company in right relationship. We contribute to the visual improvement of the enterprise—and the company provides us with the opportunity to do so. The result is a visual workplace and work that makes sense.

We are visual beings, therefore we live in a visual world—and not the other way around.

The world did not teach us to want or need visual devices—those on our roads and highways, in our hospitals and supermarkets, at the airport, and in workplaces of the world. We need these devices because visuality is a language we already speak and know. That knowing is embedded in our chemistry, in the way our mind naturally and elegantly seeks and recognizes patterns—and in the way that we think, perceive, and behave. We are visual beings, therefore we live in a visual world.

It's the same way with visuality at work. The visual workplace is a physical workplace. It exists because visual devices and visual mini-systems exist in it. Visuality is not a world of the imagination even though our imagination helps us create it. It is real, tangible, immediate, and natural.

Throughout this book, I have showed you many visual principles and practices. We have walked through a ton of visual examples. And many of you have begun to apply these principles and practices and already created a ton of visual solutions of your own.

If you are lucky, you are surrounded by people who are doing the same, applying the two driving questions, the principles of smart placement, the elements of visual where, and drilling deeper and wider into the language of visuality and visual thinking—in short applying the WTMS methodology.

If you are very lucky, your supervisors and managers are not only supporting you, they are making their own value fields speak. That makes them lucky too. And you know what? The very next book I write is going to be for them—*Visual Leadership*—so they can go even further and get even luckier.

When you apply the WTMS method, you transform your work area and your company, and in the process you transform yourself and each other—because there is no way you can gain expertise in a language without that language changing you. You are thinking and speaking visually.

An Uncommon Solution

Workplace visuality is an uncommon solution. Its rewards are both obvious and understated. The obvious part is operational transparency and the elimination of searching, errors, mix-ups, defects, rework, scrap, accidents, late deliveries, and other obvious forms of motion. As we locate work items closer to their points-of-use, we automatically reduce the distance traveled. As we make the workplace physically and psychologically safer, we begin to relax on the inside. As we embed the pattern of work in the physical landscape, operational details surface visually. We become masters of our work day.

That's when the understated rewards start. Unwanted questions and interruptions begin to evaporate. Things no longer get in our way. Struggle begins to recede. The workplace becomes our partner in delivering value to our customers and suppliers, downstream, upstream, at stream, and in the marketplace.

Over time, the area we move within becomes more focused and requires less vigilance. The order, logic, and content of work become so visual that a harmony settles in. Our movements become efficient and less scattered. We begin to notice less obvious forms of motion. We develop ways to visually minimize these as well—or eliminate them completely.

Workplace visuality turns motion reduction into a science and an art and has become the perfect ally to your other improvement efforts: TPM, six sigma, A3 Thinking, quick changeover, lean, and other methods that make up the excellence journey. Aligned with visual, they forge a powerful partnership.

As that alliance deepens, operations in every part of the company are performed efficiently, smoothly, and within the context of time, speed, safety, and quality. If you have ever observed or worked in a department that has mastered visuality, you have seen people move within a space defined by the value that gets added there—the work. The waste has been removed from the process. Motion is at an absolute minimum. In the best of these areas, work looks more like dancing. Every step and movement are choreographed, measured, fluid, and intentional.

The same can be true of all work settings, including traditional manufacturing. Whether you work in a city hospital or country clinic, a machine shop or stamping plant, on an assembly line or in purchasing, in a bank, military depot, or an open-pit mine, visuality is central to it and can create an entirely new level of work, one that blends focus, intention, and results for outputs that are superior.

As your focus becomes more precise, suddenly it's just you and your work. When the struggle has been minimized and even the tiny interruptions are removed, you can simply do your work. You are alert and relaxed as you bring a new level of your attention to the task at hand.

This state is possible at work, in your work area, in your company. You have experienced it before, but perhaps not yet at work. It is a state of intense stillness where all your resources are at your disposal and surface to assist you when and as needed. They flow in you and from you. Motion as you have known it no longer exists in any form. It is just you and the steady rhythm of your breath as value is added.

This is what you have always wanted work to feel like. This is what work is meant to be—the ease of your contribution flowing through you and into the process your company has asked you to perform. This is work that makes sense.

Appendix

Resource Section

Visual Thinking Inc. and The Visual-Lean® Institute
The Shingo Institute, Home of The Shingo Prize

Index

VIS\UAL
THINKING INC.

Mastering the Technologies of the Workplace Visuality

Under the leadership of Gwendolyn Galsworth, Visual Thinking Inc. (VTI) is the premier resource in the world for products and services that teach and support visual thinking, visual management, and the technologies of the visual workplace. Based on over thirty years of hands-on implementations in the field, our visual methodologies are robust, complete, and proven. Our clients include a wide range of industries and settings—from factories and military depots to banks, medical centers, and open-pit mines.

The Visual-Lean® Institute is VTI's educational arm, training and licensing in-house instructors and external consultants in any of the Institute's nine core visual workplace methodologies.

With licensed affiliates in the United States, Canada, Mexico, Europe, China, and Australia, VTI sets the pace for the industry with visual management/visual workplace offerings that include onsite and online seminars; workshops; complete Online Training Systems; on-site assessments, consulting, and troubleshooting; visual conversions: conferences: keynotes: and executive study missions—all with a unique visual workplace focus.

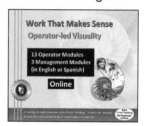

WTMS Online Training System 13 Operator Modules + 3 Management Modules *(English or Spanish)* plus a Complete WTMS Resource Folio, with WTMS Operator Booklets pdfs.

VTI offers training and certification for trainers and multi-site corporate licences world-wide in *Work That Makes Sense, Mistake-Proofing, The Visual Machine®,* and other core visual workplace technologies.

With over 100,000 visual solutions in our database, we continually refine and upgrade our instructional materials and designs. We are constantly implementing. Visit our website (*www.visualworkplace.com)* for our services and products and for Dr. Galsworth's books (also on Amazon)—plus over 100 free downloadable podcasts and articles. Join our *Visual Thinkers Club* and receive our monthly newsletter, *The Visual Thinker.* Let the workplace speak!

Visual Thinking Inc.
Website: www.visualworkplace.com

Phone: 503-233-1784
Email: contact@visualworkplace.com

Our Books

Achieving Perfect Quality Through Poka-Yoke Online Training System

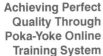

Complete Online Learning Systems

Train-the Trainer, online and onsite

Visual Thinking : The Visual-Lean® Institute Curriculum		
Track	Track Content • Courses	
Track 1	Visual Workplace/Visual Thinking & The Visual Site Assessment	
Track 2	Work That Makes Sense: Operator-Led Visuality	
Track 3	Visual Machine:® Let the Workplace Speak	Machine Lubrication: Visual & Effective
Track 4	The Visual-Lean® Office: Operational Excellence in Your Office	
Track 5	Management By Sight: Visual Displays & Visual Scheduling Boards	
Track 6	ScoreBoarding: Visual Standards & Visual Problem Solving	
Track 7	Visual Management: Metrics That Monitor/Metrics That Drive	
Track 8	Visual Leadership: Operations Template, X-Type Matrix, Systems Template	
Track 9	Perfect Quality Through Mistake-Proofing For Engineers	

Keynotes & Retreats

Conferences

Visual Benchmarking Tours

**Visual Displays
Visual Scheduling
Visual Leadership
Visual Metrics
Visual Standards
Visual Machine®
Visual Problem-Solving**

Onsite & Online

Training Tools & Supports. Instructional Wall Charts, Podcasts, Tool Kits, Resource Folios, packed with exercises, forms, checklists, hit lists, and templates you can customize.

Onsite and Online Visual Assessments and Seminars

...the Nobel Prize of operational excellence

Established in 1988, The Shingo Institute, home of The Shingo Prize, is internationally recognized as the premier award for operational excellence, providing an organizational roadmap for attaining the highest standards. Named after Dr. Shigeo Shingo, co-architect of the Toyota Production System, the award is a milestone on any company's journey to operational excellence and a sustainable cultural transformation.

The Shingo Prize is more than an award. It is a means for creating alignment, synergy, and purpose throughout an entire organization. We teach that a sustainable culture of continuous improvement is achieved by focusing on a distinct set of principles, aligning management systems, and implementing improvement techniques throughout an entire organization.

The focus is on principle-based leadership; vision and strategy alignment; employee empowerment; continuous improvement; innovation and development; quality and sustainable results.

Whether or not you plan to challenge for The Shingo Prize, there is no better diagnostic format than The Shingo Prize model and the application criteria it includes. Download both at: *www.shingoprize.org.*

The Shingo Prize & Workplace Visuality. Robert Miller, former executive director of The Shingo Prize, said this about the work of Gwendolyn Galsworth:

> *"Galsworth's visual workplace methodology is in perfect harmony with the model of Operational Excellence represented by The Shingo Prize.*
>
> *Visual concepts, tools, and thinking are essential as we pursue other guiding principles of seeking perfection, quality at the source, and the continuous flow of value to customers.*
>
> *As I learn more about this important approach, I am hopeful that it will reach the hands of all of the great experts who know their jobs so well and want to ensure that what is supposed to happen does happen."*

Index